The Social History of the Decorative Arts

Furniture 700-1700

The Social History of the Decorative Arts

General Editor: Hugh Honour

Eric Mercer

Furniture 700-1700

Weidenfeld and Nicolson

5 Winsley Street London WI

© 1969 by Eric Mercer

SBN 297 17809 1

All rights reserved. No part of this publication may
be reproduced, stored in a retrieval system, or transmitted,
in any form or by any means, electronic, mechanical,
photocopying, recording or otherwise, without the
prior permission of the Copyright owner.

Designed by John Wallis for
Weidenfeld and Nicolson Limited, London
Printed in Great Britain
by Ebenezer Baylis and Son Limited
The Trinity Press, Worcester, and London

Contents

Contents

Acknowledgements

I am greatly indebted for much assistance and advice to the editor of this series, Mr Hugh Honour, and to Miss Arlene Wolosker of Weidenfeld and Nicolson. For their help and kindness in various ways I am grateful to Mr Maurice Barley, F.S.A., Mr Norman Drinkwater, O.B.E., F.S.A., Mr John Hopkins, Dr P.J. Jones, Dr G. Schade, Mr R.E. Parsons, Mr Alec Tiranti, Mr Francis Watson, C.V.O., and the staff of the library of the Victoria and Albert Museum. I owe very much to my wife for her help in innumerable ways, and I am grateful for the enthusiastic, if intermittent, assistance of my daughters, Sarah and Helen.

The Royal Commission on Historical Monuments have kindly allowed me to reproduce photographs in advance of official publication. For permission to quote from works in copyright I wish to thank the following publishers: Jonathan Cape; Ceramic Book Company, Newport, Monmouthshire; Cambridge University Press; J.M. Dent and Sons; Anton Hiersemann, Stuttgart; Librairie Armand Colin, Paris; Librairie Hachette, Paris; Presses Universitaires de France, Paris. I have been unable to contact some publishers and to them I offer my apologies.

E.M.

Illustrations

Stools and thrones

(between pages 32 and 33)

1   King David as a harper (Musée des Augustins, Toulouse) (*Marburg*)
2   Scene of Eustace Deschamps presenting his poems to Charles V. MS. 20029 f.4v. (Bibliothèque Nationale, Paris)
3   Fold-stool from Styria *c.* 1200 (Oesterreichisches Museum für Angewandte Kunst, Vienna)
4   Sixteenth-century X-chair in Winchester Cathedral (*Reproduced by kind permission of Mrs Mary Tomlinson*)
5   Charles the Bald enthroned as Holy Roman Emperor from a mid-ninth century MS. MS. Lat. 1152 f.3. (Bibliothèque Nationale, Paris) (*F. Foliot*)
6   Monk seated on a chair, from a twelfth-century MS. MS. R.17.1 f.283v. (Trinity College, Cambridge)
7   Welsh chair with turned ornament *c.* 1600 (Victoria and Albert Museum)
8   Edward the Confessor on his throne, from the Bayeux Tapestry (*Giraudon*)
9   Detail of feasting scene; bench with demi-lion ends. Cotton MSS. Julius A VI f.4 (British Museum)
10 Christ enthroned, from a ninth-century Spanish MS. H. Y. Thomson MS. 97 second series f.13 (British Museum)
11 Phillippe VI presides at the Court of Peers. MS. Fr. 18,437 f.2 (Bibliothèque Nationale, Paris)
12 *Check to the King* by the Monogrammist B.R. (Kupferstichkabinett, Basel)
13 Mid-fifteenth century drawing of chairs by an anonymous Flemish artist (The Lehman Collection, New York)
14 Sculptured scene of Christ on a capital from Autun *c.* 1150 (Trianon Press, Paris)
15 Fold-stool-type chair from an eleventh-century south Italian ivory (Victoria and Albert Museum)
16 Chair with a half-back on a mid-twelfth century capital from Reading Abbey (*Alec Tiranti Ltd*)

Cupboards, caskets and chests

(between pages 40 and 41)

17 Twelfth- or thirteenth-century cupboard at the Obazine Church, Corrèze, France (*Musée des Beaux-Arts, Tours*)
18 The Franks casket, seventh or eighth century (British Museum)
19 Twelfth-century lead casket with silver and enamel enrichments (Fitzwilliam Museum, Cambridge) (*Alec Tiranti Ltd*)
20 Late-twelfth century casket of copper and silver (Louvre, Paris) (*Ann Münchow, Aachen*)
21 Fourteenth-century ivory casket (Victoria and Albert Museum)

Beds

(between pages 56 and 57)

13

148   *L'hyver*, engraving by Abraham Bosse (British Museum)
149   *Ladies dining together*, engraving by Abraham Bosse (British Museum)
150   *A licentious banquet*, engraving by T. B. Barentz (Ashmolean Museum, Oxford)
151   *The Schoolmaster*, engraving by Abraham Bosse (British Museum)
152   Painting by Pieter Breughel the Younger to illustrate the proverb 'Falling between two stools' (Schloss Pommersfelden) (*Marburg*)
153   Day-bed at Knole, Kent (*Royal Commission on Historical Monuments, England*)
154   Late-seventeenth century day-bed, New England, U.S.A. (The Metropolitan Museum of Art, New York, gift of Mrs Russell Sage, 1909)
155   Early-seventeenth century English chair (Victoria and Albert Museum)
156   Sixteenth-century Spanish chair (The Metropolitan Museum of Art, New York, bequest of Gwynne M. Andrews, 1931)
157   Seventeenth-century chair of north American origin (The Metropolitan Museum of Art, New York, gift of Mrs Russell Sage, 1909)
158   Early-seventeenth century X-chair at Knole, Kent (*Royal Commission on Historical Monuments, England*)
159   Sixteenth-century Italian chair (The Metropolitan Museum of Art, New York, Rogers Fund, 1913)
160   Sixteenth-century Spanish chair ornamented with enriched nail-heads (Victoria and Albert Museum)
161   Late-seventeenth century French upholstered armchair (The Metropolitan Museum of Art, New York, bequest of Benjamin Altman, 1913)
162   Bedroom scene by Crispin van de Passe (British Museum)
163   Oration to St Margaret, mid-seventeenth century engraving by Buran (Oesterreichisches Nationalbibliothek, Vienna)
164   Detail of *Le Touche*, engraving by Abraham Bosse (British Museum)
165   Late-seventeenth century four-poster bed at Knole, Kent (*Royal Commission on Historical Monuments, England*)
166   Late-seventeenth century Dutch bed (Rijksmuseum, Amsterdam)
167   State-bed at Knole, Kent (*Royal Commission on Historical Monuments, England*)
168   Mid-seventeenth century Dutch interior by Terborch (National Gallery)
169   Mid-seventeenth century ebony cabinet (Kunstgewerbemuseum, Berlin)
170   Seventeenth-century Indo-Portuguese cabinet in teak and rosewood (Victoria and Albert Museum)
171   Mid-seventeenth century ebony cabinet with painted panels (Rijksmuseum, Amsterdam)
172   Buffet of 1664 from Basel (Kunstgewerbemuseum, Berlin)
173   Late-seventeenth century cupboard from south-west France (*Studio Violle, Moissac*)
174   North German 'Diele' cupboard of *c.* 1700 (Kunstgewerbemuseum, Berlin)

1 The Middle Ages

The medieval house

In modern times changes in furniture have followed one another in quick succession, and it is possible without any very refined analysis to distinguish half-a-dozen clearly differentiated periods, and as many national styles, within the last three centuries. In contrast the seven hundred or so years between the accession of Charlemagne and the end of the Middle Ages may be treated more or less as a whole.

The apparent homogeneity of furniture over that long expanse of time may be ascribed to two major causes of equal effect but of very unequal natures. The first is quite simple and wholly negative: so little has survived that there is not the necessary material to permit an analytical sequence of styles and forms. Even when some pieces are given the benefit of the very considerable doubts about their true age – when, for example, the bench from Alpirsbach, the hutches at Valère in the Rhône Valley, the cupboards at Obazine and at Halberstadt are allotted to the late twelfth or early thirteenth centuries – they still amount to no more than a handful, and pieces of earlier date, apart from a few folding stools and caskets, are non-existent. Knowledge is not wholly dependent upon survivals and much may be learned from written documents and from contemporary illustrations, but the farther back one goes in time the scantier the documents become, and to a less extent the illustrations as well. Further, neither documents nor illustrations can provide the authenticity and the detail which are necessary for making fine stylistic distinctions. Early documents are never concerned with furniture for its own sake and refer to it only in passing; and illustrations have to be treated with care, for in the absence of verification from other sources it is not always clear whether they are representations of reality or flights of the artist's fancy. In one way, therefore, the uniformity of early furniture is the result of an obscurity in which everything is blurred, and many centuries can be subsumed under one heading not by virtue of a prodigious power of generalization, but because there is very little to generalize about.

Nevertheless, the uniformity is not wholly due to the distorting effects of ignorance and there is another reason which, if not of more importance, is at least capable of throwing more light upon the subject. The character and development of furniture is very much dependent upon the nature of the house which it is in. This is true of every period, but the dependence is closer at some times than at others, and in earlier years it was very close indeed, so close that little of any consequence can be said about the furniture of the age without a preliminary discussion of the houses which it graced and the purposes which it served.

At first sight this claimed connection may seem extremely tenuous, for over the last three centuries the dwellings of the upper classes, for example, have changed very little, until recently, whilst their furniture has undergone a long series of metamorphoses; and on the other hand in the early Middle Ages furniture had a uniform character although appearing in the houses of men of varied social positions within a society and in greatly differing societies. House forms are themselves determined by a wide variety of causes: by social organization, by interrelationships of classes, by the ways in which men earn or steal a living, by the level of economic development and by the natural environment within which all this occurs. With such multifarious forces playing each its own role within innumerable combinations it might be expected that houses throughout western Europe over nearly a millennium would show a wide range of forms. This they do and the house of an English peasant was vastly different from that of a French nobleman, from that of a French peasant and, for that matter, from that of a peasant in another part of England. Yet despite all these variations it is not necessary to conduct a detailed examination of each kind of house and of the conditions from which it sprang, for they all had one element which was highly effective in determining the amount and the nature of furniture within them.

Common to all of these houses was a main room, in many the only room, in general use by all the occupants and provided with a fire,

18

which was often the only one in the building. Houses of this form were standard over wide areas and for long periods, ranging in space over most of western Europe and in time from the neolithic village of *c.*1500 BC at Skara Brae in the Orkneys to the 'black houses' which were still being built in the Hebrides in the nineteenth century and some of which are still occupied in the mid-twentieth. This main room, known in Latin as *aula* and in the vernaculars as 'hall' or 'salle' or 'saal', was a living room, a parlour, a dining-room, a bedroom, a workshop, sometimes a court-house and sometimes a kitchen and a byre as well. Even in a large house with several rooms many of the activities of all the occupants and all of the activities of many of them went on in the hall. It was indeed far more than a mere room, it was the heart of the little community which used it. In a moving passage in his *History* Bede used it as a symbol for life itself; and compared human existence with the flight of a sparrow through the king's hall on a winter's eve; momentarily in the warmth and light, and then returning to the cold and darkness whence it came. The role of the hall was so dominant throughout much of western Europe that the word itself was often used to describe the building it was in. In Carolingian and in medieval France 'salle' frequently meant not the hall alone but the whole house and in England, and especially in northern England, many a house of some status is still known as a 'hall'. Conversely a medieval Italian chronicler, Johannis de Mussis, used 'domus' to mean both house and hall in a single sentence, and as late as the eighteenth century the main room, the descendant of the medieval hall, in many small English houses was called the 'house' or the 'house-part'.[1]

The many and varied functions of the hall affected furniture in one very obvious way: they tended to restrict the amount of it to a minimum, for with so much going on it was necessary to keep the floor space as free of obstructions as possible. This consideration was important in all halls, and it was paramount when much of the space was occupied by an open hearth in the centre of the room. The central open fire, from which the smoke was allowed to drift upwards and escape through vents in the roof or was conveyed away by a light funnel-like structure called a firehood, was not universal in western Europe in the Middle Ages, but it was very common and by no means confined to northern countries. Its use among all classes in southern England up to and beyond the end of the fifteenth century is well established; it was not uncommon in the houses of the knights and burgesses in fourteenth-century Germany; it had disappeared from the houses of the French nobility by the twelfth century but not from those of lesser men; and it was known in many Italian towns throughout much of the fourteenth century.[2]

The limitations upon furniture that such a usage entailed can be imagined easily enough, and if they cannot there are aids to assist us. Houses with a central open fire in the main room were occupied in parts of Scandinavia until a very recent date and their floor space was very restricted [Plate 34]. Of course, the hall of a medieval lord with perhaps a width of about twenty feet or over had more free space than a peasant's house, but then it had more people moving around in it. Whatever the status of its owner and whether it had an open fire, a firehood, or a chimney the medieval hall discouraged the use of all furniture which was not ranged against the wall.[3]

Those men who had nothing more than a hall would have been unable to afford much furniture in any case, but the nobility and gentry had other rooms as well in which the limitations imposed by the nature of the hall were less. Yet even the houses of these, except the very great, had scanty accommodation. Surviving small houses of medieval date, whose early occupants can be identified, are extremely rare and since they look to modern eyes like cottages, it is not always easy to appreciate quite how low were the housing standards of the gentry and petite noblesse. A good example is Plas Ucha in Merionethshire, built not before the late fourteenth century and perhaps as much as a hundred years later [Plate 33]. It had a hall with an open central hearth, a solar – a private chamber for the lord's use – and a service end with pantry and buttery. As the illustration shows, it would not be outrageous to describe its appearance as 'mean'. It is however reasonably certain that it was the home of an important family, the barons of Cymmer.[4]

Of course, it may be said that Wales was a poor and backward country and not typical, but it is clear that many a medieval French manoir had no more accommodation than Plas Ucha. E. Perroy in a recent article on the French aristocracy has emphasized how meagre were the standards of the petite noblesse, at least in the old county of Forez, roughly the modern department of Loire. Du Faïl, writing in the late sixteenth century of the houses of the petty seigneurs of about fifty years before and using a term which then meant no more than 'parlour' or 'chamber', remarked that to have two *salles-de-logis* in one house was considered to smack of grandeur. Even in early fifteenth-century

Florence, Agnolo Pandolfini in *Del Governo della Famiglia* was still of the opinion that, 'The whole family should have one roof, one entrance-door, one fire and one dining-table.' He was championing a hopelessly lost cause in central Italy by then but his nostalgic views reflect the conditions of earlier years.[5]

Most of the evidence cited above refers to the countryside but in at least some towns equally simple standards prevailed: the wealthiest burgess in the important town of Colchester in 1301 had no more than three rooms in his house, a few men had two and most had only one. Thus even in those houses which had a solar or chamber, free of the bustle of the hall and reserved for the lord's family and friends, that room still had to serve the purposes of bedroom, parlour, private dining-room and council chamber, and this varied usage, although less marked than in the hall, inhibited the use of nearly all furniture except the barest necessities. In some cases this was further compounded by the medieval habit of housing animals and human beings in the same quarters. Peasants often shared their hall with their cattle and greater men shared their chambers with more aristocratic creatures. At the end of the twelfth century Alexander Neckham laid down that a decently furnished chamber needed a perch for the falcons to roost on. At a later date, when costly furniture was common, René of Anjou in 1471 found it necessary to protect a magnificent bed in his château at Angers with a railing to stop the dogs from sleeping on it.[6]

Among the greater barons, who had houses of more consequence and with more accommodation, these considerations applied with less force, but there were others which brought about much the same result. As the owners of many manors and lordships, often scattered through several counties or provinces, great men were often on the move from one house to another and were rarely long at any; and their attendance, frequent or occasional, at an equally peripatetic court caused them to spend even less time in one place than they might otherwise have done. Some idea of the mobility of the court, and by analogy, of the households of the magnates, is provided by the record in the *Patent Rolls* of King John's movements. In a year taken at random, 1204–5, he was at nearly a hundred different places from Somerset to Yorkshire and never stayed at any one more than ten days. John was not noticeably more house-proud than his predecessors and successors, but the state documents of his time are filled with references to repairs and improvements at his many houses. If men in his position were to furnish on any

21

scale at all they had to provide furniture not for one house but for several, and in the knowledge that it would all be standing unused for the greater part of the year. Wealthy as many of them were they had to think twice about furnishing to a high standard of comfort. Nevertheless, their wealth might have been enough even for this if their comforts had been their most immediate concern: but they had more pressing problems. The position of any magnate depended upon his ability to bring armed force to his overlord's aid when called upon and yet maintain a quasi-independence of him. To do this he needed to be in command of considerable military power of his own and had to reward and support a great number of vassals and retainers who were a continuous drain upon his finances.[7]

Men have always been skilled at finding virtue in doing what they have to do and it became a matter of pride to spend money in this way. Riccobaldo of Ferrara, writing in the fourteenth century and at a time when things had changed, remarked of thirteenth-century Italy that the pride of the nobility was 'to have lofty towers, of which all the cities in Italy were full'. The same was true in other ways in other countries and there were not only good material reasons for not spending money on furniture, there were also good ideological ones for spending it on other things. Further, a man had a duty to God and to his soul as well as to his lord and his lineage and if, when all the rest had been looked after, there was still money to spare it was best expended upon charitable and religious objects, upon monasteries and churches, upon chantry priests and hospitals.

No class of men in early medieval Europe had much reason or much opportunity to spend heavily upon furniture. The lowest sections of society had little furniture because they could afford little. Those above them had less than they could have afforded because the nature of their houses precluded more. The very greatest had in proportion to their wealth perhaps least of all, because their position in feudal society demanded that they should spend most of their wealth in other ways and spread what remained over a great number of houses.

Scanty furniture

The lack of furniture in the early Middle Ages is partly demonstrated by the rarity of surviving examples, for there are very few pieces which can be certainly ascribed to a date before 1200 and not many to before

22

1300. It is sometimes claimed that this is not a reflection of the conditions of that age but of the widespread destruction of early pieces, as old-fashioned or as worn out, in the great span of time between their creation and the present day. There is some truth in this, and it must not be supposed that what has come down to us is all or even anything more than a minute fraction of what there once was. All the same, it is not the whole truth, for pieces with an exceptional purpose or from an exceptional milieu, less affected than domestic furniture by the considerations outlined above, have survived throughout the same length of time in greater numbers than any others. Further, if it were merely a question of the lapse of time then survivals ought to become gradually more numerous as we approach the present day. In fact they do not, and there is instead a very sudden increase in their numbers in the late fourteenth and fifteenth centuries.

Perhaps more important and certainly more convincing is the evidence provided by those contemporary documents such as wills and inventories which concern themselves with household possessions. None of these is earlier than the thirteenth century and most of them come from later years when furniture was more plentiful, and in consequence conclusions drawn from them may reasonably be supposed to exaggerate rather than to minimize the amount of furniture in eleventh and twelfth century houses. In late thirteenth-century Bologna there were in most dwellings nothing more than a bed and a chest, and sometimes not even a bed. In Siena at about the same period the furniture of even the best houses consisted of no more than a bed, a table, a bench, a coffer and an iron-bound or a painted chest. The furniture of Guichard Vert, the owner of three small lordships in the old county of Forez, consisted in 1287 of two beds, a table, three benches and five coffers. The tax returns of 1294 and 1301 for Colchester show that the most prosperous townsmen had no more than a bed or two and that many had nothing that even a tax-collector found worth recording. At a much later date in Germany the inventories of Burg Badenweiler of 1424 and of Prozelten-am-Main of 1483 record very little furniture, and that mostly beds. If we leave inventories with their prosaic accounts of the furniture of actual rooms and turn instead to Alexander Neckham's descriptions of the ideal furniture for a chamber we find nothing very different. Neckham could think of no more than a bed with a chair at the side and a bench at the foot and two perches – rods fixed at head-height and spanning the corner between two walls at right angles [Plate 35] – one to hang clothes from and one for the falcons to roost on. An Italian writer has remarked that 'the interior of a private house of the thirteenth century must have borne a close resemblance to that of the present day peasant's home in the mountainous districts'.[8]

One of the commonest items mentioned in early inventories is a bed, but it is extremely doubtful whether in all, or even in many, cases a piece of furniture is intended rather than a mattress and bed-clothes. Originally 'bed' in English and 'lit' in French meant no more than what we today would call 'bed-furniture' and, in later years, when a framework to place the coverings upon became common, the English introduced the term 'bedstead' and the French 'châlit' to distinguish between the bed and its appurtenances. That for many men the distinction was of no practical application for centuries after that is suggested by the fact that 'lit' was not used in its modern sense in France before the late sixteenth century and by the retention to the present of 'feather-bed' to mean what in contemporary English usage would more correctly be called a feather-mattress. As late as 1390 the accounts of Charles v of France refer to the provision of bedsteads for the 'King's servants' at the Hôtel St Pol not as a normal thing, but in order to keep the bedding off a floor which was permanently damp. Whether anything very elaborate was then provided is uncertain and it may have been no more than the bed-boards which the British army used to issue, and perhaps still does, in similar circumstances. A whole century later, in 1492, the ladies of Anne of Brittany were given 'six paillasses pour servir à metre par terre soubz six des licts des dames d'honneur, damoiselles et femmes de chambre de la dicte Dame'; a passage which incidentally serves to establish the contemporary meaning of 'lit'.

If these were the provisions made at that late date for the highborn it is not likely that ordinary men were better off either then or very much later. The plot of Chaucer's 'Reeve's Tale', in which a Cambridge undergraduate tricks the miller of Trumpington's wife into getting into the wrong bed, depends upon there being no difference between the bed hastily prepared upon the floor of the chamber for the student and that in which the miller and his wife always slept. Among the goods of some of the wealthier citizens of Barcelona in the late fifteenth century a bed is only once listed, although this may have been due more to Spanish custom than to lack of furniture. Harrison's famous description of England in 1577 is inclined to underestimate the standards of earlier

24

years and exaggerate those of his own, but he was probably not far from
the truth when he said that the beds of most men a generation or two
before had been 'straw pallets or rough mats covered only with a sheet'.
In the Peak district of Derbyshire in the mid-to-late sixteenth century
the houses of even the more prosperous husbandmen and yeomen
'rarely (had) a good table and even more rarely a chair or even a stool;
even if there were mattresses there was no bedstead'.[9]

That these conditions lasted among some men throughout the
seventeenth century is shown by evidence from the eighteenth and early
nineteenth centuries. In the great house at Cowdray in the mid-
eighteenth century the servants slept on pallets put down in the Long
Gallery at night and rolled up and removed in the morning. In early-
nineteenth century Northumberland some small farmers and their
families slept during the summer in the byre in which the cattle had
been stalled during the winter, a form of transhumance which suggests
that they had no heavy bedsteads to move around. These references
come from a time long after the Middle Ages, let alone the early Middle
Ages, but in revealing the fossilized survivals of earlier habits they
serve to confirm the conclusions which may be deduced from the
necessarily scattered and incomplete evidence from former centuries.

It must not, of course, be supposed that bedsteads were unknown
before the thirteenth century, but even those who slept upon one rarely
had it or thought of having it, to themselves [Plate 66]. Not only did husbands and wives and brothers and sisters sleep together, but total
strangers as well. Medieval chroniclers relate of more than one successful warrior that he magnanimously honoured his captured enemy with
an invitation to share his own bed. One would not expect to find much
furniture upon a battlefield and half a bed might well have seemed
better than none, but sharing of beds was a common and normal
practice at all levels of society in war or peace. Even queens of France
when not sharing a bed with a husband shared it instead with one of
their ladies. It was regarded as a sign of the munificence of William of
Wykham's foundation at Winchester and of the royal foundation at
King's College, Cambridge, that each scholar had a bed to himself; at
Eton they slept two to a bed and three to a bed at Wells choir school.
In the early sixteenth century the priests and gentlemen of the chapel
of the Earl of Northumberland slept two to a bed and the 'children',
that is the young boys, were three to a bed. The smith, the joiner and
the painter on the other hand had a bed apiece, but this was presumably

not a mark of their status, nor yet the result of everybody else refusing to sleep with such fellows, but probably because they slept in their workshops amidst their tools and materials of their trade, just as Oliver Twist three centuries later slept amid the coffins in Mr Sowerberry's shop.[10]

The widespread and in some parts long-lasting practice of sitting upon the floor is further evidence of the scantiness of furniture [Plates 36, 37 and 38]. In the East this was universal and when Robert of Normandy visited Constantinople he and his followers were surprised to find the Emperor and his suite sitting upon cushions in this way. Before joining them the Normans ostentatiously spread their cloaks down to sit upon and as ostentatiously left them lying when they rose to leave, remarking superciliously when reminded of their apparent forgetfulness, 'We do not carry our seats around with us.' Their scorn, however, was more a reflection of their provincialism than of western superiority, for they could have found the same custom in their own country. In wealthy households the floor of the chamber or solar was often richly carpeted. In the thirteenth century Ulrich von Lichtenstein describing his lady's room said, perhaps with some exaggeration, 'The floor could nowhere be seen, for it was bespread with many a fair carpet' and in the *Roman de la Charette* and in *Berthe aux Grands Pieds*, in the *Niebelungenlied* and in the *Lohengrinlied* persons of some importance are described as sitting upon a carpet. The sculpture at Chartres of Pythagoras shows him sitting upon a cushion on the floor, and there can be little doubt that some of the cushions listed in the fourteenth-century inventories of Clemence of Hungary and of Bonne of Luxemburg were meant to be used in this way. Even in the late sixteenth century Brantôme recollected that in his youth it had been usual to sit upon the floor in the Queen's presence. By the time of the first Bourbon kings it was a matter of some surprise to the French to find Anne of Austria 'sitting upon a cushion in the Spanish fashion among her ladies'. In Spain itself, however, where Moorish influence was still strong, sitting upon the floor was the normal thing. The very well-furnished house of Doctor James Torres who died in 1504 had no chairs in it and it was customary up to the end of the seventeenth century for women, at least, to sit upon a cushion or a low stool, and the very low tables peculiar to that country were intended for their convenience.[11]

26

Early medieval conditions made furniture not only scanty but ill-appreciated as well: and the scantiness helped to confirm the low appreciation and the latter in its turn intensified the former. In asserting this one cannot cite any document which positively singles furniture out for denigration, but there are many in which textile furnishings are minutely described and highly praised while furniture in contrast is ignored or passed over in a word or two. There were two main kinds of textile furnishings: hangings and carpets upon walls and floors; and the draperies upon furniture itself, such as bed-coverings and curtains, cushions and table-covers, together with the 'bankers' and 'dorsers' placed upon the seats and backs of chairs and benches. Both kinds were often highly expensive and came in for a great deal of admiration.

Medieval Europeans were nearly as fond of pageantry as modern Englishmen and hangings played a great part upon ceremonial occasions and acquired some of their prestige in more intimate settings from this function [Plate 1]. In 1317–18 Edward II ordered from a mercer of London a great hanging 'for the King's service in his hall upon ceremonial occasions'. When potentates paid state visits to towns the outsides of the houses were often adorned with tapestries, as on the occasion of Queen Margaret's visit to Aberdeen in 1511 when, at least according to Dunbar, 'The streittis war all hung with tapestrie.' By the fifteenth century a large collection of tapestries and other hangings was common in every great household, and in the early sixteenth century Cardinal Wolsey had a vast collection, of immense value. In most inventories the hangings come at the head of the list and are the most expensive items, and when Alexander Neckham was describing his ideal chamber he began not with any piece of furniture, but with curtains or tapestries to hang upon the walls. The previous quotation from Ulrich von Lichtenstein shows that carpets were equally esteemed, and Matthew Paris commented on the surprising contrast, to English eyes, between the humble mules of Eleanor of Castile's suite and their numerous rich carpets.

The distinction drawn earlier between beds and bedsteads was generally observed by medieval and even later writers who lavished words upon the bed-clothes and hangings and ignored the frame-work, if any, which they were placed upon. Ulrich von Lichtenstein was lyrical about his lady's bed upon which 'lay a fair mattress of samite whereon were two quilts of silk, better there might not be, and over all such a bed-cover as no knight ever saw a fairer. There too lay a precious bolster and two most comely pillows.' Of the bed itself he had not a word to say. There are many descriptions extant of late-fourteenth and fifteenth century beds in England, but rarely is anything except the coverings and hangings mentioned. Chaucer was not fond of long descriptions of furniture and furnishings but on one of the rare occasions when he indulged himself he described a bed in the same way:

> . . . a fether-bed,
> Rayèd with gold, and right well cled
> In fyn black satyn doutremer

So common was this attitude that beds were distinguished by the textiles upon them, and in the will of Lady Margaret de Eure of 1378 beds of 'Paris work', of 'York making' and of 'bluet' were referred to not by the material or nature of the frame but of the coverings. John, Lord Nevill of Raby, lieutenant of the Duchy of Aquitaine who died in 1386 left to his brother 'a green bed powdered with falcons, with carpets of the same set', a description in which bed and carpet are thought of as being of the same material.[12]

When the Bohemian noble, Leo de Rozmital, paid a visit to western Europe in 1465–6 he was highly appreciative of the magnificent beds, but always it was their coverings which he commented upon. The one which drew forth his highest praises belonged to a Venetian merchant and was 'covered with cloth of silver and (upon it) were placed two cushions and a pillow ornamented with pearls and precious stones'. Inventories reveal the same preoccupation, and up to a very late date. At the marriage of Margaret of Austria with Juan of Castile in 1497 the clerk who drew up the list of the couple's possessions went into detail to describe the hangings of a bed, but passed over pieces of furniture, and pictures, in a few words. At the Château of Condé in 1569 forty bedsteads were listed, one of which was of oak and the rest of fir or pine, but no attempt at a further description was made. A Roman inventory of 1538 dismisses the bed in one word but describes its hangings in detail.[13]

The very presence not so much of cushions but of carpets and other textiles upon pieces of furniture is an indication of the low estimate of most of it [Plate III]. As early as Gregory of Tours' time the benches in a well-kept noble household were expected to be covered with carpets and

in later years the provision of 'bankers' and 'dorsers' was almost universal. Early manuscripts often show an important personage sitting upon a
chair or bench which, whether plain or highly decorated, is covered
with a rich textile. One of the most magnificent of later pieces of
furniture was the dresser or buffet upon which gold and silver plate
was displayed; in its early form, however, it was generally a mere
series of open shelves covered by a rich cloth. It would be wrong to
give the impression that an appreciation of textiles necessarily meant a
denigration of furniture, for in later years both were highly esteemed,
but up to about the beginning of the fifteenth century there was a sharp
contrast between the admiration bestowed upon the one and the comparative lack of interest in the other. Havard studied many French
documents, but the earliest in which furniture was described as fully
as fabrics was the inventory of the chamber of Jeanne of Laval at the
Château of Angers in 1470.

Heavy construction

Besides being scanty and ill-esteemed early furniture was crude as
well. No one of these qualities was the cause of the others, all were the
result of social conditions and domestic habits, but each of the three
intensified the other two. The crudest pieces have had less chance than
their betters to survive, but in the churches of Milton Bryant in Bedford-
shire, of Somersham and Wistow in Huntingdonshire, of Orton in
Westmorland [Plate 39] are chests formed from hollowed-out logs.
They might perhaps be written off as insular oddities were it not that
in 1206 Pope Innocent III, when collecting money for a crusade,
directed that a 'hollow trunk' with two locks should be provided in
every parish for this purpose. There is little reason to think these
English chests were made as a result of Innocent's appeal; they more
probably represent the kind of simple, and presumably well-known,
receptacle that he had in mind.

Most early furniture was of far more sophistication than this, but
since timber at the time was almost invariably hewn with an axe
rather than cut with a saw, and since the production of thin timbers
was an extremely difficult process before the invention of the saw mill,
wooden furniture at first had to be made of timber of very heavy
scantling. Even in later years, when the technical means for providing
lighter scantlings was at hand, the conservative bias of gild regulations

sometimes worked towards the same end. In Florence the gilds insisted that any piece should be made throughout of the same wood and forbade much worked decoration, for example in the form of a cornice along the top; as late as 1384 any craftsman who wished to make a chest not of regulation size had to pay a fine for the privilege. As a result such forms as chests and cupboards were made of heavy planks in one piece tenoned into equally heavy uprights at the corners, a method of construction well illustrated by surviving chests in many churches [Plate 27]. Perhaps one would not expect furniture in a poor country church to be of the highest standards, but pieces from much wealthier abbeys and cathedrals, and sometimes of considerable elaboration, were made in the same way: the cupboard at Halberstadt [Plate 11], the hutches at Valère [Plates 31 and 32], the chest, much restored, from Chester Cathedral. In those areas where, for one reason or another, the carpenter had little competition from an upstart joiner, furniture of heavy scantling continued to be made long after more refined methods of construction had come into general use. In the Victoria and Albert Museum there is a cupboard made of hewn planks of mid-sixteenth century date, and a chest in Corfe Castle church of similar construction is dated 1672. These examples are not wholly a reflection of English backwardness, for the Rijksmuseum at Amsterdam has a plank-made chest of sixteenth-century date and of local manufacture. The influence of the carpenter is perhaps most clearly seen in Spain where early furniture is amazingly coarse. Spanish carpenters enjoyed their greatest opportunities in working upon the much admired wooden ceilings. These were not seen at close range and depended for their effect not upon any refined workmanship but upon their general design and bold decoration, and so the carpenters not only joined pieces of timber together with rough nails, but allowed the nails to protrude from the far side. The effect of this technique, or lack of technique, upon woodwork of a different purpose is seen in some pieces of Spanish furniture in which not only are nails used but their tips are allowed to stand clear of the timber in the same unfinished way.

Common pieces of domestic furniture, apart from chests and cupboards, have hardly survived at all from an early age, but their sturdy build can be deduced from other sources [Plate 40]. In many regions in which timber was scarce and an easily split stone obtainable much furniture was made of the latter material. Early timber furniture has survived less well, but its direct successors in eighteenth and nineteenth

30

century Scandinavian peasant houses probably reflect its qualities
reasonably accurately, and are of very rough workmanship [Plate 43].
Nor was this true only of peasant furniture: an illustration from a
fifteenth-century French translation of Boccaccio shows a lady of rank,
or of leisure, sitting upon a barrel chair of crude construction.

Caskets and fold-stools

But if early furniture as a whole was scarce and clumsy and viewed
with indifference there were nevertheless some important exceptions,
and they occurred in those exceptional situations in which the general
conditions of medieval society and the general influences upon the
nature of furniture were absent or were of less importance. One class
of men which was free from many of the restrictions outlined above was
the clergy, and especially the monastic and cathedral clergy. Their
collective wealth was enough to allow of ample accommodation of
various kinds within their buildings and to liberate them from the
burdens which pressed upon the great majority of laymen; at the same
time their way of life was more sedentary than that of the great magnates and the feudal calls upon their wealth were far less. In consequence
most furniture of a date before the end of the thirteenth century and
particularly the relatively immobile pieces have an ecclesiastical
provenance. It is sometimes argued that this does not show that
furniture was commoner amongst them than among laymen, and for
two reasons: in the first place abbeys and major churches were less
likely to be sacked and plundered than secular buildings and at the
same time their contents were less susceptible to the vagaries of taste
and consequent destruction or neglect; and secondly, laymen often
deposited their valuables in churches for safe-keeping and some, if not
many of the pieces now in ecclesiastical ownership, may not have belonged to churchmen originally. These points are far from trivial and
have to be allowed considerable weight, but when all allowance has
been made for them it still remains true that many other treasures
equally susceptible to destruction and even some furniture, of an easily
portable nature, have survived in secular keeping. Secular furniture has
certainly suffered more than ecclesiastical from the passage of time and
the present difference in numbers between the survivors of the two
kinds exaggerates an originally smaller contrast, but it has not created
one which never existed.

In saying this it has to be admitted at once that problems of dating before 1300 are far more difficult than in the centuries which followed. The bench from Alpirsbach in the Black Forest [Plate 46], was dated by Feulner to the thirteenth century and by Müller-Christensen to the late twelfth; Luthmer ascribed the so-called 'Bishop's Throne' at Goslar to the eleventh century, but von Falke thought that it might be as late as the thirteenth; Havard was confident that the cupboard at Obazine [Plate 17] was of the fourteenth century, whilst Jacqueline Viaux thinks it is of the twelfth century.[14]

A pretence at an assured dating of these pieces, and of others, would be in the nature of a confidence trick, but at the same time it is clear that there is a wide unanimity, apart from Havard's surprising date for Obazine, that these are among the earliest surviving examples and that they are at any rate earlier than *c*. 1300. Other pieces of which the same may be said are the cupboards at Bayeux and formerly at Noyon, at Halberstadt [Plate 11] and Chester, and the hutches at Valère [Plates 31 and 32]. Apart from their date they all have this in common: that they are either at present in ecclesiastical buildings, and as far as is known always have been, or else they have come from them, as for example the so-called 'Bishop's Throne' at Goslar which was originally in the Cathedral. All of these, and a few others which may be contemporary, do not amount to more than a handful, but they illustrate the total predominance of ecclesiastical productions amongst the surviving immoveable pieces from the earliest period.[15]

Part of the price which the clergy paid for their privileged status in the Middle Ages was to writhe under an endemic anti-clericalism. It would be unwise to believe every denunciation of the moralists and every jibe of the satirists, but there may well have been some foundation for the charge made by Villon and by the author of the *Chronique Scandaleuse* that many clerics enjoyed a level of comfort and even luxury in their style of living which was otherwise found only amongst kings and princes.

Apart from the examples mentioned above and a few others all the surviving furniture of this early period is small and easily portable. The peripatetic way of life of those men who could most have afforded to furnish inhibited the use of heavy pieces in their houses, but on the other hand encouraged the production of lighter articles which could be carried around, and one of the reasons for the wide use of textiles was the ease with which they could be packed into a travelling chest and

Stools and thrones

1 King David as a harper, from a romanesque sculpture. As befits either his rank or his favour with God he sits upon a fold-stool.

2 Eustace Deschamps presenting his poems to Charles VI of France. The king sits, as his Dark-Age predecessors had done, upon a fold-stool with lion's-head ornament on the tops of the stretchers.

4 (*opposite*) Sixteenth-century X-chair in Winchester Cathedral, supposed to have been used by Queen Mary at her marriage to Philip of Spain.

3 Richly ornamented fold-stool from Styria c. 1200: a symbol of its owner's dignity.

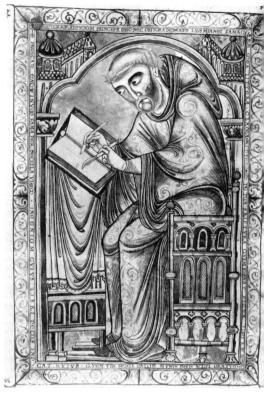

5 (*left*) Charles the Bald enthroned as Holy
Roman Emperor. His seat appears to be of
stone, with inlays of marble and metal. From
a mid-ninth-century manuscript.

6 (*right*) A monk seated on a chair with round-
headed arcading. The uprights with protruding
knobs are commoner in metalwork than in
timber. From a twelfth-century English manuscript.

7 Chair with turned ornament from Wales
or the West Country, *c.* 1600.

8 Edward the Confessor on his throne. The chair has lion-head ornament, a more realistic rendering of Plate 9; from the Bayeux Tapestry.

9 Bench with ends in the form of demi-lions, from an eleventh-century English manuscript. It is almost certain that the artist had never seen any bench as magnificent as this and was drawing what he would have liked to see.

10 Christ enthroned, sitting upon a chair with arm-rests and a back. From a ninth-century Spanish manuscript.

11 and 12 For a long time only the very great could aspire to a chair. In Plate 11 (*opposite*), from a fourteenth-century French manuscript, Philippe VI presides over the Court of Peers seated on an elaborately decorated fold-stool. The peers sit on stools or benches, the commonalty sit on the floor or stand. In Plate 12 (*left*), from an early sixteenth-century German engraving, *Check to the King*, the King alone has a chair. The courtiers stand, and even Death, belying his egalitarian reputation, has more respect for his victim than to sit.

13 Mid-fifteenth-century drawing of chairs, reserved for the great, and stools, for ordinary people, swept up together as a symbol of social chaos.

14 Sculptured scene of Christ sitting upon a chair without back or sides, on a capital from Autun of *c.* 1150.
15 Chair of fold-stool type but with a high back, from an eleventh-century south Italian ivory.

16 Chair with a half back on a mid-twelfth-century capital from Reading Abbey.

transported from house to house. For this purpose the comparatively
light and compact folding-stool, ever at hand for the comfort and
dignity of its owner, was useful and almost indispensable. A very early
specimen is the so-called 'Throne of Dagobert' in the Bibliothèque
Nationale in Paris: later ones are the mid-thirteenth century stool in
the Cathedral Museum in Perugia, that of *c.* 1200 in Vienna [Plate 3]
and the stool in the Nonnberg Convent near Salzburg, which is known
to have been given to the Abbess in 1242 and may have been made
considerably earlier.

Early manuscript illuminations, and especially those of the tenth
century, often portray rulers sitting upon fold-stools and it is clear that
these were more than merely useful household articles. They differ from
most furniture of the period in having a very long and honourable
ancestry. As a matter of interest one may mention that they were known
in dynastic Egypt, in Bronze Age Denmark and in ancient Greece, but
what is of importance for their later development is that they were
widely used by the Romans and especially by the field commanders of
Roman armies. Post-Roman specimens based upon Roman models
have survived from all the centuries of the invasions and there seems
little doubt that when the leaders of barbarian war-bands were transmuting themselves into territorial rulers they took over the Roman
commander's fold-stool as a symbol of majesty, and used it as a throne.
When Abbot Suger in the early twelfth century added a rigid back to a
stool which even then was of considerable antiquity and called it the
'Throne of Dagobert' he had no authority for ascribing it to one
Frankish king rather than another; but that it had been the throne of
an early Carolingian ruler is very likely, for it closely resembles the
chair which a contemporary illumination portrays Lothar I sitting
upon at his coronation in 843. The fold-stool was exactly suited to
serve as the chair of kings or other potentates, for it had within it all the
prestige of Imperial Rome and at the same time was portable enough
to accompany its wandering owner wherever he went. Of course, its
use was not necessarily confined to royalty. Other important laymen,
and ecclesiastics such as abbots, bishops and saints, are often shown
sitting upon a fold-stool in early illuminations, but it was still the
preserve of men highly distinguished from their fellows in one way or
another [Plate 1].

Because it had these qualities the fold-stool acquired others. The
'Throne of Dagobert' is of gilded bronze with lions' claw feet and with

lions' heads at the tops of the stretchers; the Nonnberg stool has similar decoration with the feet in bronze and the heads in ivory and with ivory inlay upon the stretchers; the one in Perugia is inlaid in ivory and metal. If the later writers of the popular 'chansons' and 'romans' are to be believed the Emir of Egypt had a fold-stool made of ivory and Charlemagne had one of gold. Fold-stools are not the only chairs surviving from a remote age: several bishops' thrones of the eleventh and twelfth centuries have come down to us, for example those of stone in the Italian cathedrals of Anagni, Bari and Canosa and the chair formerly in the cathedral at Goslar. These belonged to men who were something other than great magnates, and they serve to illustrate the differing effects upon furniture of different ways of life. The peripatetic king or great noble had a richly decorated portable seat: the more sedentary bishop had a fixed one.

The rich decoration upon fold-stools must be ascribed to their peculiar function, and although they had their origin in the years before medieval society was fully developed they, or their lineal descendants, continued in use long afterwards. Their subsequent history is best considered here because of the light that it throws upon earlier developments. In later years much other furniture was also highly decorated, but even then fold-stools continued to be the most highly decorated of all. The earliest fold-stools were made of expensive materials and were richly ornamented while the earliest fixed chairs such as Charlemagne's marble coronation seat at Aix-la-Chapelle and the 'frith-stool', probably a bishop's throne, in Hexham church, Northumberland, were by contrast very much plainer. In the mid-fourteenth century King John of France paid an immense sum for a 'faudesteuil' whose frame was covered with thin pieces of rock crystal and silver and decorated with illuminations of the royal arms and biblical scenes and characters. It has been denied that this was necessarily a folding stool rather than an X-chair – a chair modelled upon the fold-stool and with the front and back legs on each side crossing each other in the form of a letter X, but no longer collapsible or particularly light. The point cannot now be determined, but whether a fold-stool or its successor is meant in this case the aura of kingship still clung to it, for a miniature from Froissart shows Charles v of France at his coronation sitting upon just such a chair, and in another illumination of 1383, in which Eustace Deschamps presents his poem to Charles vi, the king sits upon a fold-stool with the traditional lion's head ornament on the tops of the stretchers [Plate 2].

As late as the sixteenth century X-chairs still tended to be reserved for kings and princes. When Anthonis Mor came to England he painted Queen Mary sitting in one, and the example preserved in Winchester Cathedral is traditionally said to be that which was used at her wedding to Philip of Spain [Plate 4]. Another descendant of the fold-stool appeared in the sixteenth century: an armless folding chair with a reclining back. The inventory of Catherine de Medici of 1589 has several entries which appear to refer to a chair of this sort, generally the prerogative of those distinguished enough to dine at the head of the table. Even much later, long after the fold-stool had lost its unique position, it retained its renown for luxury and the name of 'fauteuil' was appropriated for the rich and elaborately upholstered armchairs of seventeenth-century France.[16]

One form of furniture which has many affinities with the fold-stool is the small box or casket, varying considerably in size, often no more than a few inches in dimension in any direction, but never too big to be picked up and carried by one man. Caskets and fold-stools are alike in being portable, in being richly decorated and in surviving in a few instances from a very early period. The special function of caskets was to hold small valuables of all kinds: a French writer of the early fourteenth century knew them as receptacles for jewellery, an inventory of the Duke of Normandy in 1363 lists one which held spices and another inventory of 1399 described one as 'full of relics'. With this as their main purpose they were more portable than fold-stools and accompanied their owner even more closely; the plot of the late medieval romance of Lancelot of the Lake depends upon a young lady's carrying a rich and beautiful casket in front of her on her horse.

Like fold-stools, caskets enjoyed a great amount of prestige, not because of any essential connection with royalty, but because of their precious contents; and as these were often holy relics caskets had some sanctity as well. In consequence, and because, like fold-stools, they were portable, so like them, they were highly decorated. A very early example is the Franks casket of whalebone in the British Museum, probably of the late seventh or early eighth century [Plate 18]. It is less than ten inches long and is covered with carvings in low relief of episodes from Roman legend, from the Bible, and from Norse mythology, and it has a runic inscription. Its date and its origin are matters of dispute, but it is clearly from a northern milieu. Whalebone is too humdrum a material to be used for anybody with pretensions who

35

has easy access to a more exotic one, and as the working of ivory was well known at Charlemagne's court, it is not surprising that the small boxes in which he placed some relics he had acquired should have been of that material. Ivory was not the only expensive material used in this way and in the College of Audenne at Namur there is a casket of about 700 made of bronze. Wood was also used but it was embellished with other materials: a very early example of Frankish derivation was enriched with bronze, iron and bone, with interlace ornament. A mid-twelfth century example, now in the Fitzwilliam Museum at Cambridge and probably made by a craftsman from Lorraine, is of lead embellished with silver and enamel [Plate 19]. At a much earlier date Gregory of Tours claimed to have found a casket filled with martyrs' relics and made of silver.[17]

Caskets continued to be distinguished by their wealth of ornament into the twelfth century and the 'little coffer' which belonged to 'Fair Rosamund', the mistress of Henry II, was described with awe as 'made by a wonder craft . . . There it seemeth that giants fight, beasts startle, fowls flee and fishes move', a reference apparently not merely to the richness but to the liveliness of the carving as well. The Charlemagne legend was still a useful political weapon in the twelfth century and when the Emperor Frederick I was in possession of a piece of bone which was confidently asserted to be Charlemagne's arm he had a magnificent repository made for it. The casket is now in the Louvre; it is of wood covered with copper and silver, partly gilt and enamelled and carved with figures of saints beneath an arcade [Plate 20]. Equally rich in materials, in enamelling and carving is the so-called 'Cassette of St Louis' of the thirteenth century in the church of Dammarie (Seine-et-Marne). By the thirteenth century some caskets were remarkable not merely for their profuse decoration, but for their cunning use of contrasted materials as well. An example in the Minster church at Essen has richly carved acanthus-leaf and other motifs in a broad band upon the lid and sides, and a mosaic of light and dark woods; another in Halberstadt museum is inlaid in chequer-work and herring-bone patterns.

Just as fold-stools and X-chairs seem always to have kept one step ahead of other furniture in the amount of decoration lavished upon them so too do caskets. Even as early as the thirteenth century Cologne ivory workers were producing small caskets with highly decorated figure-subjects, for example of ecclesiastics and of scenes from the story

36

of Tristan. By the early fourteenth century, when carving of some elaboration was appearing upon heavy timber pieces, Parisian craftss men were turning out a great number of ivory caskets even more elaborate and sophisticated. Several examples, in the Hermitage at Leningrad, in the British Museum and in the Victoria and Albert Museum [Plate 21], are of interest both for their richness and for their continued use of the Arthurian legends with a bias towards the romantic episodes of Tristan and Isolde. Work of this sort was not wholly confined to Paris, for in the last named museum there is another casket of wood and probably of English manufacture, with two scenes from the same story, placed within panels on the lid formed by delicately ornamented iron bands. In later years, although ivory continued in favour, even more expensive materials were sometimes used: a French inventory of 1399 lists a casket of silver with enamelled scenes from the life of Christ and at Vincennes in 1418 there was one of jasper decorated with gold and with carvings at the corners enriched with sapphires, emeralds and pearls.[18]

By the end of the Middle Ages fold-stools had turned into the relatively immobile X-chairs and at about the same time caskets were beginning to lose their formerly essentially portable character. Since they were small they could, of course, always be carried, but the mention in 1507 in an inventory of Anne of Brittany of a 'box of crystal' and in the inventory of the royal furniture of Louis XIV of five such boxes, which were clearly never intended to travel around very much, reveals the change which had come over them. By about 1500 much other furniture was as richly ornamented and made of as expensive materials as caskets once had been, and caskets themselves were often plainer than before.

This development, however, was the reflection not merely of an increase in luxury among the very wealthy, but also of the spread of some comfort to lower social levels. Compared with the fourteenth-century references cited above, another of 1463 from the will of an English townsman has a more homely ring: 'a lityle grene coffre for kerchys'. The description both of the container and of its contents reveal that an article which had once been reserved for the aristocracy was being given a more sober form and was accommodating more commonplace objects for more ordinary men.

Chests

Caskets and boxes were well enough for safeguarding small articles like jewellery and precious relics, but many men had other valuables of greater bulk and for these a chest was needed. As early as the seventh century the essential connection between a chest and valuables was well established and appears in Gregory of Tour's story of the Emperor Justin, who was so greedy of money that he had iron chests to safeguard his hoard of coins. Very few men could have chests made of iron, but that wooden chests were intended as places of security is shown by the fondness for covering them with iron bands and straps. It has been argued that this was nothing more than an admission of their poor construction in early years, when the carpenters who made them knew no better joint than a mortice and tenon and in consequence used iron straps to make good the deficiencies of their skill. There may be something in this, although in Essex, at any rate, and by the thirteenth century, carpenters knew many other joints, including several sophisticated variants of the dovetail. That in any case security was at least one reason for using iron is shown by later references. The inventory of Charlotte of Savoy of 1483 lists more than forty chests and of these one was of iron and contained purses filled with coins; when Thomas Coryat visited the Mint at Venice in 1608 he was struck by the 'marvailous strong chests hooped with yron and wrought full of great massy yron nails, in which is kept nothing but money'. In some parts of France 'huche' had acquired by the late Middle Ages the meaning of 'caisse', a place of deposit of public money and 'the public chest' used to be a common idiom in English for official funds.[19]

It was for this reason that when chests were not deposited in a special place for safe-keeping, like the one which the Countess of Angoulême kept doubly-safe in the chapel of the castle of Cognac, they were lodged in the chamber or solar of a private dwelling. This room was the most difficult of access in the whole house, almost invariably on an upper floor, and reached from within the hall and often by a narrow winding stair. The practice, of course, carried its own risks, and medieval accounts of the sack of a city or a house often relate how the more knowing plunderers made straight for the chamber, where they expected to find the chests and valuables [Plate 25]. In 1455, at a time when some powerful men in England found it necessary or convenient to dispense with the legal processes by which they usually got their own way, there

38

was much plundering by the armed retainers of great lords, and James Gresham succintly described one such incident in a letter to John Paston: 'In the meantime his meny rob his chamber and rifled his hutches and trussed such as they could get together and carried it away on his own horses.'[20]

The claim that every medieval dwelling had a chest in it probably exaggerates their numbers in early years, for the Colchester inventories of 1294 and 1301 and Genoese ones of the late thirteenth century noticeably fail to mention chests, and Alexander Neckham omitted them from the list of articles in his ideal chamber. Nevertheless even in early years chests must have been very common and they were used not only for holding valuables but to transport all the household goods which accompanied great men on their journeys. This may well have been their original function for in French the word 'bahut' which at first meant the leather covering upon a wicker-work frame placed around travelling chests became in time a general word for any sort of chest. By the fifteenth century many chests were never meant to be transported anywhere and in England the portable kind came to be called a 'trussing chest' or 'trussing coffer' and its stay-at-home cousin a 'great standing chest'.[21]

Although the chest was always a common piece of furniture it is difficult to point with confidence to any early ones which undoubtedly belonged to laymen. Most of the survivors are in churches and the ecclesiastical origin of the majority of them at any rate is hardly in doubt. A smaller number has found its way into museums, but most of these may have come from the same source. It is equally difficult to say which, if any, were meant to be portable. It might be supposed that delicately ornamented furniture would suffer severely from continual travelling and that it was the plainer chests which were the portable ones. However there are some almost wholly undecorated chests, of which the 'dug-outs' mentioned earlier are extreme examples, whose provenance and limited storage space in relation to size and weight argue against their having been intended as carriers. At the same time one of the very rare early illustrations of a chest actually in transit, from the mid-twelfth century *Hortus Deliciarum* of Herrade of Landsperg, shows a very plain example [Plate 24] and it seems likely that there was a tendency, and nothing more than a tendency, for portable chests to be less highly decorated than their immobile fellows.

French documents often refer to the manufacture of chests and of as many bahuts to go with them. Originally the bahut may have been a more or less easily detachable covering, but the later and wider meaning of the word and the definition as late as the seventeenth century of a 'coffre de campagne' as one covered with leather suggests that the leather-covering before long was permanently attached not to a wicker-frame but to the body of the chest and that this practice was especially true of travelling chests. English references seem to lend considerable support to this conjecture. A very early chest, mentioned in the Household Roll for 1265 of the Countess of Leicester, was of worked leather banded with iron; it was used for packing silver vessels in and was almost certainly meant to be portable. Those rare documents which distinguish clearly between portable and immobile chests often describe the former as leather-covered: a fifteenth-century inventory of the Duchess of Suffolk lists a travelling chest 'covered with black leather and bound with iron' and a portable 'chair of estate' which was apparently carried around in 'a case of leather'. In 1556 Sir John Gage possessed 'two trussing coffers covered with black leather of Flanders making, bound with iron'.[22]

Some chests developed 'standards' or legs at the corners, presumably in order to keep the base away from a damp floor. Some of these, such as those at Valère, had long standards and were never meant to be transported any distance, although others, like the examples in the Musée des Arts Décoratifs and the Musée de Cluny at Paris, had much shorter ones. Those standards which did not positively hinder certainly did nothing to help in making a chest portable and in general they are a sign of immobility, but here again there is no absolute rule, for the chests shown in transit in the *Hortus Deliciarum* have short standards.

Large chests must have been difficult to transport in any circumstances and it is probable that most travelling examples were considerably smaller than the massive pieces to be seen in many churches today. The Duchess of Suffolk's travelling chest was described as 'square' and since most surviving chests are rectangular, and if they were as wide as they are long would be wholly unmanageable, it is likely that hers was considerably smaller than them. Sir John Gage's 'trussing coffers' were meant 'to carry upon a horse' and cannot have been of any great size. The use of smaller chests for travelling is suggested again by two entries under the year 1512 in Anton Tucher's 'Household Book', wherein a small iron chest belonging to Angelo Schawer, the Fugger agent at Rome, is compared with another which

Cupboards, caskets and chests

17 Cupboard at Obazine, Corrèze, France, of uncertain date but probably late twelfth or early thirteenth century.

18 The Franks casket, of the seventh or eighth century. It is covered with scenes from the Bible, from Roman legend and from Norse mythology, and has a runic inscription.

19 Twelfth-century lead casket with silver and enamel enrichments, probably by a Lorrainer.

20 Late twelfth-century casket of wood sheathed with copper and silver and partly gilt and enamelled; purpose-made to hold a piece of bone supposed to have been part of Charlemagne's arm.

21 Fourteenth-century ivory casket. It is carved with scenes from the *Siege of the Castle of Love*, in which the assailants and defenders pelt one another with flowers, and reflects the current cult of Romance.

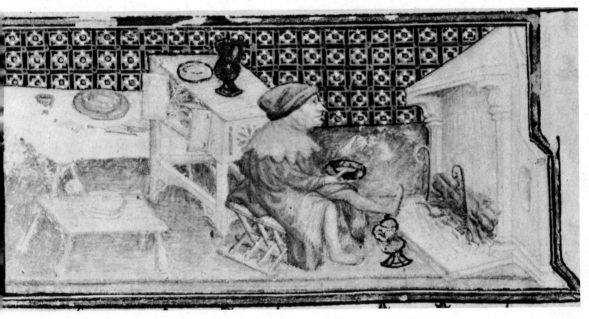

24 (*above left*) Part of the baggage train of the Queen of Sheba; a small travelling chest is slung across a camel's back. From a twelfth-century Alsatian manuscript.
25 (*above right*) *The Death of Dives*, from a late thirteenth-century manuscript. While a demon carries away the rich man's soul, another rogue steals the money-bags kept in a chest at the foot of the bed.
26 The comfort of a lightly made seat drawn up to the fire, an illustration of 'January' from a late fourteenth-century manuscript.

22 (*opposite above*) Sixteenth-century Swedish chest with lifting rings to slide a stout pole through.
23 (*opposite below*) Plank-built German chest of *c.* 1300. The front is covered with well-carved, striking and often charming animal figures, but all in a wholly unorganized design.

27 Oak chest, probably late thirteenth century; built of heavy planks and with stout cross members.

28 Medieval chest in Laneham church, Nottinghamshire, with palmette ornament and with remains of arcading at the bases of the styles.

29 Thirteenth-century chest from Voxtorp, Sweden; ironwork decoration with reminiscences of Dark-Age zoomorphic ornament.

30 Medieval chest with shields of arms painted on the inside of the lid, perhaps of *c*. 1340.

31 and 32 Hutches of softwood from Valère, Switzerland; probably early thirteenth century. The most outstanding surviving examples of the use of Romanesque architectural forms in furniture ornament.

Lucas Siczinger carried with him on his journey to Venice. In the
Hortus Deliciarum, all the chests of the Queen of Sheba's baggage train
are small and are slung across the backs of camels.[32]

Many surviving chests have or had an iron ring or handle attached
to each end and it has been suggested that this shows that they were
portable. The argument is not conclusive however, for a sixteenth-
century chest in Spaldwick church in Huntingdonshire and another of
1703 in St Ives church in the same county have similar attachments
and it is unlikely that they were ever meant to travel far. In any case,
the provision of a single ring is perhaps not much to the point, for being
made of thick planks a chest of any size was extremely heavy in its own
right; when filled with plate or armour or textiles its weight must have
been formidable and hardly to be managed by a man at each end
getting a couple of fingers through a ring. A sixteenth-century example
from Sweden perhaps better reveals how things were done: at each end
are two small rings placed some distance apart and from each an iron
bar runs to a single larger ring big enough for a stout pole to be slipped
through it [Plate 22]. In this way the combined efforts of several men
could be utilized to lift the chest and carry it to a waiting cart or
perhaps sling it between two horses. A leather-covered and iron-bound
Spanish chest of the fifteenth century appears to have had originally
an iron ring at each end of its front and rear faces, an arrangement
which would have allowed a similar use of linking pieces to two central
rings. Some of the chests with a single ring at each end may have
had similar but less efficient attachments, but if they did not it is difficult
to see how the rings were for much more than moving the chest about
within a room or at the most within a house.[24]

It would be hazardous to claim that no early travelling chests have
survived, but it seems highly probable that very few of those chests
which have survived were meant to be portable. In one way this is
merely to repeat in other words that ecclesiastical furniture has been
preserved while secular has not, for the peripatetic lay magnate might
be expected to have more portable and fewer immobile chests than the
sedentary bishop or abbot. Nevertheless this is not the whole answer,
for some churchmen also needed travelling chests and three other
reasons may be adduced. Firstly, travelling chests by their very function
were more likely than their stay-at-home fellows to suffer damage and
consequent destruction; secondly, if they were in general smaller than
immobile chests they were probably of little use for storage once

society had changed and their owners had abandoned their vagabond ways; and thirdly most of them were probably less highly decorated and consequently less likely to be preserved as objects of aesthetic value or as curiosities.

Ornament

Furniture throughout the early centuries was homogeneous not only in its environment and in the forms which that gave rise to, but in its mode of decoration as well. With rare exceptions ornament was either in overall patterning unrelated to the proportions of the piece it was decorating, or else it was applied to isolated places upon a whole surface or to isolated parts of the structure. Motifs might be few and monotonous or many and various, but they were rarely organized into a composition or a series of compositions. The chests in the Brunswick Museum and in the Kunstgewerbemuseum at Berlin [Plate 23] are extreme cases which emphasize the general tendency. Their fronts are divided into many small panels each carved with a separate subject of beasts or birds or fabulous monsters. The effect is extremely rich and it would be difficult to find more profuse decoration. Taken separately each compartment is a composition in itself, and some are very good, but all of them considered together are merely so many separate elements, unrelated to one another, uncomposed, and sadly revealing that a whole is sometimes less than the sum of its parts.

Two reasons for this are clear enough and have already been touched on: the low esteem in which most furniture was held did not encourage the expenditure of a great amount of wealth and thought upon it, and on the other hand one of the most highly esteemed forms, the fold-stool, had no surfaces large enough to be organized into a composition. These reasons, however, are not the only ones nor even the most important and for an adequate explanation one has to look beyond furniture at the state of the other arts, and particularly interior decoration and architecture.

The nature of the medieval house, and the conditions of life of its occupiers, affected the decoration upon its walls as much as it affected the furniture within them. In all houses it was expensive, and in those only occasionally occupied it was uneconomic, to line the walls with wooden panelling, and the normal practice was to cover them with hangings, which could be easily carried from house to house, or with

42

paint. By the thirteenth century wainscot was not uncommon, at least in royal houses, but it was of heavy boards and of the plainest form and was itself generally painted. The negative effect of this wide use of hangings and of paint was the absence of any incentive to the wood-workers to develop their skill in the direction of joinery and of elaborate ornament and in consequence they were unable to play much part in decorating furniture.

The positive result was of more immediate importance. Most wall painting was in the form of plain colouring or of overall patterning of the kind, for example, so beloved of Henry III of 'gold stars upon a green ground'. Many hangings were of equally simple design and so too in all likelihood were the imitations of curtains which were painted upon the walls of Westminster Palace in the mid-thirteenth century, of Francesco Datini's house at Prato over a century later and at the Ca d'Oro in Venice in the early fifteenth century. In all these cases the paint was applied to masonry or rather to a plaster rendering upon it, but many houses everywhere in the Middle Ages, and some houses over wide areas for long afterwards, were built of wood and this too was treated in the same way. Often simple colouring was employed, but sometimes, as at Ludgershall in 1245 and at Guildford Castle in 1255, paint was used to pick out the main posts in the framework or the free-standing posts of an arcade. Where paint was used in these ways, either to cover a large surface or to emphasize the structural members in a timber building, it is not surprising that wooden furniture, and especially when it was of a heavy scantling and simple form, received similar treatment, and references to the painting of it are widespread in space and time.[25]

In his *Lestorie des Engles* written sometime before 1147, Gaimar described the bed of the tenth-century Saxon King, Edgar, as having painted posts and two Genoese inventories of the late twelfth century mention painted beds and chests. The mid-thirteenth century records of Henry III's reign have several references to the painting of furniture and so too have Florentine records of the fourteenth century and they reveal that in the early part of that century there were specialized 'painters of chests'. As late as 1580-1 Montaigne noted in his travel diary that most Swiss furniture was painted and the frequency of the practice in England is shown partly by documents and partly by surviving pieces which still retain a considerable amount of paintwork upon them. In one way, of course, the painting of furniture has never ceased and much of the painted peasant furniture still common enough in Austria, Scandinavia and parts of Germany, is of the eighteenth and nineteenth centuries. The important difference however is that in early years even the best furniture of kings was often painted, while later painting was usually confined to the furniture of lesser men or to the less important furniture of the great.[26]

Although few examples have survived and detailed records are rare it seems clear that most of this painting was very simple. King Edgar's bed, if Gaimar is to be believed, was merely coloured in vermilion and so too were the legs of a chair which belonged to the Duchess of Orleans in the fifteenth century. The two early cupboards at Bayeux and, formerly, at Noyon appear to have had overall patterning upon them. A 'great chair' belonging to Charles v of France was painted with fleurs-de-lys in 1380 and a Florentine piece was enriched in 1418 with stars. At a much later date painted arabesques and running floral decoration were common motifs upon Elizabethan and Jacobean beds.

The unorganized manner of this decoration is shown by those rare documents which refer to gilding. Gilding is not quite in the same category as ordinary paint, for on the one hand it is very expensive, and on the other it has been used at many periods to enhance isolated parts of a valuable piece or isolated ornament upon it. Overall gilding, however, is in the same decorative mode as any other colouring. Naturally it was not common and even the extravagant Henry III was once moved to forbid its use upon a surface where it was not likely to be seen; but he was not always so thrifty. In 1246-7 he ordered the benches in the Queen's Chamber at Winchester to be gilt and in 1250-1 the responsible official at Windsor was warned to take care that the king's seat in the hall there should be 'completely ornamented with gold and paint'. Even in later years, and when among wealthy men furniture had acquired a very different grammar of ornament, pieces were sometimes gilt all over. De Commines reported that in the best Venetian houses of the late fifteenth century bedsteads were 'of gold colour' and in 1505 the wife of Giacomo Sanuti of Bologna owned a bedstead of 'gilded wood'. In all of these examples the influence of the plain colouring and simple patterning of early mural decoration is clear enough.[27]

The overall patterning of early wall-painting was sometimes broken up by roundels or panels with individual subjects and Von Falke has shown that the manner and many of the motifs of the painted ceiling at

44

Cologne are paralleled upon fourteenth-century German chests. On these the decoration is in relief, but it seems likely, as he suggests, that similar ornamentation was also carried out in paint. Among the commonest motifs in wall-painting were shields of arms and these can certainly be found upon painted chests. An example in the Burrell Collection at Glasgow with what are perhaps the arms of Bishop Dangerville of Durham upon it, may be of *c.* 1340 [Plate 30]. The plain chests which Italian girls took with them when entering a nunnery were often painted in a similar manner, and it is likely that this was a very common kind of decoration.

Beyond all this, however, early mural painting sometimes took the form of single figures, life-size or larger, and occasionally of considerable grandeur. The qualities which made furniture such a difficult medium for most decoration made it extremely suitable for this, for they ensured a large amount of free surface to work upon and very little extraneous ornament to distract the eye from the painting itself. The cupboard in Halberstadt Cathedral, probably of the early thirteenth century, has two of its main faces painted with a nearly life-size figure of a female saint. The painting is much restored, but it probably retains some of the qualities of the original and imparts a monumental simplicity of decoration seldom equalled in any later furniture [Plate 11]. The subject-matter in conjunction with the provenance might seem to suggest that such works were found only among churchmen, but there are grounds for thinking that they sometimes appeared in lay surroundings as well. In 1250–1 the King's seat in the hall at Windsor Castle was ordered to be painted with a figure of the king holding a sceptre in his hand, and it seems probable that what was intended was a nearly life-size figure upon a tall chair-back. On a slightly smaller scale, but still in a somewhat monumental vein, is a bed, now in a chapel of the church, from the Ospedale del Ceppo at Pistoia; it is painted with half-length figures of the Virgin and Child dominating smaller figures of angels.[28]

The best known and undoubtedly the most beautiful examples of painted furniture are the Italian cassoni of the Renaissance, but they are the products of an aesthetic milieu rather different from that of the early Middle Ages and do not help us to visualize the appearance of their predecessors. Perhaps more helpful are the numerous pieces of eighteenth- and nineteenth-century peasant furniture which have survived in parts of Germany, Austria and Scandinavia. In their forms, in their choice of motifs, and in their use of paint they differ immensely from those which have been discussed so far, but their lavish and vivid colouring can give us some idea of what much medieval furniture looked like. This, of course, is not wholly fortuitous, for in many ways the peasantry in those countries at that time had arrived at much the same housing standards that the upper classes of western Europe had reached five or six centuries earlier.

The use of so much paint upon furniture was doubtless due in great part to the cheapness of that medium, but it reflects as well the inability of most wood-workers to develop the ornamental qualities which lay within their material in the absence of any general demand for them to do so. The commonest method of working upon wooden furniture was by turning. It has been argued that this was a direct legacy from the late Roman Empire, shown for example in the ornament upon a sixth-century sarcophagus of an Alemannic chief. It may well be that a copying of Roman models played a part here, but it was the very ease with which turned ornament could be produced which made the copying possible. Long after it had vanished from the furniture of the wealthy and fashionable, turned ornament was still common upon that of minor men in remote areas [Plate 7]. In earlier years, however, turning was prevalent upon the furniture of the very greatest. Illuminated manuscripts, ranging in time from the 'Benedictional of St Aethelwold' of the tenth century to a psalter from Peterborough of the late thirteenth, have innumerable representations of thrones and chairs of estate decorated in this way, and a mid-thirteenth-century book of Old Testament illustrations, in the Pierpont Morgan collection, shows no knowledge of any other form of ornament for the uprights of wooden furniture. It appears to have been the turners who first separated as an independent craft from other wood-workers and there was a turners' gild in Cologne by 1180. It was about that time, or a little later, that a very early surviving example of their craft was made: the bench at Alpirsbach, in the Black Forest, with turned uprights and supports and turned billet ornament upon the back of the seat [Plate 46]. Undoubtedly the use of turning reflects a certain level of skill among wood-workers, but the prevalence of it shows as well that the level was not a high one.[29]

Wood has been so widely used for furniture for so many centuries now that it is perhaps difficult to realize that some earlier pieces and many of the more cherished ones, were made of other materials, of ivory and metal. Sometimes, and especially when iron was used, there

46

were practical reasons for this. The iron 'chair of estate' which belonged to the Duchess of Suffolk in 1446 had a 'case of leather' to go with it: it was clearly meant to take to pieces for ease of carriage and was probably made of iron for that reason. So too perhaps were the 'four iron posts for the hangings of a bed' which were at Leicester Castle in 1322–3. In 1328 Clemence of Hungary had a 'chair of leather garnished with iron and with an iron back' and this too was probably meant to be easily dismantled. In some cases iron seems to have been preferred to wood for a less happy reason. Parisian iron-founders of the late eighteenth century were advertising their beds as free from bugs and an English traveller in Italy in 1767 commended the iron beds in the hospital at Florence because they had no crevices to harbour such creatures. Medieval men were not as indifferent to vermin as we sometimes think and in 1393 the *Ménagier de Paris* discussed the use of iron beds as a precaution against bugs and fleas. [30]

In most cases, however, metal was used for its prestige and for its decorative potentialities. It will be remembered that Charlemagne's fold-stool was said to have been made of gold and when Leo de Rozmital visited England in 1465–6 he saw, or said that he saw, Elizabeth Woodville sitting at dinner on a golden chair. If Benedict of Peterborough and the author of the *Chronicle of Bertrand du Guesclin* are to be believed, the daughter of Henry II in the twelfth century had a table-top and trestles of gold, and in the late fourteenth century Peter of Castile presented the Black Prince with a table-top of gold inlaid with precious stones. Caskets, as small pieces, were often made of silver, but so too, according to Froissart, was the cradle of the Count of Flanders.

It is clear from the way in which they are described that such pieces were rare, but a less expensive metal such as bronze was probably widely used. The 'Throne of Dagobert' is made of it and so too is a reliquary of *c*. 700 in the College of Audenne at Namur. The uprights of many of the seats and beds which appear in illuminated manuscripts are heavily ornamented with large knops protruding boldly beyond the plane of the main shaft [Plate 6]. These are well known upon brass lecterns and, on a smaller scale, on silver chalices, but to work them upon a solid piece of wood involves a great amount of labour and a great waste of timber. Illuminators were not always upon oath and they may often have indulged their fancies in drawing furniture, but the frequency of illustrations of this ornament suggests that many pieces

47

were made of metal, and generally of less precious metals such as brass or bronze or even iron.

The gold table-tops mentioned above were less probably of solid metal than of wood covered with thin gold plates in the manner of the copper-covered wooden reliquary in the Abbey of St Benoit-sur-Loire, and it is likely that metal was most widely used in this way; as inlay, and in the form of worked ornament affixed to a prominent part of a piece of furniture. A very early example of the second usage is the Frankish casket of wood mentioned above, with inlaid iron and bronze ornament. The Salzburg fold-stool of 1242 or earlier is inlaid with ivory and has lions' feet in bronze at the bases of the stretchers. A similar practice seems to be revealed by many early illuminations which picture pieces presumably of wooden construction but with ornament in a different material upon them. An eleventh-century manuscript in the British Museum has a fanciful representation of a wide bench presumably of wood but with full size lions' heads and foreparts of a different material forming the ends [Plates 8 and 9]. An early wooden casket in the Louvre is covered in copper and silver partly gilded and enamelled, and the so-called 'Cassette of St Louis' in the church of Dammarie (Seine-et-Marne) is of wood with enamelled plaques upon it of figures in relief. Even some of the elaborate stone thrones of the period had metal adornments and in 1236–7 Henry III ordered that his marble seat in Westminster Hall should have two brass leopards at the sides.

In all of these cases metal of some prestige or of a bright colour was used, and iron decoration only became common at a later period. It differed also in having a primarily utilitarian purpose, as in the bands around a chest, but despite this it was the applied metal which was decorated and not the body of the piece itself. The two chests of the early thirteenth century in the Musée Carnavalet and the Musée des Arts Décoratifs in Paris are quite plain, but the iron bands upon them are formed into decorative patterns. The peak of achievement is probably the richly decorated fifteenth-century chest in the museum in Barcelona. More ordinary examples are a chest in Icklingham Church, Suffolk, and the cupboard at Obazine [Plate 17]. Even the mid-fourteenth century casket in the Victoria and Albert Museum with scenes from 'Tristan and Isolde' carved upon it, which reveals a very advanced stage of wood-working technique, has its panels formed by decorative iron bands. The tendency to apply decoration – of

48

The medieval house and its furniture

33 Plas Ucha, Llangar, Merionethshire; the fourteenth- or fifteenth-century home
of the barons of Cymmer, much altered, but typical of the houses of the lesser nobility
in the later Middle Ages.

34 Interior of a Swedish peasant house with an open
hearth in the middle of the room.

35 Early sixteenth-century woodcut showing a perch;
a rod is fixed to the wall at head height and serves as a
wardrobe.

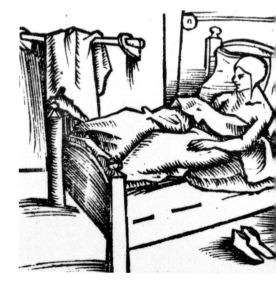

36 A medieval assembly, where Royalty sits upon a bench and others sit on the
ground or stand. From a fifteenth-century French manuscript.
37 and 38 A medieval congregation sits upon the floor and the apes
at school do the same in imitation of their human cousins.

39 Medieval 'dug-out' chest at Orton Westmorland.

40 A peasant feast in 1493. The bench on which the diners sit is made up of a plank into which three pairs of roughly shaped legs have been dowelled.

41 Dinner-time in the fourteenth century, a scene from the Luttrell Psalter. The diners sit at a bench against the wall, the table is a board laid upon trestles and removed when not in use.

42 (*opposite*) Trestle-table placed against the wall while a meal is being served. From a fifteenth-century French manuscript.

43 Even in the advanced Low Countries and in the seventeenth century the furniture of those who had to get a living by hard work was as crude as ever. Notice the roughly mended settle in this water-colour by A. van Ostade; or the cut-down barrel used as a table in the painting by Reuter (*opposite*).

44 The Great Hall at Penshurst; a table-dormant in
position along the side-wall.
45 Peasants at an inn; painting by Willem Reuter.

46 Benches of secular origin of
twelfth- or thirteenth-century
date at Alpirsbach in the Black
Forest. Large, and built of
heavy timbers, they are as near
to immoveable as any non-
fixture can be.

47 A built-in wall-cupboard
fitted with an iron-bound
wooden door. From a twelfth-
century English manuscript.

48 (*opposite*) A room in a fifteenth-century house; notice the double window-seat
contrived in the thickness of the wall. From a French manuscript.

49 Ornate stone sideboard of the early fourteenth century, formerly in a house in Lincoln.

51 (*opposite*) Stone sideboard or buffet at Dirleton Castle, East Lothian.

50 Interior of a neolithic stone house at Skara Brae in the Orkneys. All the furniture – bednooks, cupboards, two-tier dresser – is of stone.

52 (*above left*)
Bartonbury Farmhouse,
Down St Mary,
Devon; panelled
partition in the hall.
The chamfers on the
uprights stop about
two feet above floor
level, showing that a
bench was intended
here from the first.

53 (*above right*) Door
of a spice-cupboard in
a house at Strickland
Roger, Westmorland;
of the late seventeenth
century, but with
old-fashioned Jacobean
ornament.

54 Cupboard of 1674 built into a partition wall,
in a house at Troutbeck, Westmorland.

55 A settle used as a bed, an illustration of the 'Story of Tobit' from the late fifteenth-century *Bible Historiale*.

56 Swedish peasant house with a wide bench serving both as a seat and a bedstead.

57 and 58 Box-bed of 1712 contrived beneath the stairway in a house at
Baldersdale, Yorkshire; shown open and closed. The ventilation panels are similar
in form to those in some contemporary pantry-cupboards, and in function to the
tracery openings of some late medieval beds in noble houses.

59 (*opposite*) Swedish box bed with cupboards beneath and above the bed space
and at the foot.

60 Late fifteenth-century canopied bed with bench-chest at side; from *The Birth of The Virgin* by M. Reichlich.

paint, of ivory, of metal – to wooden furniture instead of working

upon the material itself is in marked contrast with the carving of decoration upon ivory caskets throughout the period, and even upon the early Franks casket of whalebone. It is a direct result of employing wood-workers almost wholly upon carpentry rather than joinery and of the consequent lack of refinement of their techniques in comparison with those of some other crafts.

This contrast was not peculiar to furniture. The refinement of Merovingian and early Anglo-Saxon jewellery and of Northumbrian stone carving from the early eighth century is not reflected in the rare timber objects which have survived. Even so venerated a work as the wooden coffin of St Cuthbert of *c*. 698 is extremely crude in comparison. The difference however did not arise from the nature of the material, for early stone carving was equally crude, as the close similarities between St Cuthbert's coffin and the stone slab from the Hypogeum at Poitiers attest. It arose from circumstances which allowed stone carvers to develop the skilled technique of the Northumbrian crosses and inhibited a parallel development amongst wood-workers. Stone carving like metal-work earlier was largely independent of the nature of domestic buildings, in a way in which wood-work and furniture was not, and its practitioners were presented with problems and in consequence with opportunities which were denied to the wood-workers.

The function and the form of individual pieces, the manner of interior decoration, the comparative lack of skill of the carpenters, and the greater skill of craftsmen in ivory and metal – each of these played a part in determining the nature of furniture in early years, but all of them in conjunction are still incapable of providing a complete explanation of it. For that it is necessary to turn to a consideration of the influence, or rather of the lack of influence, of architectural conceptions. Architecture was an admired art from early times and Eddi, the chorister and biographer of St Wilfred, was at great pains to communicate to his readers some idea of the beauty and magnificence of the buildings erected by his master. Until the coming of the Romanesque style, however, the achievements of architecture in the new kingdoms were scanty and limited and it was far from having that supremacy above other crafts which it later attained. In consequence those men who might have acquired some conception of organizing space by integrating a wall-surface into a whole were little able to

D

affect interior decoration, and less able to affect furniture than the admired craftsmen who worked in other media upon a much smaller scale and within the confines of a traditional manner of decoration.

At the same time, because of the undeveloped state of the art and because it was still far from having created a grammar of ornament it had far less than the other crafts to offer in the way of individual motifs. It is true that the Carolingian renaissance led to an interest in classical architecture which lasted for a long time and that this was occasionally revealed in furniture. The Bishop's throne at Goslar has columns with acanthus-leaf capitals at its sides, early manuscripts sometimes illustrate pieces of furniture with similar decoration, and a ninth-century Latin gospel, in the style of the school of Rheims, has a chair whose back is flanked by columns carrying an entablature and pediment. What is however noticeable is the great rarity of motifs of this sort and their absence from contexts in which later craftsmen would not have been able to resist using them. The Bayeux Tapestry has several pictures of pieces of furniture with substantial corner-posts which could well have been treated, but never were, as columns or piers, or could at least have been given architectural capitals; instead they remain plain posts with some applied decoration at top and bottom.

In this at least the tapestry is typical of many other sources of evidence and of those rare pieces which have survived. The commonest motifs were those which, while not necessarily of Dark Age origin, were easily assimilated to the zoomorphic patterning of Dark Age art. The animal and human heads upon the tops of the stretchers of fold-stools, and of the uprights of other pieces, and their accompanying lions-claw feet are ultimately of classical origin, and it was in this that much of their appeal lay, but it lay as well in their similarities with barbarian motifs. Upon smaller pieces the interlace pattern of Dark Age jewellery and of the Northumbrian manuscripts and crosses remained popular over many centuries, and even the inhabited vine-scroll occasionally appeared. It is possible that they were common upon larger pieces as well, for the bronze parts of the Goslar throne are decorated with a form of interlace and with a motif which resembles the peltae so beloved by the makers of the enamelled hanging bowls of the British Isles. In Scandinavia, where stone buildings were rare until a very late date, old motifs lingered and a derived form of the traditional Jellinge and Ringerike ornament appears upon a thirteenth-century chair in the University Museum at Oslo, and on a chest in the Historical Museum at Stockholm [Plate 29]. Its influence is also clear upon the elongated animals on chairs of Norwegian and Icelandic origin in the National Museum at Copenhagen. By the end of the twelfth century the Romanesque style had achieved its greatest successes and had left its mark upon most of western Europe, and it was at that time that a new form of architecturally-derived ornament began to be common upon furniture.

This change, however, did not come all at once and many pieces of furniture still retained old motifs side by side with new. A chest of pine in León Cathedral in Spain combines architectural forms with traditional decoration, in this case not of northern European but of Moorish origin. It has a gabled roof with Gothic crocketting upon it, but the main face is ornamented in a mudejar technique, that is with straight strips of wood nailed to the framework in the shape of stars and rectangles and other geometric figures. This unusual specimen has been claimed as the work of a Moorish prisoner in Christian hands, and it may well owe some of its character to these or similar circumstances, but it is only an extreme example of a combination of old and new forms of ornament which was widespread in the thirteenth and fourteenth centuries. There is, for example, in Laneham church in Nottinghamshire, an iron-bound chest with palmette ornament and with the damaged remains of round-headed arcading at the base of the styles [Plate 28].

Among the earliest and finest examples of the influence of Romanesque architecture upon furniture are the hutches from Valère in the upper Rhône Valley [Plates 31 and 32]. These are probably of early thirteenth-century origin, are of common local woods such as pine, walnut and larch, and were almost certainly made by local craftsmen. The largest of them – three and a quarter metres long – is decorated with blind round-headed arcading, with a form of nail-head ornament upon it, springing from short double-columns. The hutch itself is carried upon six short legs formed out of whole planks, and the three front legs are carved in the form of round columns with capitals and bases. A smaller and perhaps slightly later example again has blind arcading upon the hutch, with bird-headed grotesque ornament. The legs are no longer solid, but have been worked into a series of superimposed openings, in which a single arch below carries two smaller ones above; a direct copy of the baying-system of some Romanesque cathedrals. The remaining three hutches at Valère differ again in detail but are all alike in their display of architectural motifs.

Probably slightly earlier than these and of far less sophistication, is a chest in Westminster Abbey. The styles and central muntins have been continued downwards to form legs and upon these curved shafts have been worked and provided with a cap and base. Earlier again, but an illustration and not a survival, is a chair from the 'Eadwine Psalter' of *c.* 1150 at Trinity College, Cambridge. Its thin uprights decorated with bulbous knops are in a more primitive tradition, but its back is formed of three tiers of round-headed arches and it shows clearly the beginnings of architectural influence. There are so few survivals from before 1200 that certainty is impossible, but it seems likely that the Romanesque style had almost run its full course before it began to affect furniture at all powerfully.

2 The survival of primitive forms

Immobility

In the modern house there is, or was until recently, a clear distinction between furniture and fittings and the former comprises in essence objects which are moveable but not easily transportable. In the early Middle Ages a very different distinction existed. Furniture in the modern sense was not unknown but it was not common and most pieces were either easily portable or were wholly or largely immobile. The portability of early furniture was ascribed in the last chapter to the nature of the medieval house; the directly opposite quality of immobility is to be ascribed in the main to the same cause.

It was explained earlier that the hall of a medieval house was the site of multifarious activities and with or without an open fire in the centre its floor space had to be kept as free as possible. As a result furniture in it was relegated to the sides, and tucked tightly and ranged lengthwise along the walls. Even in the solar, in those houses which had a solar, this consideration although of less weight was still important.

Furniture disposed in this way, and intended to be kept firmly in its place, was likely to be fixed to, or contrived within, the wall it was ranged against, and this likelihood was increased in both stone and timber buildings because of the dominant part played by the mason in the one and by the carpenter in the other. It was both an ease and an economy to allow the builder to plan the furniture from the start, and in the absence of joiners and joinery there was little reason to prevent him from doing so. As late as 1525 and in so stately a home as Hengrave Hall the building contract specifically referred to the inclusion of cupboards and detailed the form they were to take. In the United States as late as *c.* 1800 it was customary for the carpenter of a timber house to build the furniture as well.[1]

There was however yet another reason for restricting the amount of moveable but not easily portable furniture. Despite the very varied uses to which many rooms were put they often had one or two constant ones for which part of the room was reserved. The upper or dais end of the hall, for example, was reserved for the lord to dine at or conduct formal business. Just as the bishop's throne in many cathedrals, although well away from any wall, was a heavy or even a fixed piece because it was in constant use and for one purpose only, so too in many secular halls the chair and high table on the dais were immoveable. At first this was not a very usual arrangement and a trestle table which could be cleared away when not wanted was in general use [Plates 41 and 42]. In later years the heavy permanent table, the 'table dormant', became very common [Plate 44], even among men of no very high social standing and Chaucer could say of his Franklin that:

> His table dormant in his halle alway
> Stood redy covered al the longe day.

Other pieces in other rooms and in other kinds of buildings acquired the same fixed character for similar reasons.

The lack of any clear distinction in medieval times between furniture and fittings was a direct consequence of the attachment of much furniture to the building it was in. And this attachment has contributed to the rarity of survivals from the early Middle Ages, for nearly all the domestic buildings of those centuries have disappeared, and their fitted furniture with them. Those few houses which have not vanished have lasted only because they could be put to new uses and the new use has generally entailed the elimination of the old fittings. As a result the evidence for this once common kind of furniture is largely dependent upon documents and illustrations and upon inferences from the pieces to be found in those areas where a primitive type of house has survived.

Immobility sometimes resulted from the sheer weight of the material of which a piece was made, especially when the material was stone. The use of stone was referred to in a general way in a previous chapter: here it is necessary to emphasize its curious social distribution, for it

54

was commonly employed by the highest and lowest social classes but not so often at intermediate levels.

Fragments of a stone table of thirteenth-century date have recently been recovered from Westminster Hall, and in 1262–3 Henry III ordered an old bench and chair, presumably of timber, to be removed from the hall at Silverstone in Northamptonshire and replaced by stone ones. Ecclesiastical stone pieces in the form of pulpits and bishops' thrones were, of course, not uncommon and have been mentioned in an earlier chapter. According to Montaigne, the abbey of St Feron at Meaux had immense stone tables in the refectory. The Westminster Hall fragments retain traces of elaborate Gothic carving, and it may be supposed that expensive ashlar was often used, partly because of the ornament which skilled masons could work upon it [Plate 5].

When stone was used by those at the bottom of the social scale it was for precisely opposite reasons, because it was the cheapest and most easily obtainable material. In areas where timber was scarce houses were often built of dry-stone walling and in many places a stone was available which could be split into long thin slabs suitable for a variety of domestic usages. This was an age-old practice and at Skara Brae in neolithic times bed-nooks were formed by dividing off a part of the room with large stone slabs set on end, and dressers were made by laying horizontal slabs upon short bearers [Plate 50]. Similar nooks were contrived in a similar way in the late Dark Age house excavated at Mawgan Porth on the north Cornish coast, and a stone bench and a stone support for a seat or bed were found in the thirteenth-century platform house excavated at Garrow Tor on Bodmin Moor. In the lean-to dairy attached to the rear of many a farmhouse in northern England similar slabs, raised upon short stone bearers, were used into the nineteenth century. This was partly because stone was still a convenient material, and partly, and in the sunken 'cold room' of many a more pretentious house wholly, because it was thought to keep milk and other foodstuffs cooler than a wooden shelf.[2]

It was not only free-standing stone furniture which might be immoveable but also, although to a lesser degree, wooden pieces as well, both because of the great size of many of them [Plate 46] and because of the weight of the large timbers employed. Apart from chests and cupboards, wooden chairs, for those few people who were entitled to them, were often of this nature. Although most private buildings had to serve many purposes, public ones, that is those owned or occupied by institutions and societies, often had one purpose or contained special purpose rooms. The commonest buildings of this kind, in which furniture needed neither to be portable nor to be restricted to the side of the wall, were probably the chapter-houses of cathedrals and monasteries, and it is not accidental that one of the earliest English chairs to survive comes from Little Dunmow Priory in Essex and probably formed part of a set of stalls. It is built of heavy timbers with solid sides and is ornamented with arcading of thirteenth century character. Laymen as well as clerics belonged to corporate associations, and the throne of fifteenth-century date, for the three joint masters of the united Gild of St Mary, St John and St Catherine at Coventry is a survival from a similar but lay milieu [Plate 95].

Mobility is a relative term and there are many gradations between the immobile and the easily moveable piece. One of these was the settle, a long high-backed bench, and the use made of it in northern England is revealing and characteristic of much medieval furniture. The central open fire was certainly rare and may have been wholly unknown amongst ordinary men in the north; instead the fire in the main room was generally made against a cross wall and beneath a fire-hood which projected several feet from that wall and was carried on a transverse beam. The fire-hood was flanked on one side by the exterior wall of the building and on the other by the 'heck', a timber-screen which cut off the fire from the entrance into the room. In this way a heated space was enclosed on three sides. In summer the settle was ranged against a side wall, but in winter it was placed across the fourth side, facing the fire and forming a kind of inner room. In one sense it was moveable since it occupied different positions at different seasons of the year; in another sense it was immoveable since it stayed in the same position throughout the whole of the summer or winter.

Built-in furniture

The commonest kind of immoveable furniture in the houses of wealthy men, and probably the commonest furniture of any kind in most others, was the piece constructed as a part of the building it was in. Stone seats built into or against a wall are a well known feature of chapter houses and of the choirs of some churches, but similar seats in stone or timber were common, perhaps almost standard, in many domestic buildings

Beds

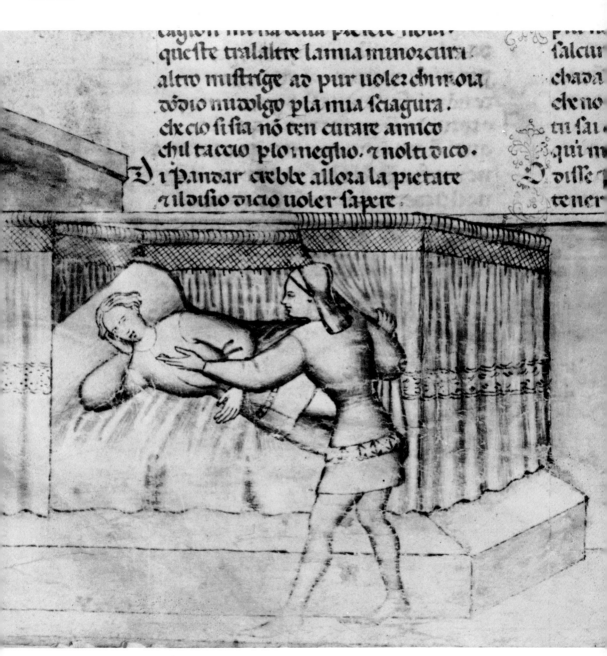

61 Late fourteenth-century bed with curtains carried on a surrounding frame.
From an illustration to Boccaccio's *Filostrata*.

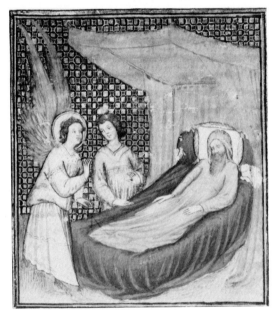

63 (*above left*) Bed with mattress slung on leather thongs and with a curtain suspended from hooks in the wall. From a twelfth-century Alsatian manuscript.

64 (*above right*) Twelfth-century bed with a tent-like canopy and with a screen at the foot. From the Winchester Bible.

65 (*below left*) Bed, with textile canopy and curtains, set in the middle of a wall and projecting into the room. From a late fifteenth-century French manuscript.

66 (*below right*) A medieval inn at bed-time; notice the sharing of beds and the medieval habit of sleeping naked.

62 (*opposite*) Bed in the form of a shallow box upon short legs. From a tenth-century English manuscript.

68 *The Birth of the Virgin* (1510), by Juan de Borgoña, in the chapter-house of
Toledo Cathedral. The bed shown is set in an alcove which can be curtained off
from the rest of the room and is provided with its own window.

67 (*opposite*) Bed of 1626, set in a corner and built-in with the panelling. From a
house in Dordrecht, Holland.

69 Bed from the Château de Villeneuve, Auvergne. The panelling at the head and along one side shows that it was always intended to stand in a corner.

70 Late fifteenth-century bed with textile canopy from Carpaccio's *Dream of St Ursula*. The bed posts appear to be of metal, and contrast with later elaborately carved posts of timber.

and throughout many centuries. When Beowulf and his companions visited Hrothgar's hall they sat upon benches around the walls, as did many other men in many other Dark Age halls, and it is reasonably certain that these benches were fixtures. In most surviving houses of early date the original furniture, fixed or not, has long vanished, but in one or two Devonshire farmhouses some evidence still remains. At Bartonbury, Down St Mary Parish, and at Newhouse Farm, Christow, both of which were originally of manor house rather than farmhouse status, the sixteenth-century panelled partitions in the hall still have benches attached to them [Plate 52]. It is true that the present benches are clearly later than the partitions, but that they are renewals and not additions is shown by the mouldings upon the partition panels; these are not finished in the usual way with an ornamented stop above the floor or groundsill, but are returned at seat level and it is clear that a bench permanently in this position was intended from the start. Even in the seventeenth century fixed benches in houses of considerable pretensions were not unusual. At Ford House near Newton Abbot an oak bench fitted into the window-recess and carried on turned balusters was built about 1630 and in 1600 at Ingatestone in Essex a bench at the upper end of the hall was described as 'lyinge upon bracketts'. When a fourteenth-century building, formerly part of Little Dunmow Priory in Essex, was altered and improved in the sixteenth century care was taken to provide a fixed bench in the newly contrived main room.

In peasant houses, and especially in areas where social change was slow, built-in benches were standard until very recently. In houses in the Alpine valleys they were fitted near the stove in the main room, and in the more primitive Scandinavian houses they ran along both sides of the room and generally returned along the end as well. In Denmark all through the eighteenth century the commonest form of seating in a peasant house was a bench fixed to the wall, and the table in front of it was sometimes supported upon poles let into the ground.[3]

Even among the upper classes the tradition died hard, and there are a large number of late seventeenth-century upholstered benches with elaborate ornament upon one long side and upon both short sides, but with none at all upon the other long side. These were no longer physically attached to the wall, but it is clear that they were always meant to stand against it.

All the fixed seats so far mentioned were in a more-or-less public

57

71 (*opposite*) Early-sixteenth century bed with timber canopy, from the Charterhouse at Basel

room – the hall of a house or the meeting room of a society – but among the wealthy they appeared in the solar as well, often in the form of a seat in a window-recess [Plate 48]. There was a thirteenth-century example on an upper floor at Millichope in Shropshire and in the royal accounts for 1253–4 the officials at Clarendon Palace were ordered to make a window with a seat in it. Fourteenth-century examples still survive in some numbers, as at Dacre Castle and Preston Patrick Hall in Westmorland. In German town houses by the end of the fourteenth century they were apparently almost a standard fitment. [4]

Benches and seats were not peculiar in being fixed, and cupboards built as part of the wall were very common for a very long time. Their raison d'être was the same; in great houses to keep as much as possible of the floor space clear, and in lesser houses in stone areas both for that reason and because if planned from the beginning they were cheaper than a separate piece of wooden furniture. With Skara Brae in mind one may suspect that in stone houses they are of immemorial antiquity, but little certain evidence appears before the twelfth century. A manuscript of that date in the British Museum illustrates an elaborate example, with four fitted shelves and closed by a wooden door profusely ornamented with ironwork [Plate 47]. There survived until the mid-nineteenth century in a house in Lincoln what appears to have been a built-in sideboard of early fourteenth-century date. It was probably sited in the screens passage – the passage which ran between the hall and the kitchen – and was a very highly decorated stone recess with quatre-foil tracery and, it would appear, ball-flower ornament [Plate 49]. Its purpose was probably the same as the less magnificent piece at Gillingham referred to in the royal accounts for 1261–2 – 'a certain bench between the King's hall and kitchen to arrange the King's dinner on'. Furnishings of this sort were not peculiar to England nor yet is it merely a deduction that these recesses in houses were intended for cupboards. The accounts of the town of Amiens for 1401 specifically refer to 'Aumailles qui sont dedans le mur en ladicte maison'; and in the Great Hall of Dirleton Castle in East Lothian there still survives a decorated stone recess which served either as a dresser or as a sideboard [Plate 51].

Like much other fixed furniture they began to disappear from the houses of the wealthy by the end of the Middle Ages but were common amongst other men for long afterwards. In any small stone-built house

erected as late as the early nineteenth century in the north of England
one may expect to find cupboards recessed into the walls. Well-known
examples of these are the 'spice-cupboards' of the Westmorland
'statemen's' houses of the late seventeenth and early eighteenth
centuries. Housewives of the period had the problem, not unknown to
those of today, of keeping spices dry in the damp English climate and
they had no air-tight tins or cellophane wrappings to aid them. Their
solution was to have a recess provided in the wall against which the
fire was made and beneath the fire-hood; since the fire burnt every day
of the year its heat kept the contents of the cupboard dry, and the
cupboard immediately near the only fire in the building was con-
veniently placed for using the spices in cooking, eating or preserving.
The cupboard was given a tight-fitting wooden door which was often
the object of the most elaborate carving in the house, and generally in
an out-of-date Jacobean style [Plate 53].

Perhaps the best known of all furniture of this kind is the built-in bed
contrived in a recess or even in a purpose-built outshut. In houses with
fixed benches around the walls there can be little doubt that most
people did as Beowulf and his followers did in Hrothgar's hall: they
spread bedclothes upon the benches when it was time to go to sleep.
Even in the Dark Ages however greater men had something better than
that, and two divergent, but not easily separable tendencies in the
development of the bed were already appearing: the one arising from
its presence in a room of public use, but of less public and much less
general use than a hall; the other from its presence in the main or only
room of a small house. For the moment it is the second development
which concerns us, one which arose from the need or the desire to
protect the bed as much as possible from the muck and mess of daily
life. There were several ways of doing this; at Skara Brae and Mawgan
Porth upright stone slabs were used to screen off a small area of the
floor space. In the thirteenth-century settlement at Hound Tor on
Dartmoor a different method may be deduced. The houses there all
have byres divided, if divided at all, from the living quarters by a
flimsy partition and during the winter the muck of the byre must have
become liberally scattered over the floor of the main room. At that end
of the room which is farthest from the byre is a platform raised about
one foot above the general level, and we may surmise that here the
bedding was spread, the platform serving as a primitive bedstead. Beds
like these are known only from excavations, but similar ones still

59

survive in the black houses of the Hebrides, which are built with low dry-stone walls five to six feet thick. Narrow tunnel-like bed-niches are contrived within the thickness of the walls, generally one on each side of the open-hearth fire and sometimes another in the wall of the byre itself.

In small houses without an attached byre the problem was less one of keeping the bed off the dirt of the floor than of keeping it away from the area of daily activity. The simplest way of doing this was to continue the Dark Age practice of spreading bedclothes upon fixed benches and to make more or less elaborate arrangements for keeping them in position. Nothing of this sort has survived from an early period but it seems likely that here again Scandinavian peasant houses of the eighteenth and nineteenth centuries have preserved older ways. In some of these dwellings the seat of the bench is divided into compartments of about six feet in length by split logs or shaped pieces of timber spiked to the surface, and another piece of timber similarly fixed along the outside edge of the seat makes the fourth side of a shallow box in which the bedding is laid [Plate 56]. In other Scandinavian examples which are later in form if not in time, a framework is constructed above the bench and curtains are hung from it to make enclosed spaces; when doors and panelling replaced curtains a true box-bed appeared.

Box-beds are known from many other countries, but elsewhere as in France and England it is the box-bed alone – the end product – which has survived; in Scandinavia the full development can still be traced. It is clear that this development reflects a change in material conditions and a rise in the living standards of the population as a whole, but at the same time it reflects the failure of those standards to rise very far. Because the accommodation is still much the same as before, because there is still one main room used for multifarious purposes, the bed may develop from a rough bench into a piece of sophisticated furniture, but it is still without a room of its own and is wall-bound. Box-beds were once common in several French provinces. In the sixteenth century Du Faïl described an example in Brittany which was placed in a recess against the fireplace in the only room in the house, and most French examples appear to come from dwellings with very limited accommodation. At a small house in Baldersdale in Yorkshire which originally had only a main room and a dairy on the ground floor a bed-cupboard dated 1712 was sited beneath the upper part of the stairway [Plates 57 and 58]. When blocks of tenements, each

60

with one room, were designed for weavers at Bannockburn near Stirling around 1780 built-in box-beds were provided and in the two-room tenements built shortly afterwards at New Lanark each room had a box-bed. Indeed in Scotland bed-cupboards or bed recesses are not so uncommon in town tenements today.[5]

With much wall-bound furniture it is not easy to decide whether the furniture is a part of the wall or the wall part of the furniture and the previously mentioned confusion between furniture and fittings was paralleled by one between furniture and fabric. In a house at Stavely, in Lancashire, north of the Sands, the wall between the main room and service room is partly made up of a panelled partition and partly of an elaborate cupboard, dated 1639, attached to, and prolonging the line of, the partition. In Westmorland many houses of the late seventeenth and of the eighteenth centuries have a highly ornamented cupboard forming part of a wall in the main room [Plate 54].

It may be surmised that much free-standing furniture as well served as a partition wall. In those houses in the north of England wherein the settle was placed in winter against the heck and opposite the fire-hood, it served in that position as the fourth wall of an inner room contrived within the main room. That the area divided off was essentially another room, and was thought of as such, is shown by the almost invariable provision of a small 'fire-window' in the external wall to light the enclosed space. In a house at Corscombe in Somerset this use of furniture still survives, or survived up to a few years ago, and an immensely long settle stretching from one lateral wall to within three feet of the other serves as a partition shutting off the main room from a passage running transversely through the house. In Northumberland in the early nineteenth century the one-room dwellings of the labourers on the extensive farms were often partitioned into two, not by any fixed structure but by large press-beds whose backs and head pieces served as a wall. A similar usage of beds and of dressers was common in North Wales and in Ireland until at least the beginning of this century.[6]

To our eyes this may seem an extremely primitive way of dividing a building into rooms, and it may be thought that it was never common at higher social levels. It is, in fact, a comparatively late and sophisticated method. In the great stone towers of the eleventh and twelfth centuries rooms were often made merely by separating one space from another with hangings and curtains. Many of the bed-alcoves discussed

61

above, and more elaborate forms which appeared later, were thought of as separate rooms, although divided by nothing but a curtain, and in Italy the word 'camera' was actually used to mean the space enclosed by the canopy and curtains of a bed. As late as 1399, when the French and English ambassadors met at Leulinghen in the Pas-de-Calais to arrange a truce and were accommodated for a long period in the church, separate rooms were provided for them and their suites by hanging tapestries across the building. The idea of forming a smaller space within a large one by using very temporary partitions continued long after this, and in the second quarter of the seventeenth century Madame de Rambouillet held her salon in the famous Blue Room of her Hôtel in an area intimately screened-off from the rest of the room. The employment of furniture to divide a space into rooms is a more permanent form of this practice, and one which survived in peasant houses because more primitive conditions there prolonged a more primitive use of furniture and a use of more primitive furniture.[7]

Multi-purpose furniture

Just as furniture in general was often used as a fitting within a house, or even a part of the fabric, so particular pieces were often used for many different purposes. Even today, of course, a bed may be sat on or a chair slept in, but this is an exceptional response to exceptional and usually temporary circumstances. In former years, in contrast, it was seldom that any piece was reserved to only one use.

It has already been noticed that beds and bedsteads rarely occur in early inventories. In part this was because many people had nothing but straw to sleep on, but in part it was because they used other pieces of furniture as beds [Plate 55]. If an inventory had been taken of Hrothgar's hall it would probably have had nothing to say about beds and bedsteads, but this does not mean that his guests had nowhere to sleep : as we know, they slept upon the benches. This practice continued, so normal that it went largely unrecorded, for many hundreds of years. French inventories of the late sixteenth and early seventeenth centuries speak of 'deux petits bancs servants de lietz' and of a 'banc à coucher', and as late as 1708 there was in Mme de Maintenon's ante-chamber at Versailles 'un banc à lit de bois de chêsne'. Similarly, inventories from the north of England ranging in time from the mid-sixteenth to the mid-seventeenth century refer to 'a long settle with a bed' and 'a settle

with a mattress upon it'. It is clear that the distinction between a bench
and a bed was often a very fine one and in those Scandinavian houses
mentioned earlier it is not easy to decide whether a bench is being used
as a bed or a bed as a bench. Most men, unless they were charged with
drawing up an inventory, probably never distinguished one from the
other.[8]

Very often, too, an undoubted bed was used as a seat, and not only
in poor houses in which the very rare furniture had of necessity to serve
several turns. When Ulrich von Lichtenstein in the thirteenth century
visited his lady in her chamber, 'she sat there upon a bed and greeted
me right modestly', and this was no clandestine lovers' meeting, which
there might be good reasons for beginning in this way, for 'eight ladies
stood by her side'. Similarly, when Chaucer's Troilus visited Cressida
he sat beside her upon the bed, but not because he was, or was hoping
to be, her accepted lover, for when Pandarus visited him they too sat
together upon the bed.

In most chambers the bed was the normal seat of the owner, at least
when he or she had visitors and its use in this way was so well recognized
that it very early became a kind of 'chair of estate' in which great men
received suitors and delegations. When Jordon of Ciano, a Franciscan
from Germany, went to Rome in 1238 the Pope received him in bed,
and over a century later Froissart presented a book to the king of
England by laying it ready on his bed. In later years this function of the
bed was heavily emphasized and played a large part in developing it
into an elaborate and ostentatious piece of furniture.

Chests as well as beds were often used as seats. Feulner has pointed
out that Italian cassoni with flat tops have sides sloping inwards to the
base and has suggested that this slope was intended to prevent the
elaborate decoration upon the front from being damaged when they
were being used as seats. It was perhaps a cassone of this sort that
Boccaccio had in mind when he described two lovers as 'seated upon a
curious chest at the bed's foot'. A French document of 1471 speaks of
two 'coffres servans de banc', and two centuries later chests were still
being used as benches in ante-chambers; for when Vitry waited upon
the maréchal d'Ancre at the Louvre in 1659, 'il demeura longtemps
dans la Salle des Suisses assis sur un coffre'.

Chests could be made to serve other purposes as well and were sometimes used as tables, especially as writing tables. Late medieval illustrations of town life often show merchants using chests as counters and as

writing desks, and it is perhaps not accidental that the only indigenous piece of Spanish furniture – the vargueño – was essentially a chest with a drop-front which could be used to write upon. The chest was too short to be used as a dining-table and for this purpose a bench was often pressed into service. When Gregory of Tours was summoned to Chilperic's presence he found the Frankish king in a rude tent, made of the branches of trees, with a bench before him upon which bread and meat had been laid. Nearly a thousand years later a French inventory of 1583 listed 'ung banc ... servant pour table'.

A development of this habit of using one piece of furniture to serve the purposes usually demanded of another was the apparently later practice of constructing a piece with the express intention that it should have more than one use. An early reference occurs in an inventory of the Duke of Bourbon of 1507 which lists eight benches of which one was so made that it could be used as a bed: 'dont il y en a ung qui est fait pour servir de couchette.' In what way it differed from its companions is not clear, but it is probable that a folding or sliding board could be raised along the front to form a shallow box within which the bedding was placed and held in position. Inventories of the early seventeenth century from northern England sometimes mention a 'long-settle bed' or a 'long-settle bedstead' and, in contrast with earlier accounts of benches and settles with 'beds' or mattresses laid on them, suggest that there too, at a later date, some furniture was purpose-made for several functions.

The distinction often made in sixteenth- and seventeenth-century documents between a chest serving as a seat and a seat serving as a chest perhaps had little significance to contemporaries, but is of considerable importance to us. A chest used as a seat may or may not have been made to serve both purposes, and all one can do is to infer from its form, as in the case of some cassoni, that such an intention was in the maker's mind. A seat that is to be used as a chest, on the other hand, for example, an Italian cassapanca, must have some kind of receptacle built into it at its inception and the intentions of its maker are beyond doubt [Plate 109].

Fifteenth-century documents sometimes speak of chairs with chests in them and of benches serving as chests, and one may guess, from later surviving examples, that the chair or bench had a solid front and sides, and that the seat lifted up on a hinge to reveal an enclosed box-like space beneath it. By the early sixteenth century the inventory of the

64

1 (*opposite*) The splendour of medieval hangings is shown in this scene of the Duke of Lancaster dining with the King of Portugal; the furniture, in contrast, is plain. From a fifteenth-century French manuscript

Duchesse de Valentinois, the wife of Cesare Borgia, could refer without any apparent need of an explanation to 'a little bench' containing some of her clothes, and later reference to 'closed chairs', to 'closing chairs', and to 'chairs with a lock' show that the form had become common enough to acquire a terminology of its own. At about the same time Gilles Corrozet in his hymn to the comforts of domestic furniture spoke as a matter of course of the

> chaire bien fermée et close
> Où le musc odorant repose
> Avec le linge delyé[9]

Many other multiple uses were possible and a very long-lasting one, if Europe as a whole is considered, was the combination of a bed or a seat with a cupboard. An early example is in the church of St Germain l'Auxerrois. Richly decorated with linen-fold panelling of the late fifteenth century it is basically a cupboard in two stages with three compartments to a stage, but in front of it is an attached bench, with side panels, whose back is formed by the lower stage of the cupboard and whose seat serves as the lid of a chest. It may have been used as a bed as well, for a Parisian inventory of 1628 mentions a bench serving as a bed and having the form of a cupboard. At the highest levels of society such pieces probably went out of use fairly rapidly, but at others they lasted for a very long time. The built-in beds of peasant houses in Brittany and other parts of France often had a bench in front of them, which served in part as a seat, in part as a step to climb up into the bed and in part as a chest. This, too, was a perpetuation at lower social levels of what had once been common practice at the highest; a free-standing part-canopied bed with similar bench-chests at the side appears upon a late-fifteenth century painting in the Pinakothek at Munich [Plate 60]. In Scandinavia very elaborate box-beds were being built in the eighteenth century which had a tier of cupboards above the bed-opening and a cupboard in several tiers and rising nearly to ceiling level at the ends[10] [Plate 59].

It is possible to list other combinations of function in purpose-built furniture, some of which, such as table-chairs, lasted even in well-provided houses to a very late date. Their interest, however, lies less in their variety than in their common revelation of housing standards. On the one hand they reflect still primitive conditions, in which rooms are few, in which space in any room is seriously limited by the many

65

11 (*opposite*) Cupboard in Halberstadt Cathedral, probably thirteenth century, monumental both in form and in the style of ornament

activities carried on there, and in which furniture is often in the way. On the other hand, however, early double-pieces indicate a change in social conditions, for they were made to serve their intended purposes and no others and to that degree mark a movement away from former conceptions of undifferentiated furniture towards the more modern one of every piece to its own function.

3 The end of the Middle Ages

Changes among the upper classes

Few people would dispute that the differences between medieval and modern Europe are so immense that the conventional division of European history into two main periods is well justified: and it will be widely agreed that the dividing line between the two falls somewhere in the sixteenth century. At the same time it will also be agreed that the transformation, cataclysmic though it was, had a long gestation behind it and took a long time to mature.

It now seems reasonably clear that from about the middle of the fourteenth century medieval society was undergoing changes which – whether or not we think of the age in terms of a 'general crisis of feudalism' – were turning it into something very different from what it had been. The causes of the process are a matter of debate, but at least some of its effects are well known. Not all of these are of equal importance to us, but there are three which may be singled out for the part which they played in influencing the development of late medieval furniture: the formation of large territorial groupings, the dominance of a patriciate in the towns, and the tendency among some of the landed classes to engage in urban pursuits.

By the mid-fourteenth century the mechanics of government, simple though it was by modern standards, was far more complicated than in earlier years when a peripatetic court carried many of its administrative personnel and their records around with it. As it became more complicated government tended to become centralized, and although kings and princes still had many houses they spent more of their time than formerly in a selected few. On a smaller scale a similar process was occurring on the estates of those greater nobles who required an administrative service of their own. As a result great men no longer needed to scatter that proportion of their wealth they devoted to their comforts among many houses, but could concentrate it upon some of them. At the same time, a more or less permanently based court meant that many men found it necessary or convenient to build or acquire a house nearby, to occupy it for long periods, and to furnish it to a standard not below that of their peers. The outward result of this was perhaps most clearly seen in England where a centralized administration began early. By the end of the fifteenth century almost the whole of the way between the court at Westminster and the city of London had been built over by the town houses of the great nobles along the Strand.

The existence of a patriciate in the towns – of an oligarchy which held effective control over the town's policies, whatever popular form the government might take – is well attested from nearly all parts of western Europe long before the end of the Middle Ages. As early as the late thirteenth century Philippe de Remy, the Seigneur of Beaumanoir, in describing the legal customs of the Beauvaisis said firmly: 'The rich men possess rule in the towns', and in Florence, for example, at that time they held at the least a considerable amount of power. Townsmen, however rich, generally had no need for more than one house and if they had a taste for comfort could indulge it within a narrow compass. It is something of a commonplace amongst German writers that the increase in the amount of furniture, and of the money spent upon it, in the fourteenth and fifteenth centuries is directly traceable to the greater wealth at that time of urban merchants and bankers. Undoubtedly there is some truth in this. Genoese inventories of the late thirteenth century reveal more, and more diversified, furniture in the homes of wealthy citizens than any other contemporary and many other later inventories, and it is probably not accidental that this happened in the years when, according to the Genoese chronicler, Jacopo d'Orio, the city 'outshone all other cities in Italy in wealth, in glory and in power'. Nevertheless, there is very little evidence which supports, and a considerable amount which controverts, the idea that even wealthy townsmen had much furniture before the end of the Middle Ages, or which suggests that they had more than other men of equal wealth. No simple explanation will suffice here.[1]

Because they did not live under the same conditions as feudal landowners, merchants were not subject to the same constraints in furnishing their houses; but they were subject to others peculiar to themselves. The merchant class of the late Middle Ages was the product of a long and painful process of capital accumulation in which the best way of securing present gains had been to re-invest them in the business which had provided them. Landlords might have wealth to spend; merchants had had only capital to employ. By the fourteenth century, however, matters were different. Up to then medieval economy as a whole was expanding, often rapidly, but about that time in many parts of western Europe there was a slow-down, sometimes even a stagnation, in economic development and merchant capital was tending to seek other outlets besides trade and finance. Urban investment in land had been known before, but it seems at this time to have reached a new level of intensity, of which perhaps the most striking evidence is to be found in Venetian history. In the middle of the fifteenth century, under the doge Francesco Foscari, Venetian foreign policy made a sharp break with its past and prejudiced the defence of the city's over-seas possessions, and of much of its trade, in order to achieve large territorial gains on the Italian mainland. In part this was a response to the menace of hostile coalitions of mainland states, but in part it was the result of a deliberate preference for the small but safe returns of land ownership over the immense but risky profits of commerce. If therefore the great increase in domestic furniture in the fourteenth and fifteenth centuries is partly to be ascribed to the new needs of rich merchants, nevertheless these needs arose not because they were merchants nor because they were rich, but because they were in the process of changing into something other than mere merchants.[2]

This change, however, coincided with a change in the nature of the land-owning classes. Despite all their affectation of contempt for trade the nobility of western Europe were never averse from soiling their hands with its profits, so long as those profits were big enough and easily come by. As the towns developed, so too did the connections of the nobility with them. The upper classes of fourteenth-century Florence were a mixed lot, but a large proportion of them were of noble origin, and much the same was true, to a greater or lesser degree, of other towns, not only in Italy but in Flanders and elsewhere. With business interests in the towns these men needed houses in the towns and, to take an example from what was then almost the edge of the world, the best house in fourteenth-century Shrewsbury belonged to

the Charltons, Lords of Powys and sheep farmers and wool dealers as
well. With many of their interests concentrated in the town some
landowners tended to spend much of their time there and had thereby
the opportunity, if no more, to provide themselves with permanent
comforts. Unlike an urban bourgeoisie, which had had to develop the
virtues of thrift and foresight, these men had little inhibition, when
trading profits came their way, of converting some of them into the
delights of luxury. [3]

Almost simultaneously, therefore, urban merchants and noble
landowners found the previous restrictions upon comfort in their houses
less pressing than they had been. But this occurred amongst classes who
were living not merely side by side but in close association with each
other, who were inter-marrying freely and mingling not merely their
blood but their habits of life as well. The sons of nobles who married
merchants' daughters were acquiring bourgeois wealth without acquiring the whole range of bourgeois motivation, and tradesmen marrying
into landowners' families were picking up some of their in-laws'
standards without forgoing any of their own wealth. As a result not
only town houses but country houses as well were being built and
provided with more comforts than previously. This was very noticeable
in Italy and especially in central Italy and in Florence in particular,
where developments of this kind were occurring before the end of the
thirteenth century. It was not confined to Italy, however, and one of
the most famous English houses of the fourteenth century – Penshurst –
was built by a London merchant.

The increase in domestic comfort among the upper classes in the
late Middle Ages occurred at a time when the economy was, at least,
less buoyant than it had been, when government was becoming more
centralized, and when the urban patriciate and the rural noblesse were
modifying their ways of life and coalescing with each other. Every one
of these changes contributed to the development of furniture, but no
single one was the unique cause.

The decline of the hall

Although the hall remained the most important room in a house of any
pretensions up to and beyond the end of the Middle Ages, there were
clear signs well before then that it was losing some of its importance.
As early as the thirteenth century an outraged moralist complained of

the habit of some great ladies of dining in the bower or solar and coming into the hall later only as a formality. The rules laid down in 1458 for the regulation of the English royal household attempted to enforce the old custom, but it is clear from later events, as for example the banquet given to the ambassador of Charles of Burgundy in the queen's chamber, that they were of slight effect. In Germany from about 1300 onwards many of the uses of the great 'Saal' were being usurped by other rooms, and in some of the smaller houses of south-eastern England of the late fifteenth century the hall was of no greater area than the solar or service rooms. In larger houses the hall continued to be of considerable size, but it was no longer accompanied by a single chamber but by several. Before 1377–8 Leicester Castle had been provided with a 'dancing chamber'; in the late fourteenth century Charles v had in his Hôtel de St Pol in Paris not only a 'chambre de retraite' but an 'étude' as well; Francesco Datini's house at Prato had three guest rooms by 1405; and the fifteenth-century merchant's house known as Hampton Court at King's Lynn had, besides other rooms, a separate 'counting-house' with its own entrance.[4]

The decline of the hall increased the number of rooms which were free from the restrictions imposed upon the hall itself and at the same time lessened the pressure upon the formerly lone solar. But this occurred in conjunction with, and very largely as a result of, the new attitudes to domestic comfort and convenience among the upper classes and in consequence it now became both materially possible and socially commendable to expend large sums upon adequate and ample furnishings.

The new conditions are well illustrated by Datini's house. While the hall was furnished merely with trestle-tables and two reed chairs, the main bedroom had a bed with benches, a chair, a painted coffer, three chests with locks and a cupboard; and the guest rooms had, besides beds and truckle beds, walnut trestle-tables and several chests. In contrast the richest inventories from late thirteenth-century Genoa show the halls furnished to much the same standard as Datini's hall, but the other rooms falling below the level of his. In 1470 Jeanne of Laval's chamber at Angers had a great bed with low footstools, probably used as chests, a smaller bed, a great bench, two smaller benches, a cupboard and a small low table. By the early sixteenth century a person of any consequence had very much furniture in his or her chamber and the inventory taken in 1514 for Louise Borgia, the daughter of Cesare Borgia and his French wife, listed a great bed, two smaller beds, a table, a buffet, a small bench and three 'escabelles' – low short benches – a large settle and no less than seven chests.

Furniture and fittings

The increase in importance of the chamber and the decline of the hall had an important effect upon the very nature of furniture. The chamber was less of a public place with a daily routine than the hall, and it had less need of unencumbered floor-space in the middle. Consequently furniture began to lose its connection with the wall and its character of a fitting, and became more or less free to move around. This emancipation was shared by many forms, but it can perhaps be most clearly seen in the development of the bed in upper-class houses.

As early as the barbarian invasions there were differences between the bed furniture of ordinary men and of the great. While Beowulf's followers slept upon benches in Hrothgar's hall, Hrothgar himself and his nobles seem to have slept in their separate 'bowers', and presumably upon something other than a communal bench. Just what they slept upon is not clear, and one must begin a discussion of the history of the bed at a humbler social level.

The well established development of the bed in peasant homes was sketched in an earlier chapter: from the bedding spread upon a bench attached to the wall to the bench divided into shallow boxes to hold the bedding and thence to the bed placed in a recess of one kind or another. It is apparent that in all these cases an attempt is being made to clear the bed away from the restricted floor-space of the living quarters and, within the limitations imposed by lack of means, to turn the bed-space into a separate room, or at least into an area physically distinct in some way from the room it is in.

The first stage of this development is un-recorded (if it ever occurred) amongst the upper classes, and the earliest surviving records are of beds of some elaboration. Those shown in pre-conquest English manuscripts, such as the *Benedictional of Archbishop Robert*, are in the form of shallow boxes upon short stumpy legs and are placed, in those cases in which their position can be determined, lengthways along a wall [Plate 62]. Beds of this sort appear in twelfth-century illuminations from most of western Europe and one is shown upon a marble relief on the tomb of Pope Clement II in Bamberg Cathedral. In some of these

72

III *(opposite) The Annunciation* by Roger van der Weyden, probably before 1440. Notice the textile canopy above the bed and the covering of the Virgin's seat

later examples the legs are longer, a head-board and a base-board appear, and the sides of the box are richly ornamented with balusters or with arcading; but in essence the form is unchanged.

Nevertheless, by the twelfth century new forms were appearing and these are illustrated in manuscripts and can be inferred from documents. In the *Hortus Deliciarum* a bed of conventional form set lengthways along the wall has curtains suspended from hooks on the wall [Plate 63]. The bed in which King Edgar lay when Dunstan paid his early morning call must have had tall bed-posts, for the archbishop leant against, or supported himself, on one of them, and it was perhaps these which carried the curtains which surrounded the king. A late-twelfth century Bible in the library of Winchester Cathedral shows a bed, again with short legs and with a canopy suspended from hooks in the wall, with a tall partition at its foot screening it off from the doorway into the room [Plate 64].

In all of these the advance towards separating the bed-space from the room is clear, but a more definite step was taken when bed-niches were introduced. In a set of verses written about the year 1100 for the daughter of William the Conqueror, Baudry of Bourgeuil described an ideal chamber in which the bed was placed in an alcove with a curtain in front of it. A twelfth-century sculpture at Chartres, which Feulner interprets as a bed with a tester above, appears in fact to be intended as a bed in a coved niche, for the bed is ranged along the wall and the coving runs the whole length of it. An eleventh-century manuscript from Hereford with individual portraits of the Evangelists shows each of them writing at his desk in front of a curtained recess which may be supposed to have held a bed. In the aisled halls which were a common house-type, at least in England, until the fourteenth century it is likely that part of the aisle was curtained off into bed-spaces, and some illuminations of the twelfth and thirteenth centuries show, in a conventionalized form, a series of aisle spaces with curtains hung in front of them. In a fourteenth-century French illustration of the interior of an inn a line of separate bed cubicles is arranged along one wall of a large room.[5]

Not only amongst the mass of the population but also amongst the wealthy the practice of separating the bed-space from the room continued for a long time. The castle of Meran in Germany has, or had, a fifteenth-century bed intended for a corner position, screened on one of its free sides by a curtain and on the other by a timber partition

73

IV (*opposite*) The painted scenes upon fifteenth-century Florentine marriage chests, or cassoni, were often works of art in their own right
Above, 'The Death of Procris' by Piero di Cosimo, and *below*, painting of a marriage ceremony

pierced with the ventilation tracery that was more usual in food
cupboards. When Juan de Borgoña carried out the decoration of the
chapter-house of Toledo Cathedral in 1509-11 he painted a birth scene
in which the bed was set in an alcove projecting from the room and
provided with a window in its lateral wall [Plate 68]. As late as 1626
in a house in Dordrecht a bed-space was partitioned off in a corner
and its free sides were decorated to the same design as the wainscot
elsewhere in the room [Plate 67].

As long as houses had few rooms and their single chamber had many
uses the temptation to clear the bed out of the way was often powerful
enough to over-ride any other considerations. It is, of course, for this
reason that examples of the earlier practice are seen most clearly not
in any very old houses, but in those comparatively modern peasant
dwellings wherein unchanging conditions perpetuated old habits into
modern times. Amongst the very wealthy, as houses acquired more
rooms and some individuals their own separate accommodation the
limitations upon space which had forced the bed into a corner, or out
of the room altogether, were steadily relaxed. This, however, happened
at a time when furniture was commoner than before but still not
plentiful and the bed was not merely a piece of furniture to place a
mattress and bedclothes upon, but something like a more private
chair of estate or quasi-throne, whence the most important occupant
of the room issued commands, or offered hospitality to friends and
honoured guests: When John Donne told his mistress 'This bed thy
centre is' his words had only one possible meaning, but if someone else
had said the same to a woman two hundred years earlier she might not
have read any sexual connotation into it, for the bed was then the
centre of many activities. Therefore, when it was brought back into the
room it was given the most prominent place and in more and more
instances it was put not along a wall, but against it and projecting
into the room.

The newer practice is revealed in part by illustrations [Plate 65], in
part by such literary references as Boccaccio's description of a bed as in
the centre of a room, and in part, and for the first time, by what may be
deduced from surviving examples. The bed in the Davanzati Palace,
mentioned earlier, is made to have benches along the front and the
two sides and could never have been intended to stand in a corner or
lengthwise along a wall. That in the Ospedale del Ceppo at Pistoia has
painted figure decoration upon the head and foot boards and this,

while not invisible if the bed is put into a corner, suggests that it was
intended to project into the room. These are isolated examples, for few
early beds have survived; but the change, or at any rate the tendency
to change, is illustrated by a comparison of an early-sixteenth century
bed in the Musée des Arts Décoratifs at Paris with another of equal age
in the Historisches Museum at Basel. The first is in the old manner,
panelled to tester height at the head and along one side and clearly
intended to stand in a corner [Plate 69]; the second has a panelled
head-board, a short canopy projecting from it, and decoration in low
relief around the foot and both sides [Plate 71]; in contrast with the
first it was always meant to stand free and away from a wall except at
the head.

In general it was the drapery around and above the bed, the curtains
and tester, which was more highly regarded than the frame and this
too, like the bed, slowly emancipated itself from the wall. In early
illustrations, it will be remembered, the hangings are suspended from
hooks or rails in the walls, sometimes in the form of a tent. Hangings of
this sort remained in favour for many centuries, appear in engravings
of about 1600 by Crispin de Passe, and were not unknown in Swedish
houses two centuries after that. Increasingly, however, they were
superseded by curtains and testers suspended not from a wall but
carried by the frame of the bed itself. The change came slowly. The
new form was probably not dominant before the end of the fifteenth
century, but as early as 1322–3 the Leicester Castle inventory mentioned 'four iron posts for the hanging of a bed' and an illustration
of 1380 from Boccaccio's *Filostrata* shows a bed with curtains hung from
rails carried by the bed-posts [Plate 61].

The same increase in the importance of the chamber and in the
number of chambers also brought into being a new kind of bed. When
an important man attained his own separate room he needed, or felt
that he needed, to have an attendant with him during the night, and
for his part the attendant felt that he needed something to sleep on
when his services were not immediately required. A bed of the same
kind as his master's, even on a smaller and less luxurious scale, would
have encroached upon the so recently won free space of the chamber,
and the solution was found in the truckle-bed. It was built very low off
the ground, as lightly framed as possible and reasonably easy to move;
and during the daytime was slid out of the way beneath the great bed.
As its conveniences became more widely appreciated it was used by

many more people than those in night-time attendance upon a lord, and became common among humbler men.

The bed was not alone in developing from a fitting into a piece of furniture, and one of its companions was, of course, the chair, for most men sat upon a bench, or upon a settle – a bench with a high back [Plate 96]. It is perhaps possible to exaggerate the scarcity of chairs in the early Middle Ages. That they were not so rare as is sometimes said is suggested by a twelfth-century English illumination in which musicians sit upon low chairs with short backs; and it will be remembered that Neckham recommended a chair by the side of the bed in his ideal chamber.

Nevertheless, they were in general reserved for very important people or, rather, for the one most important person in a household. It was said earlier that 'chairs' and 'thrones' were at first almost synonymous, and as late as 1548 the town council of Lyons, in ordering an important work from a goldsmith, asked for it to be decorated with a representation of 'a king sitting upon a chair'. Even in much later times chairs were often reserved for honoured guests, and it was long a matter of some concern to status-seekers that they should be offered one. In 1673 the high-born ladies of Charles II's court quitted his presence in indignation when he ordered a chair to be brought for the Duchess of Modena, and failed to show the same consideration to them. At the marriage banquet of George II's eldest son, Frederick Prince of Wales, the delicate question of whether a stool or a chair should be offered to the bride provoked much ill-feeling all round. The practice of giving a chair only to the foremost member of any company has long passed away in Europe, but the memory has remained; in a university it is only a professor who has a 'chair' and in England the ultimate authority in any assembly, from a Royal Commission to a trade union branch, is still that of the chairman [Plates 11 and 12].

The lack of chairs was in part one aspect of the paucity of all furniture, in part a reflection of the hierarchic form of medieval society and in part a direct result of the permanent dais in the hall. Many chairs were no more than the elaborate centre-piece of a seat which accommodated several people, of whom one was in authority. Such was the lord's seat in the middle of the bench before the high table or the Abbot's seat in a chapter house. In the mid-thirteenth century the officials at Henry III's houses at Geddington and Silverstone in Northamptonshire, when preparing the buildings for the king's visit,

were ordered 'to make a chair in the middle of the great bench in our
hall'. When the hall lost its old pre-eminence the need and opportunity
arose for more seats of some distinction in other rooms. Since those
rooms had less of a public character than the hall, the chair or chairs
in them needed neither to be tied to one place nor to be arranged as
the centrepiece of a series, and as early as Henry III's reign there was a
'moveable chair' in the King's chamber at Havering. In consequence
the decline of the hall and the proliferation of other rooms not only
released the chair, like the bed, from its attachment to the wall, but by
releasing it helped to multiply its number.

In early illuminations even such exalted persons as the Deity and
the Virgin, when they sit upon a chair at all, usually sit upon one which
has a low back or none and is in form little different from an immobile
fold-stool [Plate 14]. Early representations of other forms are rare. In
a ninth-century Spanish illumination, Christ sits upon a chair with
arm-rests and a back [Plate 10], and an eleventh-century ivory,
probably of south Italian origin, shows a fold-stool with a high and
presumably fixed back [Plate 15]. Even manuscripts of a date approach-
ing the end of the Middle Ages almost uniformly illustrate chairs
without backs. So long as great men sat upon fold-stools in the course
of their peregrinations, and upon seats in the middle of a bench in their
halls, even such chairs as there were tended to have an un-chair-like form.

No early examples have survived, but chairs with half-backs and
with arcaded or pierced panelled sides were probably becoming common in the course of the twelfth century. On a wooden sculpture in
the Louvre the Virgin sits upon a chair with a half-back and with
rudimentary side-pieces formed by a length of round-headed arcading.
Similar chairs appear in sculptured scenes upon capitals at Autun and
from Reading Abbey which are not later than *c.* 1150 [Plate 16].
Among a set of twelfth-century chess-men in the British Museum the
piece representing the king has a chair with a solid half-back and small
solid side-pieces. It is not however until the end of the thirteenth
century that representations of chairs with a full back and full sides
become normal and appear, apart from the thrones of royal and divine
personages, in any number.

The separation of furniture from the wall, which helped to make
chairs commoner and more chair-like, almost created the domestic
cupboard. There had been earlier cupboards which were contrived in,
or built as part of, the wall, and free-standing ecclesiastical cupboards

had been known long before the fifteenth century; but it was only then that the cupboard detached from the wall became common in men's homes. It then became so numerous, not only among princes and magnates but among men of no eminence as well, that it has come to be widely regarded as a typically 'bourgeois' piece. As we have already seen, there are reasons for regarding this view not as incorrect, but as inadequate.

At the same time attempts have been made to derive the cupboard, especially in its common two-tiered form, from two separate chests placed one upon the other and given openings in a long side instead of at the top. It is possible that it was evolved in this way; although if so one would expect early examples to be long and low, whereas they tend to be tall and narrow, like the very early piece in Halberstadt Cathedral. But even if this should be the true account of the formal development of the cupboard, it is still one which tends to obscure rather than to reveal its origins. As a piece that was never meant to travel the cupboard is in principle the direct opposite of the peripatetic chest, and its appearance in large numbers at this time cannot be divorced from the changes which were occurring in contemporary life and in contemporary houses. One of those changes was the beginning of a sharp distinction between furniture and fittings, and the replacement of the wall-bound cupboard and the primitive chest by the free-standing cupboard is only one part of a wider development.

Specialized forms

Side by side with this, and sometimes in part as a result of it, there was an increasing specialization of furniture in two ways: in the restriction of established pieces which formerly had several functions to one alone, and in the development of new forms. So long as chairs and benches, for example, were fixed to the wall they were often used not only as seats but as receptacles as well and were provided with solid bases and hinged tops for this purpose. This double usage, both because of the thick scantling of the timber and the greater amount of timber required, made them heavy and massive and since mobility had now become a desired, or at any rate a useful, quality there was a tendency to sacrifice the secondary function and make the piece in a way which would most efficiently serve the primary.

Of greater importance, however, was the development of specialized articles formerly unknown, or very little known. The free-standing cupboard was a specialized piece itself, but it soon developed specializations within it. One of these was the buffet or dresser. As more wealth was spent upon domestic comforts and luxuries it became fashionable to show off the family plate and at first the simple sideboard which served to place the dishes on was used for this purpose. As early as the late fourteenth century, however, the *Ménagier de Paris* was distinguishing between the 'dressouer de sale' and the 'dressouer de cuisine' and a late medieval English romance, *The Life of St Werburge*, was referring as a matter of course to 'the cupboard with plate shyning fayre and clere'. The essential feature of the buffet was that it was not a cupboard in the modern meaning but a stand of open shelves; but these were generally combined with closed compartments, and the fully developed buffet or dresser often had open shelves at the top, a closed cupboard at intermediate level, and a base stand upon which the less valuable utensils were placed [Plates 73 and 74]. In the late fifteenth century, the custom of dining in the chamber was becoming increasingly common. It was not unusual to entertain visiting notables there rather than in the hall, and the dresser developed into a very splendid piece indeed in aristocratic houses; and not only there. By the early sixteenth century Gilles Corrozet describing the furniture of less exalted dwellings apostrophized the chamber as 'garnye d'un beau buffet', and the abundance of dressers in the Low Countries is shown by the mention in a document of 1462 of eleven different kinds.[6]

Further evidence of this specialization is the appearance in English documents from the early fifteenth century of references to 'gardevyans' or food or 'livery' cupboards. They were sometimes kept in the chamber itself and were intended to hold the food and drink to be consumed by a guest before retiring, or as a breakfast snack upon waking up. Sometimes the closed compartment of the buffet itself was used for this purpose, but the provision of cupboards specifically for food is attested not only by documents but by the survival of pieces with open-work tracery decoration intended to serve for ventilation [Plates 72 and 76]. In France 'garde-manger' usually meant a separate room, although in a small house it might be only a cupboard; at Bordeaux in 1422 there was one made of iron.

It was at this time too that tables became common and diversified. There are some early illustrations of small and of round tables [Plate 79], and in the chapter-house of Salisbury Cathedral is an elaborately decorated round table which appears to date, in the main, from the fourteenth century [Plate 77]. Nevertheless, most medieval examples were merely long boards placed upon moveable trestles, and in many vernaculars the earliest word for a table was a 'board'. Writing in about 1449 to her husband, Margaret Paston told him that she had found his signet ring 'upon your board' and implied, intentionally or otherwise, that he had been careless to leave it lying there. The form and the name continued for a long time, for so long in fact that in English 'board' came to be used – and still is – as a collective noun for almost any body of men of affairs who sit at a table and exercise authority. Most early tables were set up in the hall for dinner and were meant to accommodate the diners sitting in a long row upon benches against the wall, and in consequence they were long and narrow. The table, in fact, was a very subordinate article of furniture and Gilles Corrozet again stated its position plainly:

Tout ainsi la table se jecte   (The table defers to the bench as
Vers le banc, comme à lui subjecte.   though subject to it.)

Even at the end of the century the long and narrow proportions of early tables was taken for granted by many men, and Montaigne complained of those in private houses in Basel that they were 'very large, both round and square, so that it is difficult to place the dishes upon them'.[7]

Nevertheless, by the fifteenth century tables were in regular use for other purposes than dining, for this is the clear implication of the mention in a Bolognese inventory of 1405 of 'une tavola da mangiare'. Late-fifteenth century Spanish inventories include such highly specialized forms as chess-tables; in 1470 Jeanne of Laval had in her chamber a basset – a small low table; and in 1446 the Prior of Durham owned 'une mensa de Prusia cum foliis', a description which suggests that at least something more than a mere board was intended.[8]

By the end of the century, or very shortly afterwards, tables in the modern sense were sufficiently common in southern Germany and the surrounding lands to have survived in some numbers, and with very diverse forms, as shown by engravings and by examples in the Historisches Museum at Basel, the Landesmuseum at Zurich and the Victoria and Albert Museum [Plates 78, 80 and 81].

As well as beds and cupboards and tables, other articles of furniture became more specialized at this time and chairs, benches, counters and

writing desks began to assume some very particular forms; but while it
is necessary to emphasize these novelties it would be a mistake to
exaggerate their importance. If European society as a whole is considered they are more significant as portents of the future – in some
cases a very far distant future – than as evidence of the living standards
of most men. To a considerable degree they were confined to a small
ruling class and many to a few persons even within that restricted
milieu. Furniture developed very rapidly at this time in many ways,
but on a limited scale and it was not until after the Middle Ages that
the new comforts of kings began to spread, not to ordinary men, but to
men who were something less than princes and potentates.

Furniture of estate

At the highest level furniture was becoming a matter of prestige as well
as comfort. Those potentates who were turning themselves into the
absolute rulers of large territories were anxious to dazzle meaner eyes
with their splendour and magnificence and were using furniture,
among other things, to this end. The Burgundian court of the fifteenth
century is perhaps most famous for display, but others had begun the
game earlier. The buffets which were set up for special occasions, such
as that erected in 1389 upon the entry of Isabella of Bavaria into Paris,
were probably little more than rough platforms, admired not for their
own beauties but for the plate upon them. By the end of the next
century, however, buffets were carefully wrought and expensively
decorated, and had developed from purely utilitarian articles into
'meubles honorables'.

For the very wealthy, indeed, some furniture was made for no other
purpose than display. As early as 1403 Margaret of Flanders was
buying two cradles for her child, one for it to be nursed and cossetted
in, and one for show on ceremonial occasions. In an English manuscript, probably of the fifteenth century, *The Christening of a Prince or
Princess*, the need for two cradles was stressed, of which one, the 'cradell
of Estate', was to be larger and more richly decorated than the other.
Cradles were not the only pieces intended for show, and in 1471 at
Angers there was a buffet with a canopy above which was expressly
described as 'de parement'.

It is 'estate' and 'parement' that account for the ubiquity of canopies
at this time. They probably originated, in a fixed form, as an occasional

comfort in an open hall. In 1249–50 Henry III commanded wainscot to be fixed for the length of six couples of rafters above the high table in his hall at Clarendon. This has been interpreted as an order to affix the wainscot to the rafters so as to alleviate the discomfort of a leaky roof. In fact, wainscot so fixed would be small protection against even a drizzle and it seems fairly clear that what was meant was a canopy set above a dais and intended to protect the diners from the soot and dirt of the smoke-blackened roof. On a fourteenth-century fresco in the lower church at Assisi a wainscotted wall is depicted with a table and bench in front of it, and over all a projecting canopy. Canopies of this sort were common as late as the end of the fifteenth, and perhaps into the sixteenth century, in the aisled halls then being erected by wealthy clothiers around Halifax; at Ovenden Hall – a small house long since converted into tenements – an almost complete example survived until 1963, and a restored example still survives at Thornhill Lees Hall near Dewsbury [Plate 82].

It was probably because of its early connection with the high table that the canopy became such a common symbol of rank and majesty. In most early manuscripts temporal rulers, and even the most saintly persons, are seated upon fold-stools or on elaborately decorated chairs with low backs; in later ones they almost invariably sit upon high backed chairs beneath a timber or cloth canopy [Plate 83]. Fixed canopies of cloth or of timber were also set up above the places where great men habitually sat, and they were such a normal feature above the high table in French houses that 'dais' and 'ciel' became interchangeable words [Plates 75, 84 and 86].

Canopies of cloth, easily dismantled and easily carried, were often provided as a mark of respect for important visitors, and especially for sovereigns [Plate 85]. An inventory of the possessions of Charles V of France, taken in 1380, lists canopies which were especially intended for use at important functions and festivities. When Queen Margaret of Scotland visited Aberdeen in 1511 there were chosen, in Dunbar's words,

> . . . four men of renown
> In gownes of velvet, young, abill and lustie,
> To beir the pall of velvet cramase
> Abone hir heid, as the custom hes bein.

Canopies used upon the most solemn occasions came to be known as 'cloths of estate' and were regarded with some awe. In 1540 English legislators found time to pass a law forbidding any but the king's children to sit next to the cloth of estate in the Houses of Parliament.

It was probably because the canopy had acquired such an aura of dignity and majesty that it was sometimes placed above other pieces of furniture as well as chairs and thrones. It was quite common, at least in illuminations, above prayer-desks. In an 'Annunciation' from an English manuscript of the fifteenth century, the Virgin is at a prayer-desk [Plate 87] which is placed against a wall and beneath a projecting canopy, and in a psalter of perhaps slightly earlier date, originally made for the Earl of Warwick, is a scene with a similar desk. Beds were often used as chairs of state and there are a few survivors with canopies above them instead of full-length testers and curtains: an example of 1470 is in the National Museum at Munich and another of somewhat later date in the Historisches Museum at Basel was referred to earlier. So pronounced was the concept of the canopy as a sign of rank that it was also placed upon furniture which was never intended for the use of any one person, but was meant to be a prestige-piece. The 'dressouer de parement' listed at Angers in 1471 was distinguished by the canopy above it. Canopied buffets occur in illuminations [Plate 88] and an English example survives at Badminton [Plate 89].

The notion that rank could and should be expressed in furniture had gone far enough in France in the fifteenth century for a would-be codifier and lawgiver to arise. In *Les Honneurs de La Cour* Alienor de Poitiers laid down what forms were appropriate to all social degrees from knights' ladies up to queens. Buffets of mere ladies were to have two shelves only, countesses could have three, princesses four, and queens five. Further the cloths draped upon them were also subject to regulation, and a queen could have crimson cloth of gold, while a countess had to content herself with velvet. It is not likely that anyone except their authoress took these rules very seriously – in fact she complained about those who broke them – but they illustrate in an exaggerated form some of the attitudes towards furniture to be found at high social levels.[9]

In a less exaggerated form the new standing of furniture is revealed in legal documents and in travellers' accounts. Although inventories still paid far more attention to rich textiles than to furniture, they no longer ignored the latter; Jeanne of Laval's inventory for example went into some detail in describing individual pieces. Even in England the new feeling is apparent in the Duchess of York's will of 1495, wherein a piece of furniture other than a bed was mentioned – 'my chair with the covering' – and was obviously a much prized possession. In a Bolognese inventory of 1505 the gilded framework of the bedstead was described in more detail than the coverings, and in his descriptions of the costly palaces of the Venetians, de Commines singled out the magnificence of the ceilings, the chimney-pieces and the gilded bedsteads.[10]

This appreciation had begun much earlier, and its first stages are revealed as early as the late fourteenth century by an international trade in furniture. In 1384 Francesco Datini wrote from Avignon to Florence to order some chests for his customers and asked that they should be 'handsome and showy and of good workmanship . . . spend on them seven or eight florins a pair; the finer and better they are, the better I can sell them'. At this time not only Florentine but Catalan chests from Barcelona were being imported into southern France and between 1388 and 1402 'bois d'Irlande', presumably Irish bog oak, was coming in as well, and probably for use upon pieces intended to be richly ornamented. By the fifteenth century Flemish chests were reaching a wide market on the continent, and were entering England in such numbers that in 1483 the gild of cofferers obtained an Act of Parliament which forbade the trade; but failed to hinder it.

The golden age of timber

Late medieval furniture differed from earlier in many ways, and especially in its method of construction. Instead of thick hewn timbers of large scantling and great weight it was made up of thin panels fitted into a well-jointed framework of uprights and cross-rails, and a far more sophisticated mode of ornament could be worked than was possible upon the plank-like structures of earlier years. The change was momentous and its causes have been much debated. On the one hand there has been a tendency to see the invention of the saw-mill in south Germany in the early fourteenth century as almost a sufficient explanation in itself, and to suppose that it created a demand from which all the other consequences flowed. On the other hand it has been argued that it was the desire for lighter and more easily ornamented furniture that brought about the introduction of sawn timbers. There is something to be said for both these views, but neither is wholly adequate.

84

That the saw-mill did not wholly create the demand which it satisfied is shown by the early emergence of gilds of furniture-makers anxious to exploit demands and develop skills which were beyond the capacities of the carpenters. The organizational development was not uniform throughout Europe. In Holland carpenters and joiners were in the same gild until the early sixteenth century and in south Germany apparently even later. Nevertheless by the late fourteenth century a gild of 'huchiers-menuisiers' had been founded in Paris, there is evidence that as early as 1280 in Rostock and 1200 in Zurich some craftsmen were specializing in the making of chests, and there seems to have been a turners' gild at Cologne by 1180. It is probable that a differentiation between carpenters and furniture-makers was appearing well before the fourteenth century, and it seems reasonably certain that, whatever the forms of organization might be, there was a tendency for some craftsmen to become highly specialized and to develop exceptional skills in order to satisfy a growing demand both for more furniture and for better furniture.[11]

It is unlikely, therefore, that it was the invention of the saw-mill which created a demand for new forms of furniture, but on the other hand it seems equally unlikely that the demand was responsible by itself for the invention of the saw-mill. It is noticeable that furniture-makers were not everywhere quick to avail themselves of the products of the saw-mill. Datini, in his previously quoted letter of 1384, was asking his Florentine correspondent for chests and coffers of light wood, but most of the surviving pieces which can confidently be assigned to the fourteenth century are constructed in the old manner, and it was not until the next century that the new came fully into its own. The conditions which were encouraging the production of furniture were also encouraging that of wainscot. Wainscot was well known long before the fourteenth century, but while the upper classes maintained a peripatetic way of life it was more convenient to cover walls with portable hangings than with fixed wainscot, which could serve only one house, and only one room within it: when a more sedentary existence became common the greater efficiency and durability of wainscot in covering walls and excluding the weather became apparent. At first, however, while thick panels had to be laboriously split it was extremely expensive, and sawn timber, which was at first little more than a convenience in furniture-making, was essential to wainscot if it was ever to be produced in the quantities, and at a price, to meet the growing market. The saw-mill did not bring about the desire for lighter and more sophisticated furniture, but it played a large part in intensifying and widening the demand which it satisfied. That demand, on the other hand, did not of itself lead to the invention of the saw-mill, but alongside of the demand for wainscot contributed towards it.

The new status of furniture had in part been made possible by the technical advances which enabled joiners to work in wood with a skill and artistry which had previously been attained only by masons and by the craftsmen who worked in precious materials. As a result wood was more widely employed and more commonly displayed than before in a number of ways. In the first place wooden members which had previously been hidden by the rich fabrics draped over them, were now made to be seen and admired. The change in the meaning of 'bed' and 'lit' from the old connotation to the modern one is a reflection of this. Bed-hangings never lost favour, but increasingly they had to share it with the highly decorated framework of the bed. Thus agreements with furniture-makers of Pistoia in 1468 and 1488 go into immense detail about the ornament and intarsia to be applied to bedsteads; and early in the next century the bill for a walnut bedstead for Henry VIII shows that six carvers worked upon it for ten months, and when they had finished the gilders got to work.[12]

Secondly, ornament was more and more produced by working upon the wood itself. Many early wooden pieces had their decoration carried out in paint, as for example, the cupboard in Halberstadt Cathedral, or relied upon the patterns formed by the iron bands which encompassed them. Many of the most highly ornamented early pieces were not chests but caskets, and even when these were of wood their enrichments were often in another material. From the late fourteenth and fifteenth centuries however there survive many chests, of French, German, English, Spanish and Low Country origin, lavishly carved with a variety of motifs and subjects, and in many styles [Plates 90, 91, 92 and 93]. Similarly, fold-stools, whose wooden framework had often been covered with precious or semi-precious metals or stones, were superseded by chairs of estate, equally magnificent, but relying for their ornament upon the elaborate carving of the timber [Plates 94 and 97].

Thirdly, there was a greater use of wood for purposes which had more usually been fulfilled by fabrics. The most widespread instance of this is the employment of wainscot in place of hangings. For canopies the development is not easy to establish in detail, for it is a matter of a

86

change in the proportions in which the materials were used rather than the ousting of one by the other. If the interpretation given earlier of the wainscotting above the royal chair at Clarendon is correct, timber canopies were not unknown in the thirteenth century. But when canopies are depicted at all in early manuscripts they are of fabric, while in later years timber and fabric ones are illustrated in about equal numbers and the two kinds figure side by side on a page from a French manuscript of *c*. 1470. Except in the box-bed of generally humble circles and the wooden testers of the sixteenth and seventeenth centuries, wood did not often replace bed-hangings, but beds with a timber canopy at Basel and Munich will be recalled, and the fifteenth-century bed with curtains on one free side and wainscot on another in the German castle of Meran has been mentioned before in a different connection.

The Gothic style

Despite the enhanced prestige of their products and their own ability to exploit new techniques, there were limits to the freedom of furniture-makers. It will be remembered that by the mid-twelfth century Romanesque architectural motifs were appearing upon furniture, and by 1200 had eliminated earlier ones from all but the more retarded pieces. The victory of Romanesque in this sphere came slowly, but the advent of Gothic architecture was reflected very quickly indeed upon furniture. That the change was sudden was in part because it was at first superficial, and early Gothic furniture differed from late Romanesque in decorative detail and in very little else: shallow-cut round-headed arcading, for example, was superseded by equally shallow arcading with two-centred heads, and nail-head and billet ornament gave way to cusping and crocketting. Before long, however, the passage from one style to the other brought about an increase in the architectural control of furniture. This is revealed in the appearance of pieces which are not merely vehicles for a display of detail, but are conceived as minute buildings in themselves.

This was not confined to furniture, and the erection of 'aedicules' – small stone structures with a special purpose, such as shrines and tombs – within larger buildings is a feature of the age; and these probably provided the prototypes for furniture. The very early cupboard at Obazine has been described by Jacqueline Viaux as 'un monument réduit à l'échelle de l'homme'. Reliquaries and treasure-chests in precious and semi-precious metals, generally of ecclesiastical origin, provide some of the clearest instances; for example the silver and copper gilt caskets at Bouillac (Tarn-et-Garonne) in the form of a church with clerestory, transepts and central tower. The now vanished cupboard from Noyon Cathedral had a crenellated parapet and a gabled roof with a gabled dormer in it. A cupboard in Brandenburg Cathedral was made with false dormers in the gabled roof, and another cupboard from Lübeck had a false front with a crenellated parapet and a large trefoil-headed door.[13]

When the new lighter furniture appeared there was already a long tradition among furniture-makers of copying architectural motifs; and this was reinforced by the accidental similarity between the principles of construction of the new furniture and of contemporary building. In classical architecture the walls are load-bearing and the stability of the structure depends upon them; in Gothic architecture, as in most modern building, the walling is merely a curtain to keep out the weather, and stability is provided by the framework – of stone in the Middle Ages, of steel or concrete today – to which the walling is attached. In early furniture all members were of the same heavy scantling and bore what weight there was equally: the new furniture was of thin panels held together by a stouter framework. In consequence, furniture-makers, like master-masons, thought of their productions as consisting of so many structural members with an in-filling in the bays between them. Whatever motifs they might employ, their work resembled that of the masons by its very form. With the prestige of masonry what it was, with the wood-workers facing the problem which had previously confronted masons – of evolving an ornament for large surfaces with no structural function – it was not surprising that the motifs already to hand were taken over.

It is perhaps possible that furniture might nevertheless have produced a distinctive ornamentation of its own, but for the effect upon it of its relationship with wainscot. Wainscot and furniture were very much one flesh at this time, and it is significant that when, at the very end of the Middle Ages, wood-workers invented an ornament of their own, of intarsia in the south, of linen-fold or 'parchment' panelling in the North, the same forms appeared simultaneously or in quick succession upon both wainscot and furniture [Plate 96]. But wainscot was very much under the direct influence, if not the control, of the masons and

The Gothic style

72 Late medieval English livery cupboard. The ventilation panels are formed, and ornamented, by open-work tracery.

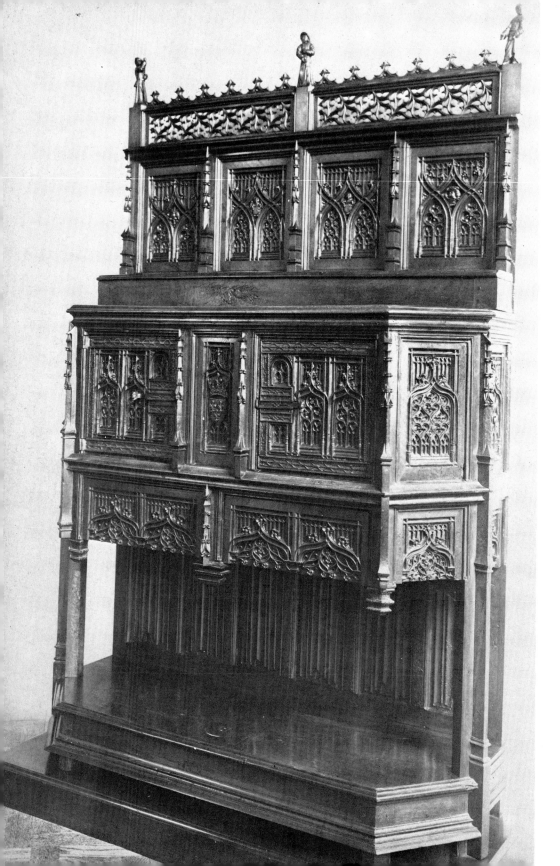

73 (*opposite*) Late fifteenth-century buffet of French origin, with tracery ornament above and linen-fold below. The intermediate compartment could be locked, the plate stood on the upper shelf and the less valuable utensils on the lower shelf.

74 Early sixteenth-century French buffet with Renaissance ornament but still with Gothic mouldings to the shafts.

75 *Balshazzar's Feast*, from the late fifteenth-century *Bible Historiale*. Notice the chair of estate, and the buffet at one side.

76 Cupboard of *c.* 1500; some of the ornamental tracery panels are left open for ventilation.

77 (*opposite above*) Round table in chapter-house of Salisbury Cathedral, in a fourteenth-century style. The top is modern.

78 (*opposite below*) Softwood table of south German origin, with low relief ornament.

79 *The Annunciation* by Robert Campin, early fifteenth century. The small table in the middle gives the room a cluttered un medieval appearance.

80 *A Ball*, engraving of *c.* 1500 by Mark Jezinger. In contrast with Plate 79, what little furniture there is, is ranged against the wall. The table, with its richly carved stand, is set in an alcove.

81 Table of *c.* 1500 with the arms of Abbot Henry of Mandach, from Rheinan Abbey.

82 Timber canopy above the hall dais, still surviving at Thornton Lees Hall near Dewsbury, Yorkshire.

83 X-chair with a textile canopy of state above. The canopy is carried on wooden brackets framed into the uprights of the chair-back. From a fifteenth-century French manuscript.

84 (*opposite*) Charles the Bold, presiding at a chapter of the Order of the Golden Fleece *c.* 1473, sits beneath a splendid canopy.

Er comence le second liure de la thoison dor

tresexcellent prince
et tresreluisant en
puissance et vertu
et mon tresredoub
te seigneur monsr

Charles par la grace de dieu duc de
bourgongne de lothrich et de bra
bant/ de lembourg et de luxem
bourg, Conte de flandres, dar
tois et de bourgongne. palatin

85 Henry VIII, in
procession to open the
Parliament of 1512, walks
beneath a canopy of state.
From a contemporary
Roll in the library of
Trinity College,
Cambridge.

86 Pope Urban II gives
an audience to St Bruno.
By the time of this
painting, by F. Zurbaran,
the Pope sits upon a
chair of no great
distinction, but still
beneath a canopy, the
saint sits on a stool with
nothing but a halo
above him.

87 (*above left*) The Virgin at a
canopied prayer-desk. From a
fifteenth-century English
manuscript.

88 (*above right*) Richard II holding
court from Jean de Wavrin's
Chronique d'Angleterre. The buffet
has a textile canopy above it.

89 Canopied buffet at
Badminton House, with linen-fold
ornament.

90 Late fifteenth-century French chest elaborately decorated with flamboyant tracery and architectural motifs.

91 Fourteenth-century French chest, with a tilting scene on the front.

92 Fourteenth-century German chest, carved with foliage and with animals in roundels.

93 Fifteenth-century Spanish chest, with elaborate tracery ornament.

94 Late medieval chair with open tracery on the back and on the seat front, much restored, in Ketteringham Church, Norfolk.

95 The chair of the Master of the united gild of St Mary, St John and St Catherine at Coventry, a heavy piece which was meant to stay in its permanent place on the Dais.

96 Early sixteenth-century settle with linen-fold ornament.

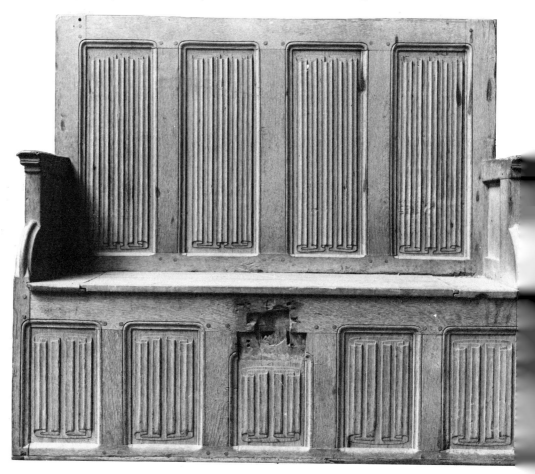

97 Chair with a high back, with tracery ornament and cusping, from a late fourteenth-century English manuscript.

98 Early sixteenth-century Tyrolean cupboard, the ornament provided by low-relief carving and by elaborate ironwork.

architects whose ends it served and whose productions it covered. The results may be seen in many late-fifteenth and early-sixteenth century pieces of wainscot and furniture which appear to be copying not, as earlier, a whole building, but one or more bays of the façade of a building. The surfaces of a late-fifteenth century chest in the Victoria and Albert Museum, for example, are worked in this form and a buffet which once belonged to the Dukes of Burgundy has its back divided into separate panels carved to resemble the fenestrated bays of contemporary building.[14]

It is in this way that furniture in the later Middle Ages is most closely controlled by architecture, and the more obvious use of architectural motifs is only a symptom of this. All kinds of masonry ornament, from base-mouldings to crocketting, were applied to it and such constructional forms as arcading and vaulting carved upon it. Nevertheless that these were of less significance than the over-riding influence of the baying system of Gothic building, is shown by the later profusion of the wholly unarchitectural 'linen-fold' motif upon furniture and wainscot which never lost an architectural form.

Regional variations

It was not until the end of the Middle Ages that furniture first began to reveal differences in style and approach between one region and another. In one way this is quite simply because it is only from this time that sufficient examples survive to allow conclusions to be drawn about differences of any kind. There is, however, more to it than that. A superficial but extremely obvious difference between late medieval English and French furniture is the ornamental use of perpendicular tracery upon the one and of flamboyant tracery upon the other. By that time English and French schools of masonry had developed very clear national characteristics and, as furniture-makers in both countries copied their own masons, a national style in furniture began to be evolved parallel with that in architecture.[15]

Of course, it would be wrong to think that all European countries of the time were as far advanced towards nationhood as England and France, and in Italy there was a very marked difference between Lombardy, for example, and Tuscany. Gothic architecture never had much of a welcome in Italy and was never indigenous there, as it was in most of northern Europe. Further, its career in central Italy was

99 (*opposite*) Early-sixteenth century cupboard of softwood from south Germany; with shallow carving

cut short very early by the Renaissance and there is an almost total lack, except in the north, of Italian examples of the highly decorated Gothic furniture which became common in the fifteenth century throughout most other regions of western Europe.[16]

In northern Italy, however, at least for most of the fifteenth century, furniture developed along very much the same lines as in southern Germany and the Alps. There such motifs as roundels, tracery, a running vine scroll, were almost universal. They were carried out in a very flat technique and the decoration was concentrated more upon the uprights and cross-pieces than upon the intermediate panels [Plates 98 and 99]. North Italian practice was not greatly different from this, and even when it preferred non-Gothic motifs it still worked in the same technique: there are a number of fifteenth-century chests from the Adige district with a more Italian ornament but carried out in the flat manner typical of southern Germany, and some Venetian chests of about 1500 have their closest relatives in the Tyrol.

While southern German furniture resembled that of northern Italy it differed in many ways from that of northern Germany, where ornament was in deep relief, where an architectonic form was given to all pieces which could bear it, and where the intermediate panels between the structural members were highly decorated. These features were not peculiar to Germany, but were to be found throughout most of northern Europe where the general principles of construction and decoration were remarkably uniform; and national differences revealed themselves in ways no less important, but much less easy to delineate. Thus, French furniture tended to be even more architecturally conscious than the others. It was rarely without richly worked tracery and cusping, and yet by the end of the fifteenth century was also remarkable for the profusion of its sculptured ornament. In northern Germany on the other hand there was a longer-maintained devotion to Romanesque ornament, a heaviness of proportion, and a liking for a display of fantasy in details. Flemish furniture was perhaps remarkable in two ways: for its fondness for sculptured representations of religious scenes; and for developing a form of ornament – the famous 'linen-fold' – which gave a rich effect and yet could be more or less mass-produced to meet the demands of a very wide and swiftly expanding market. English craftsmen arrived late and tended to copy French and Flemish examples, but with their own peculiarities of ornament upon forms which were of generally lighter construction. The Spanish, too, were

importing much Flemish furniture, but native craftsmen, while not
disregarding new forms and techniques, were fond of the old, and continued a use of coloured woods, of gilding, and of elaborate iron-work
ornament.

The most obvious of all these variations was between south and
north or, to put it in a meaningful way, between the furniture of the
mountainous regions and that of the north European plain and its
peripheral uplands. In the north furniture was treated architectonically
and embellished with deeply-cut sculptured ornament; in the south
ornament was in low relief and was applied equally to structural and
non-structural members. This division over-rode national boundaries
and human institutions; it was the direct result of different environ-
ments producing different kinds of timber. In the north hardwoods,
and especially oak, were easily available and could be treated sculp-
turally; in the south craftsmen had to use soft woods, such as larch and
pine, which were unsuitable for high relief and imposed a flat manner
of ornament upon furniture. It will be remembered that the impressive
hutches at Valère in the upper Rhône valley are made of larch, pine
and walnut. The significant difference between them and any typical
product of north Europe of the fifteenth century does not lie in the
presence or absence of architectural ornament or in a difference of
style, but in the contrast between the deeply-cut volume-conscious
ornament of the hard woods and the flat and almost two-dimensional
ornament of the softer woods.

It was because north Italy and south Germany had at least one
feature of their environment in common – the nature of the timber
available to their carpenters – that they formed a single furniture-
province in the late fifteenth century. However, it must be remembered
that this occurred at the meeting place of two countries which, for
whatever reasons, were unable to create a nation-state for many
centuries and which in the years before 1500 were far removed from
even the embryonic nationhood of such countries as France and
England. In the course of the sixteenth century, however, a sense of
Italian nationality was appearing, revealing itself most clearly perhaps
in Machiavelli's heartfelt pleas for unity. And it was in this century
that forms and styles which had originated in Tuscany spread into
northern Italy and gave its furniture a character which distinguished
it clearly from that of southern Germany.

There is perhaps some need to labour this point, for while it would be wrong to ignore the effect of the natural environment upon furniture, it is equally wrong to exaggerate it and to fall into a kind of geographic-cum-economic determinism. The situation along the Italo-German border was exceptional. Elsewhere regional styles in furniture were coinciding with the appearance of more or less mature nation-states. The state was not the only begetter of the style, but the two were closely related and both were the result of a long historical process in which the environment was one element among many others.

The furniture which has just been discussed – distinguished by elaborate decoration and the most advanced techniques – belonged, of course, to men at a very high social level. Among those of lower rank furniture also varied from place to place, but the variations were not so much in ornament as in form, and they did not always follow national boundaries. The box-bed, for example, was well-established in some French provinces by the early sixteenth century, but appears to have been wholly absent from others, and on the other hand was well known in several countries outside France. Some other kinds of furniture, however, seem to have been very localized indeed. Thomas Coryat was quite a seasoned traveller, but was very much surprised to find that the beds in Savoy were so high off the ground that 'a man needed a ladder to get up'. Montaigne, too, commented on what he considered the peculiar south German custom of dispensing with tables in bedrooms and providing a hinged flap at the foot of the bed to serve in their stead. In Spain some provinces developed forms quite peculiar to themselves.

Not all peculiarities of form, however, occurred at a low social level and in restricted areas. The highly individual 'vargueños', for example, were purely Spanish, but were known in every part of the country and were pieces that only the very wealthy would need or could afford. In essence they were travelling chests, but of a very specialized kind. They were covered in leather ornamented with metal studs and had iron handles for lifting at both ends. The top was fixed, but one side dropped down to reveal an elaborate arrangement of compartments, shelves and boxes. The dropped side could be held in a position level with the base, and the whole, placed upon a separate table, was then used as a writing desk [Plates v, 119 and 128]. Most surviving examples came from a later period than the one we are discussing, but the type was in existence by the end of the Middle Ages.

The furnishings of the upper classes and those of the population as a whole were thus alike in varying from place to place, but were very different in the ways in which they varied. Upper class furniture was more or less uniform in any one country and differed from that of other countries not in its form, but in its style of ornament. More popular furniture was much less related to political boundaries. Within any one country it varied from region to region, but at the same time the furniture of any region often closely resembled that of some regions in other countries. Moreover, differences expressed themselves less in ornament than in form and usage.

These attributes of the furniture of ordinary men reflect, as for example in their lack of decoration, a lack of wealth; but they reflect as well – and very directly – regional differences in the natural environment, in the way of life and in the general standards of the people. At this level these were still of far greater effect than the unifying tendencies of the new states. The ruling classes, however, were very far removed from the immediate tasks of production in different natural conditions and in consequence their furniture had little regional variation of any sort within one country, and little variation in form from country to country. On the other hand they were very closely connected with the formation of the new political entities which were appearing in Europe at this time. They were not, except very indirectly, responsible for the national schools of masonry and ornament which had been developing for many years, but they alone were able, and predisposed, to exploit the creations of these schools to the full. In consequence, it is upon their furniture that national characteristics, over-riding local variations, are first discernible.

Cassoni

Italian marriage chests or 'cassoni', especially associated with Florence, are the best known of all pieces with a restricted distribution. They are outstanding for much else besides: they illustrate many of the forces which played a part in the development of furniture in general; they blend a modern style of decoration with an archaic form: they have aesthetic qualities far above those of any other furniture of any other period, and they often embody the work of the foremost artists of their time. Because of this, a brief account of their origins and development may be useful.

To say that marriage chests with painted figures and scenes upon them were peculiar to Italy would be an exaggeration. Examples are known from elsewhere. In Vannes Cathedral there is a late-twelfth-century marriage casket with a parchment covering upon which is painted a series of small-scale scenes of peace and war [Plate 100]. During the late fourteenth century Florentine merchants in Avignon were importing Catalan chests from Barcelona, some 'of fine gold and painted in fine azure with figures of ladies and knights and some painted with the story of King Priam'. A Danish marriage chest of 1605 has full-length figures of the bride and bridegroom painted upon the inside of the lid, as they are upon some cassoni [Plates 101 and 102]. But all of these, and others, are negligible in comparison both with the great number of Italian and especially Florentine examples which have survived in whole or in part, and in comparison with their very high artistic achievement.[17]

The changes in the composition and way of life of the ruling classes, which affected furniture throughout western Europe, appear to have been well advanced in central Italy at a very early date. By the end of the thirteenth century at least the Florentine ruling class was an amalgam of feudal and merchant families who were already acquiring town and country houses of some convenience, although often restricted in their comforts by the needs of defence. About a hundred years later Datini's villa at Prato with its well furnished rooms had reached a high level, and throughout the fifteenth century the standard of accommodation of upper class families rose steadily. By the early sixteenth century the Florentines had become a by-word among their neighbours for their luxurious country-houses, and the Venetian ambassador remarked that 'they have this weakness that they go about the world to make a fortune of 20,000 ducats, and then spend 10,000 on a palace outside the city'. Before long his own countrymen were to be equally marvelled at for their magnificent villas along the Brenta, but the Florentines had anticipated them, and others, by at least a century.

By the first decade of the fifteenth century the Florentine ruling class had successfully terminated its quarrel with the papacy, had survived the threat from Milan, and had rid itself of the terrifying menace of the Ciompi and of a political system controlled by popular forces. It was at this time that the Renaissance acquired a new dimension in Florence. The origins of that multiform movement are not within our purview, but it must be noted that it appeared and developed

94

at a time when, both before and during the Medici regime, the city was controlled by, or in the interests of, a small number of wealthy families. In their intercourse with one another they placed great emphasis upon marriage ties and upon the splendour of their marriage ceremonies. In recording the festivities at the wedding of his son with Nannina de Medici in 1466, Giovanni Rucellai was smugly eloquent about the richness of the credence and claimed that it was the finest ever seen on such an occasion. In these displays of status cassoni had an important role and when Rucellai drew up a list of the articles in the bride's dowry it began with a 'pair of chests'.[18]

It was, therefore, not surprising that cassoni were the object of some care and were as richly decorated as means allowed. Means, however, were not always immense. The Florentine oligarchy were not numerous in relation to the population as a whole, but yet they were relatively far more numerous than territorial magnates in other countries. Their collective wealth was considerable and cassoni were made for them in large numbers; between 1446 and 1465 two manufacturers alone are known to have turned out nearly two hundred separate chests for leading Florentine families, and there were about ten such workshops in Florence in the first half of the fifteenth century. With production on this scale the amount of wealth, and of time, which could be expended upon any one piece was limited, and in consequence there was little incentive to depart from the old, and comparatively quick, process of decorating with paint or with coloured stucco.[19]

These old decorative media were therefore still being used at a time when wholly new concepts of painting had been established and when new methods of construction were providing large panels to work upon in place of the many small panels of earlier furniture. This occurred at the moment when the Renaissance had bred in Florence a great number of talented men able to exploit the new opportunities and to ornament cassoni not with diffuse late Gothic scenes and figures, but with organized Renaissance compositions. It occurred also in that comparatively brief period when medieval craftsmen were transforming themselves into modern artists. Writing less than a hundred years later, in the mid-sixteenth century, Vasari found it necessary to explain to his readers that earlier artists had felt no shame in exercising their talent upon the decoration of furniture. In the fifteenth century painters and sculptors had not wholly established a new status for themselves and were not averse from tasks which would later come to

95

be considered beneath them. In consequence many cassoni can be attributed, with varying degrees of confidence, to such highly esteemed artists as Botticelli, Filippino, Pollaiuolo, Piero di Cosimo, Uccello, and Donatello. Francesco Pesellino was the most patronized of all cassoni painters in the years before 1460, and the demand for his products was such that he specialized in this work.

The mention in an early fourteenth-century document of a 'pittor coffanorum' shows that the painting of chests was a full-time occupation by then. The painter in question may have done no more than patterned decoration, but it is clear that by 1390 far more ambitious matters were not uncommon for there is a reference in that year to 'an old chest with figures'. Up to about 1400, however, Florentine cassoni probably differed little from the painted chests of several other countries. An example of about that date in the Victoria and Albert Museum has its sides and lids divided into small panels each with figures of ladies and cavaliers on horseback and probably similar to the Catalan chests imported into Avignon with their 'figures of ladies and knights' [Plate 103].

From about 1400 a new style appeared in which the painted decoration was organized into a single scene or a series of connected scenes, and was carried out in an up-to-date manner. At first this occurred in conjunction with old forms and an early chest in the Bargello at Florence has illustrations of the *Decameron* within quatrefoil panels, and a companion has scenes from the story of Actaeon and Diana. Quite early dentilled cornices and classical bases appeared upon fronts which were divided into panels not by any extraneous ornament but by their architectonic make-up. Before long all traces of the Gothic style disappeared from Florentine cassoni which are distinguishable in this way, and in others, from other Italian, and especially north Italian examples. Cassoni had reached perhaps the summit of achievement in Florence by the last decade of the fifteenth century: they were classically designed and beautifully proportioned pieces of furniture, enriched with painting which was always of the highest competence and sometimes reached the level of such a masterpiece as Piero di Cosimo's *Death of Procris* [Plate IV].

The iconography of these paintings is wide-ranging, but is mainly from profane sources [Plate 104]. Religious themes were not unknown, but probably the commonest was the story of Tobit; and Tobit appealed to Florentines because so many of them were business-exiles and looked

Cassoni

100 Late twelfth-century marriage casket, made of wood with a painted parchment covering, in Vannes cathedral.

101 and 102 Danish marriage chest of 1605, the figures of the bride and bridegroom painted upon the inside of the lid.

103 Late fourteenth-century Florentine cassone, painted with 'figures of ladies and knights'.

104 Fifteenth-century Florentine cassone panel, with a painting of a tournament in the Piazza S. Croce.

105 Fifteenth-century Florentine cassone, with a painting of the meeting of Solomon and the Queen of Sheba.

106 Fifteenth-century Florentine cassone, with a painting of *The Triumph of Love*.

107 Mid-fifteenth-century cassone, with a painting of a nude woman on the inside of the lid.

108 Mid-sixteenth-century Roman cassone with carved ornament in high relief.

109 Florentine cassapanca of *c.* 1550, the seat lifts up to reveal storage space below.

forward to their homecoming. Most of the other religious subjects seem to belong to ecclesiastical furniture. Taddeo Gaddi's panels of the lives of Christ and St Francis, now in the gallery of the Florentine Academy, originally formed parts of cupboards in the church of Santa Croce, and the Thebaid scenes – of hermits in the desert – on panels in the Uffizi are less likely to have come from a cassoni than, as Schubring thought, from a sacristy chest. Even when religious stories do appear upon cassoni they are often, in Schubring's opinion, nothing but a dramatization in another garb of popular tales [Plate 105].[20]

At first most subjects were drawn from very popular sources. For reasons which again are outside our purview, Italy, or at any rate Tuscany, had produced a vernacular literature very early and its themes were widely used throughout the fifteenth century. Illustrations of scenes from the *Decameron* have already been mentioned, but other popular *novelle* were also exploited and so too were portrayals of the 'Triumphs' which Petrarch had once made so fashionable [Plate 106]. Classical themes were also common, but often, for example in the *Death of Procris*, they were not taken directly from antiquity, but from popular contemporary dramatizations of antique stories.

It is perhaps not surprising that love-themes were common and that Ovid was the most popular of classical authors, so popular that Savonarola inveighed against the fondness for decorating marriage chests with Ovidian subjects. Eroticism sometimes revealed itself in paintings on the inside of the lid. An example from mid-fifteenth century Florence now at Copenhagen has scenes of a siege and allegorical figures of Faith and Justice on the outside; on the inside of the lid, not visible to the ordinary visitor, is a reclining naked woman raising her hand in a gesture of invitation [Plate 107]. However, it must not be supposed that every painting on the inside of a lid was erotic, and in the Musée des Arts Décoratifs at Paris there is one with an *Annunciation*. Masculine eroticism was often accompanied by exaggerated masculine praise of feminine chastity. Typical of this are panels in the Ashmolean Museum of the *Vestal Claudia* and of the *Marriage of Antiochus and Stratonice*, and the latter subject appears again on a chest in the Huntington Art Gallery in California.

These last are a sign of the changes in cassoni by the end of the fifteenth century, changes which culminated in the destruction by the later Renaissance of an art which its earlier self had helped to create. Several forces worked to this end, but perhaps the most important was

97

the increasing prestige of painting. On the whole very little other
furniture was painted in the manner of cassoni, but there were some
examples. A panel of 1486 in the Musée des Arts Décoratifs of *Jason
and Medea*, attributed by Schubring to the studio of Ghirlandaio,
appears to have been painted for the marriage bed of Lorenzo
Tornabuoni and Giovanna Albizzi. Commoner and more important
than such decoration was the practice of painting wainscot and the wall
above the wainscot. In the form of an imitation of intarsia and other
expensive processes it had been known for a long time and the 'spalliere
molto ricchi' noted at the Rucellai marriage in 1466 may have been of
this sort. In later years, however, it became normal to treat wainscot
in the same manner as cassoni. According to Vasari, Francesco
Ubertini, who had painted chests and chairbacks in the chamber of
Pier Francesco Borgherini, painted for another patron small figures
upon the walls of the ante-chamber, and Francesco Caroto decorated
an entire room with small-scale figured scenes. These were probably
upon wainscot as were the scenes, painted in his villa, of Lorenzo
Tornabuoni hobnobbing with the 'Seven Liberal Arts' and of his bride
being greeted by 'Virtue'.

Apart from the documentary evidence there are many surviving
panels painted in a cassoni manner which are too large to have come
from any chest or other piece of furniture. As Schubring has shown –
and he has listed many examples – they were originally fixed to the
wall above the wainscot. Sometimes it is quite impossible to be certain
of the origin of a surviving panel, and two early-sixteenth-century
scenes from *Orlando Furioso*, attributed to Girolamo da Santa Croce,
may have formed part of a wall decoration or may have been applied
to the fronts of two companion chests.

When wainscot and the wall-space above the wainscot was treated
like this, then the painting upon cassoni became of less importance. It
was now only a minor piece of organized decoration in a much greater
whole and no longer stood out from the rest of the room. Further,
painters now had new opportunities of displaying their skill upon the
much larger surfaces of wainscot and walling. It was probably for this
reason that in Venice, where there was much more wall painting,
there were few painted chests, if any, during the fifteenth century.
Cassoni painting was beginning to become small-scale work and
increasingly beneath the attention of men who aspired to cover whole
wall-surfaces and ceilings with their compositions. The increased

size of their work had an effect upon style and iconography.

This change did not occur by itself, but in conjunction with others. It would be naive to suppose that the oligarchs who ordered cassoni in the fifteenth century were men of the people, but that they had a more or less popular background of thought and culture is shown by the iconography of the early cassoni. It is now generally agreed that from about 1450 onwards, with the appearance of new courtly societies and nobilities in many Italian states, the Renaissance began to acquire new qualities. These revealed themselves upon cassoni in two ways. Firstly, by the early years of the sixteenth century there were two kinds of chests: those for use in bedrooms or other private chambers, and those for show in such public rooms as the Sala and Antecamera. This display was more noticeable in a city like Venice, where it was not unusual for leading families to have as many as two dozen chests, but it occurred in Florence as well. Secondly the effect of a more learned classicism remote from ordinary men became apparent. Cassoni were more and more embellished with classical ornament and given the appearance of a classical monument, a form well illustrated by the Strozzi chest of 1512. At the same time the subject matter of the paintings upon them was drawn, far more than before, directly from classical sources; and such recondite themes as the marriage of Antiochus and Stratonice, Horatius, and the denunciation and retirement of Scipio replaced the more popular ones of earlier years. As Schubring says, 'Die Novelle und das Genre verschwinden vor dem kanonischen Mythus. An Stelle der frischen Improvisation sprechen Hexameter und Alexandriner.'

In combination these developments destroyed the 'intimate domestic art', to use Schubring's phrase, of earlier cassoni. They eliminated painting, partly because it was a non-classical element within a classical framework, partly because it was of minor importance upon cassoni against the new background of interior decoration, and partly because it was beneath the attention of artists newly conscious of a higher status. In its place they introduced the richly carved and elegant pieces of the mid-sixteenth century, splendid in themselves, but wholly different from early cassoni [Plate 108].

4 The sixteenth century: modern men and modern homes

The modern house

Developments which had begun during the fifteenth century reached a new level in the next, when throughout much of western Europe absolute monarchies were establishing or had already established their power and prestige. Feudal nobles who had formerly been 'over-mighty subjects', either individually or in association with others, were ceasing to be semi-independent vassals in command of a military strength of their own and were beginning their long decline into mere titled owners of large landed estates. As a result their homes had fewer purposes than before and were freed from many of the restrictions once laid upon them. There was no longer any need for houses that were partly fortresses, partly seats of administration, and partly centres of economic activity providing for the large population of clients and retainers which the first two functions brought into being. Military strength and accessibility to supplies, therefore, were not of importance any more, but instead comfort or prestige or aesthetic design, or all three in conjunction, determined the form and character of a great house. The way in which these new elements affected building varied from country to country. In Spain the nobles moved into the towns; in England they built large, and the gentry built small, country-houses; in France the Crown and uniquely important families like the Guises and the Montmorencis, together with such wealthy and favoured financiers as Bohiers and Berthelot, built the châteaux of the Loire and of the Paris hinterland. The new houses were far from uniform, but much as they differed from one another, they differed from their predecessors far more; as may be seen when Plas Ucha, mentioned earlier, [Plate 34], is compared with its later compatriot of similar status, Vaynol Old Hall [Plate 110].

That the change was clear enough and significant enough to be understood at the time is shown by contemporary comment. In a letter to Pirckheimer, Ulrich von Hutten spoke scornfully of the old practice of building for security rather than for comfort, of living in low-ceilinged dark chambers and of lodging human beings almost cheek by jowl with the cattle and horses. In France, Henri Estienne accused earlier generations of designing their houses as though they were meant to be prisons and of neglecting all the conveniences which his own times rightly demanded. William Harrison in 1577 described the comforts and luxuries of the homes of his wealthier contemporaries with a complacent sense of superiority over former ages which was more indicative of the new conditions than all the criticisms of Hutten and Estienne, for he took for granted what they still found it necessary to urge: that houses should be built as pure residences and as nothing else.[1]

One effect of this change was that the hall, which had been almost a house in itself, became little more than an entrance vestibule. At first it lost none of its magnificence, indeed in some ways it became more imposing than ever, but it forfeited nearly all of its earlier functions; and these were taken over by other rooms. Instead of dining publicly in the hall, or on more intimate occasions in the solar or chamber, great men now took their meals in a dining room reserved for that purpose alone [Plate IX]. Equally they no longer used the hall for giving audiences or conducting business in; if they were mighty enough they had an audience chamber for the first, and for the second most men had a parlour. Some even had two parlours, one for winter and one for summer. The solar as well, which had once played several roles, acquired the name of the Great Chamber or the Saloon, ceased to be much of a bedroom and was used mainly as a sitting room. It was usually accompanied by a Long Gallery, in which the residents could get the benefits of exercise without having to meet the perils of the open air, and often by another chamber for the use of the lady of the house and her attendants. Not every home had all these rooms and even in those of some pretensions the hall might still contain a bed, and the parlour very often did so; but all the same this conversion of the house, from a centre of economic activity into a residence, was occurring at social levels far broader than those that had been affected by previous developments.[2]

In one way, of course, these changes followed from others of earlier years and it is possible to claim that the sixteenth century was no more than the fifteenth writ large. But while it would be difficult to say at exactly what point the medieval dwelling-cum-fortress-cum-workshop-and-farm turned into the modern residence, the metamorphosis amongst the upper classes and amongst townspeople was complete by the end of the sixteenth century. Furniture had shown some symptoms of change in the late Middle Ages, but the effect upon it of the consummation of the 'housing revolution' was enormous.

Where conditions had formerly inhibited its use they were now encouraging proliferation and specialization upon the one hand, and on the other were turning individual pieces from items of baggage or fixtures into furniture in the modern sense. The change in the nature of the house would have been enough by itself to cause an increase in the amount of furniture; but it did not occur by itself, for it was one aspect among many others of the transformation of feudal lords into royal courtiers. Whatever the pains of that process may have been, one of its compensations was clear: since great men no longer had to expend their fortunes upon maintaining private armies and fortresses and upon lavishing rewards upon likely supporters and bribes upon potential enemies, they could, although they now had many new demands upon their purses, devote more of their wealth than formerly to their comforts and luxuries. This, however, took place when the Renaissance was making men with any pretensions of belonging to the élite conscious of the need to be conscious of Art and to display Taste. One of the recognized ways of demonstrating both qualities was to build and decorate and furnish in the sumptuous manner that the age approved of [Plate 122]. Thus it happily turned out that the need for more furniture coincided with the ability to provide it, and both with the wish to do so.

It is a commonplace amongst sixteenth-century writers, whether critics or panegyrists of their times, that much furniture was to be found in houses of no very great distinction. Gilles Corrozet was something of a worshipper at the shrine of domestic comfort and his descriptions are not to be taken as typical of every French house, but his ideal chamber was immeasurably better furnished than that of Alexander Neckham in the twelfth century; although, since both rooms existed only on paper, their costs were exactly the same and Neckham was talking of the highest social level and Corrozet of relatively modest ones. How little Neckham was content with was related earlier; Corrozet wanted, besides the bed, a buffet, a bench, a table, a chest, an imposing great chair and an assortment of low stools and benches. He was not singular in these demands. In purporting to describe the contents of an ordinary German house Hans Sachs listed over three hundred different articles of household use and among them an impressive array of furniture. In England Harrison took some delight in lamenting the luxuries of furnishing and equipment which were demoralizing the lower orders to the detriment of their betters.

There was a large element of exaggeration in all of these writers, but matter-of-fact inventories paint a similar picture, and reveal amongst the wealthiest an almost fabulous richness of furnishing. The inventory of Lord Lumley's possessions drawn up at his command in 1590 is a good example. Lumley's pride in his ancestry was so inordinate that it drew a tart remark from James I, but despite, or because of, this he played no very great role in affairs. He was, however, in possession of a large fortune from his first wife and was a man of considerable culture who collected books and works of art. In what he was and what he was not he embodies some of the qualities which were affecting furniture at the time.

Like many of its predecessors the inventory opens its account of the household goods at Lumley Castle with the hangings, of which there were still a great many. It then lists five gilt bedsteads, twenty-three bedsteads of walnut or of marquetry and another forty which were of mere 'wainscot'; it continues with seventeen chairs and fifty-seven stools of walnut or marquetry, twenty-five tables of the same materials and a further fifteen of marble. A slightly earlier inventory of the goods of a man of far lesser standing – of Robert Atkinson, a fisherman of South Shields – lists in the hall two cupboards, a counter, a chair, two forms and a long settle, and refers to bedstocks and chests elsewhere in the house. Atkinson's furniture would not have fitted out a single one of Lumley's rooms, but it was not so much less than that which a great lord would have had in his hall in previous centuries. [3]

The homes of the French petite noblesse of the early sixteenth century were still far from luxurious, but they were better furnished than before. In the manor of Ruilly near Jargeau in 1527 the main room had a bench, three oak chairs, seven stools, a table of walnut and a buffet 'de salle'. It appears to have been almost standard practice in these houses to have a buffet of two stages, and upon it – in place of, or as

103

well as, plate – a copy of the translation of the Bible ordered by Charles V. The inventories of the 'rebel' burghers of Haarlem drawn up on Alva's orders in 1567 show that the richer Dutch townspeople owned a great amount of furniture. It may be surmised, too, that in France by the end of the sixteenth century some prestige pieces had become common enough to be almost mass-produced, for some of the large and expensive cabinets of the time are, apart from a few variations in detail, near replicas of one another.[4]

The proliferation of furniture is shown in another way by some of the provisions in the will of Ralph Collingwood of Titlington in Northumberland. When he died in 1570 he left a new-made cupboard to his eldest daughter and the cut timber for new cupboards and chests to his younger daughters. Many houses had held more than one cupboard or chest, but they had been a part of the house and were individual possessions only in the sense that they belonged to the head of the family. When large pieces could be owned by other members of the family, and even by younger daughters, then furniture was becoming very common indeed.

Moveable furniture

As important as the increase in the amount of furniture, was the greater diversity of its forms. Nearly all the types found in the sixteenth century had been known in principle during the fifteenth, but in practice examples had been rare and there had been little opportunity to develop potential variations. Now, however, the new wealth available for domestic comforts allowed and encouraged an increase in all kinds of furniture. New houses, accommodating new men, found new uses and therefore new forms for many established categories, called previously unknown ones into being, and at the same time checked the development of others.

Chests which had for centuries shared with beds an almost complete dominance of the household scene were summarily deprived of their status. In the changed conditions they were of no outstanding utility and although they continued to be used, and to be made, throughout the sixteenth and seventeenth centuries their importance declined in the same proportion as that of less portable but more convenient receptacles increased. Amongst the latter were cupboards which had been known in some countries, for example in southern Germany, for

The modern home

110 Vaynol Old Hall, Pentir, Caernarvonshire, a house of much the same status as Plas Ucha (Plate 33), but built about two centuries later and with much more accommodation and comfort. The far wing is a modern addition.

113 Lightly built caquetoire of the mid-sixteenth century.

114 Venetian sgabello of *c.* 1560, an easily moveable chair suited to the new houses with more rooms.

111 (*opposite above*) *The Last Supper*, sixteenth-century engraving by Wendel von Olmutz. Although most of the diners still sit on benches, three of them are given light chairs, and of three different kinds.

112 (*opposite below*) *L'Accouchée*, engraving by Abraham Bosse. The recently delivered mother is visited in bed by her friends, who sit upon light and easily moveable chairs.

115 Court cupboard of *c.* 1600, with canted central compartment.

116 (*above*) Draw-table of *c.* 1600, adapted to more varied uses than the medieval table-dormant.

117 (*below left*) Late sixteenth-century octagonal table, ornamental in itself and adapted to many uses.

118 (*below right*) Early seventeenth-century English chair-table. The table top hinges downwards to become the back of a chair.

119 (*opposite*) Vargueño in closed or travelling position, shown open in colour (Plate v).

120 A late medieval writing-desk; the writing platform has an elaborate mechanism for adjustment.

121 Early sixteenth-century oak writing 'till' with inlaid ornament.

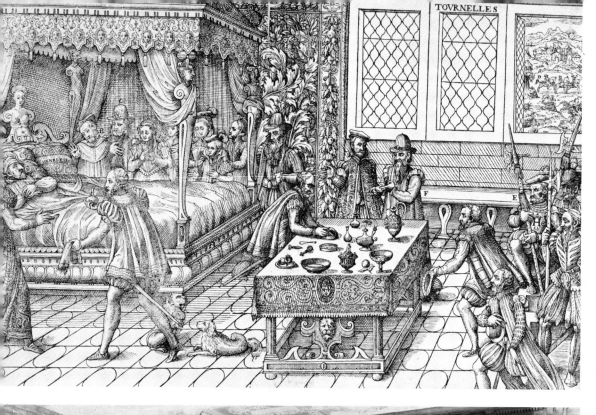

many years, but which now, and for the first time, became common and variegated.

The new cupboard was in part the old buffet in a new form, and cupboards with one or more stages unenclosed were still being made in the seventeenth century. The English term 'court-cupboard' was not very strictly used even as long ago as the reign of Elizabeth I and has been quite indiscriminately applied since, but its essence was the retention of an open stage or platform on which to display plate. In Spain and in Italy cupboards were rarely of two stages before the end of the sixteenth century and were more sideboards than anything else, with low closed compartments beneath a flat top intended again for the display of plate. In northern Europe two stages were more common and in the 'dining parlour' it was not unusual for both stages to be enclosed. A type very common in England and well known in northern France and in the Low Countries has a wholly open lower stage and a closed compartment with canted sides in the middle of the otherwise unenclosed upper stage [Plate 115].

This however was a vestigial feature and the wholly enclosed cupboard became more and more fashionable. Inventory-makers of the time were very conscious of the doors and shutters which enclosed some or all of the compartments. An English list of 1567 is typical in its references to 'an almerye with iiij doores' and 'a presse ... with v doores'. In its usual form the cupboard was divided horizontally into an upper and lower compartment and this functional division was generally reflected in the design of the front, with two doors to each of the two stages. There were, of course, many variations and an English cupboard with five doors and two 'floores' may be supposed to have had a threefold division and only a single door to one of them. A very large cupboard which belonged to Catherine de Medici appears to have had three doors running vertically from base to cornice and to have been divided into no less than forty-four compartments. The prevailing Italian type throughout most of the century, low-built and of one stage only, generally had two doors; but some Sienese examples have three.[5]

In the late Middle Ages very small chests of long and low proportions had occasionally appeared and had been intended to hold valuables or such minor articles of dress as gloves and ribbons. In France they were known as 'layettes', and as life became more sedentary the layette was attached to a larger and immobile piece of furniture and was metamorphosed into the drawer. As early as 1471 René of Anjou had in his

122 (*opposite above*) The death-bed of Henri II, 1559. By the mid-sixteenth century the macabre practice had developed of moving a dying potentate from his own bed to a 'bed of estate', where he could lie perhaps in more comfort before his death and certainly in more splendour after it

123 (*opposite below*) The Great Bed of Ware; a piece of furniture which had achieved popular fame within a few years of being made

château at Angers à cupboard 'a deux guischez et à une léaité'; that is, with two doors and a drawer. This, however, was very precocious for a secular piece, and most early examples are probably of ecclesiastical origin. A German one made by Ulrich Auer in 1458 was probably a sacristy chest as was also a cupboard of 1531 with an enclosed upper stage and three drawers below. But by about 1550 drawers were common in domestic surroundings. A cupboard in the Burrell collection with late-Gothic ornament upon it has closed compartments at top and bottom with drawers at half-height. Florentine cupboards were rarely of two stages but a cassetone of *c.* 1600 was advanced enough to have two half-drawers above a low closed stage. The previously-mentioned English 'almerye' which had four doors also had two 'shoots' or drawers and many court-cupboards incorporated drawers in the highly ornamented friezes of the upper and lower parts.

While the proliferation of cupboards and of other fixed containers was a direct result of a less peripatetic society, the parallel multiplication of such articles as tables and chairs was brought about indirectly, and in some cases through the provision of special-purpose rooms. The effect upon furniture of setting aside a room for no other use than to eat in was very great indeed. So long as men had dined in the hall the many purposes of that room had often caused the dining-table to be a mere board, laid upon moveable trestles when needed and dismantled when not. Even when there had been a 'table dormant' the needs of the household had relegated it to the sides or the end of the hall and had ranged the diners on benches against a wall. With the advent of the 'dining parlour' the table was moved into a permanent position in the middle of the room and there acquired a dignity which it had not had before.[6]

It acquired new forms as well. Dining parlours were smaller than the great halls which they superseded and fewer people were eating in them than had dined in the hall. In consequence, although a large table was still sometimes needed, it was a convenience to have a small one on most occasions. What might otherwise have been an intractable dilemma was solved by the invention of the 'drawing-table' with pull-out leaves [Plate 116]. Its earliest use is unrecorded, but by the end of the century mere merchants in such far-away towns as Newcastle-upon-Tyne had 'tables with leaves' or 'drawing tabills of waynskot'. A highly ornate example described in an inventory of 1600 still survives at Hardwick Hall. In some circumstances the new fashion of furniture in

106

conjunction with older habits of dining led to the use of permanent but easily movable tables. Montaigne noticed when at Innsbruck that the sons of the Archduke of Austria took their seats 'at a short distance from the table and it (was) moved up to them ready laden with viands'.

The migration of the dining table to the middle of the room also affected the furniture which the diners sat upon. The long benches which had been both a convenience and a necessity when people sat against the wall were a nuisance when moved away from it, and each diner now had to be provided with his own seat. At first only the head of the family had a chair and nearly everybody else had to make do with a stool. In one way this left many people worse off than they had been, and so it was not long before chairs became common in the houses of wealthy men. In France, it will be remembered, chairs with a reclining back were often given in the late sixteenth century to those who dined at the head of the table and this was probably an intermediate stage on the road to chairs for all.

The 'Dyning Parlor' was not the only new room in the new kind of house. The Solar underwent an even deeper decline than the Great Hall, and by the middle of the century the Great Chamber, or the Saloon, and the Long Gallery were the places where leisure was spent and guests entertained. With such ample accommodation available for those purposes, and for those alone, furniture was doubly emancipated; it no longer had to be kept out of the way and it could be made for one use and one only. Instead of the occupants having to go to what little furniture there was because it was fixed and served several purposes, the furniture could now come to its users in the form of lightly-made pieces each with its own specialized use. Small tables and seats of various kinds were therefore made in large numbers and of such a nature that they could be moved from place to place within a room or even from room to room. The inventory of the contents of the Hôtel de Montmorency taken in 1556 speaks of pieces which were intended for use in many parts of the house and to be moved as need arose from room to room: ' ... quatre douzaines d'escabelles servans pour tout le logis ... huict demyes tables servans tant pour lad. salle du Roy que ailleurs.'[7]

In all countries the more varied social life of the upper classes was demanding a more flexible use of accommodation and of the furniture within it; in northern countries the demand was intensified by natural conditions. Southern Europe is not blessed with the paradisal climate that travel agents would have us believe in, but the winter is less of a problem, or a problem for less time, than it is, or was, in the north. There the most important comfort in any room was the fireplace; the overmantel above it was the dominant element in any scheme of decoration; and many pieces were sited to get as much warmth from the fire as possible [Plate 26]. In summer, however, or when considerations other than keeping warm were paramount, it might be desirable to be a long way from the fireplace and this, when most furniture was a fixture or was too heavy to move with ease, could cause considerable difficulties. The problem had existed to some extent in medieval times and ingenious but not wholly successful attempts had been made to provide articles which should somehow or other contrive to be in two places at once. Within the solar these shifts might serve, but as other rooms came into general use a different solution was necessary. The answer was to have many small light pieces in place of a few massive ones and the most obvious aspect of this change was the replacement of the communal bench by individual chairs for ordinary people [Plate 111].[8]

The increased role of women in social life also played a part here. On the whole feminine influence upon furniture was exerted indirectly, but the appearance, or at any rate the appearance in large numbers, of lightly-made seats and chairs was hastened and intensified by women's need and desires. By the early sixteenth century upper-class women had achieved at least this much independence in some countries: that they had social occasions of their own from which men were excluded either by request or, if recalcitrant, by intimidation. In France and Italy, for example, it was customary for a woman to give a party to her friends a few days after the birth of her child. The hostess received her guests in bed and they sat upon moveable chairs, which seem to have been designed for these or similar gatherings [Plate 112]. As early as 1514 Louize de Borgia had in her chamber a 'petite chaise à femme' which was contrasted with her 'grante selle', a ceremonial chair of medieval derivation. It is likely that similar chairs were known in England for a 'woman's chaire' was referred to in 1547; and the Italian 'sgabello', in essence a light stool with a back, was also mobile and was used for similar purposes [Plate 114].[9]

The French word for chairs like these was 'caquetoire'. It is said to be derived from one meaning 'jollity' and to be intended to refer to the gossip and giggling which went on, or was alleged by men to go on, at these essentially feminine encounters. It is possible that the term

108

included light armchairs, but in general it seems to have referred specifically to a chair with a low seat; in 1589 Catherine de Medici had 'une petite chaise basse autrement dit caquetoyres' and in 1599 Chancelier Hurault had 'une petite chaise basse caquetoire' [Plate 113].[10]

Chairs of this sort were probably common in many houses in France and Italy, but in northern Europe stools were still widely used instead. Chairs which resemble the caquetoire were not unknown there and one in the Rijksmuseum at Amsterdam with arm-supports and a reclining back is comparable in many respects, but although it is built without the usual closed sides of most northern chairs and is easily moveable, it is very much heavier than a caquetoire. Furniture in the north was developing in the same direction as in France and Italy, but not so quickly.

Other forms than chairs were also lightly made, even including some cupboards, or at least some of the smaller kinds which were in fact part-cupboard and part-sideboard. The order given when the hall in Capulet's house was to be cleared for a dance has often been quoted to illustrate this point: 'Away with the joint stools, remove the court cupboard, look to the plate.' It is probable that few cupboards could be treated as light-heartedly as that, for most of them were very big. Tables were a different matter, however, for although many were as massive as ever, small and light ones were multiplying rapidly in sympathy with the multiplication of rooms. As the Great Chamber and the Long Gallery took over some of the duties with which the Solar had formerly had to cope single-handed, more uses for tables emerged than merely to serve meals upon, and at the same time there was more space to accommodate them.

Not the least important of the many purposes for which they began to be used was the display of their own beauties. Catherine de Medici's inventory of 1589 refers to several kinds of small table, including round, oval and folding pieces and in the following year on the other side of the Channel no less than eighty-nine tables were recorded at Lumley Castle, of various kinds and innumerable forms: square, rectangular, round, hexagonal, octagonal, and standing upon one, two, four or six legs [Plate 111]. Of course only the very rich had as many as that, but men of moderate wealth now had more than at able-dormant in the hall or a board and trestles. The small table became indeed so common and useful an article that it was sometimes made with a hinged top which turned on its side to reveal a seat and to serve as a back rest to it

[Plate 118]. Tables like this were being made by about 1500, but it was in the second half of the sixteenth century that they began to appear in some numbers. They were, of course, of greatest use to men of limited means and in one way they represent a reversion to multi-purpose furniture; but they differ in three important aspects from that of earlier years: they are very lightly made, they achieve their dual function through the exploitation of highly-skilled joiners' techniques, and they appear in dwellings socially far below those which housed their predecessors. Indeed among the classes in whose homes multi-purpose furniture had once appeared, tables of very specialized purpose and of limited use were now popular. Often large and expensive tables were made for no other purposes than for playing games; in 1514 the Duchess of Valentinois had 'une grant table à jeu de billes couvert de drap vert' and among the illustrations which accompany the Lumley inventory is one of a richly ornamented table with an inlaid chess-board. By the next century richly-inlaid tables were common [Plate 130].

The New Learning

The increase in the amount of furniture and its greater specialization are in part directly attributable to the new mode of life and the more spacious houses of the upper classes which followed from their changed social functions; in part however they are the indirect result of consequences flowing from the intellectual developments which accompanied the social movements of the time, in particular of a classically-educated ruling class and of a slight but significant rise in the status of women. Today when nearly every country in western Europe is, or is becoming, seriously alarmed about the inadequacies of its educational system we are learning again what our ancestors knew: that a country's general development is dependent upon its level of education and that, with the exception of the direct producers, the schoolteacher is the most important person amongst us. Those societies which have been too down-to-earth to bother with the airy nothings of learning have had to learn the hard way that earth has nothing to offer the unlearned. The schools and universities of medieval Europe, apart from those of the Italian cities, had been designed to turn out clerics, engaged in furthering the ideas of the Church or in the day-to-day administration of the estates of a great feudatory or of a wealthy institution. The new monarchies needed far more than that and in the course of the sixteenth century an educational revolution occurred in many countries and not only in Protestant ones. Many educational institutes were founded and many others remodelled to educate a far larger proportion of the ruling class than before and to provide, as well as learned clerics, a great number of classically educated laymen able to keep abreast of the humanist developments of the age. Such men mingled with their intellectual equals and colleagues not in a monastic 'parlour' or in a college hall but in their own homes.

In the first flush of enthusiasm for humanism many women as well as men were educated to a high standard. In France, it has been claimed, women were the more learned, and certainly such highly-educated women as Margaret of Navarre, the Duchess of Guise, Catherine de Medici and, for a brief span, Mary Stuart played a large part in setting the tone of high society. Elizabeth I of England was held in some awe and respect for several reasons and not least for her command of ancient and modern languages. She was not unique among her countrywomen for her erudition. She had been preceded by the unfortunate Lady Jane Grey and among her subjects were the learned daughters of Sir Anthony Cook, one of them the wife of Burghley himself and the other the translator of Bishop Jewel's *Apologia* and the mother of Francis Bacon. At the opposite end of Protestant Europe, in far-away Königsberg, where the Hohenzollerns were undergoing their metamorphosis from masters of the Teutonic Knights into territorial magnates, Duke Albert of Prussia obtained the services of a renowned humanist that his daughter might learn Latin.[11]

One must, of course, be careful not to exaggerate the extent of feminine learning, or of masculine for that matter. Most upper-class women in France, for example, were probably more interested in the love-affairs of Amadis of Gaul than in the philosophy of Greece and Rome. Nevertheless, the effect of any education at all could not be wholly set aside, and in the last years of the sixteenth century the fondness for 'concetti' in Italy, for the productions of the 'précieuses' in France and for Euphuism in England were local manifestations of a common European literary movement which appealed to women, but to women with sufficient culture to appreciate the conceits and allusions of those styles. However deep or shallow their learning, women were influencing fashionable literature in much of Europe and in so doing were helping to determine some of the specific forms of good society.[12]

In Italy social relationships in the most advanced circles were very much under feminine sway. The ladies who figure in Castiglione's book were not merely the feminine counterparts of the Courtier, they were also his creators; and the whole concept of such a man is meaningful only when he is set against a background of cultured women. Not every country had reached the level of the little state of Urbino when Castiglione wrote, but to shine in company, or at least to conduct oneself with decorum, was becoming an essential quality amongst all those who aspired to belong to the élite. Erasmus' *Civitas Morum Puerilium* had been translated into many languages and had gone into many editions by the mid-century and one of the reasons for its popularity was that it was essentially a book of etiquette.[13]

Here too one must guard against exaggeration both because many of the forms of the new society were still cast in the old mould and because the influence of women upon them was only one among many. But with all qualifications made, and without denying that the mere increase in accommodation was by itself enough, or nearly enough, to multiply both the amount and the varieties of furniture, the greater influence of women upon social intercourse intensified the effects of other factors and in particular altered the character of that furniture which appeared in the Saloon or Great Chamber, the successor to the medieval Solar.

Prestige pieces

The spread of literacy and the new thirst for classical knowledge not only affected furniture in general but helped to develop specific kinds. By the end of the Middle Ages the writing desk had apparently evolved into a large and elaborate object. It is known from contemporary illustrations that some examples had the refinement of adjustable tops [Plate 120] and that many had cupboards for books below the desk itself, and were so designed that writing materials could be obtained from within the desk without lifting the lid and disturbing everything upon it [Plate 48]. They appear, in short, to have been highly specialized and efficient instruments, well fitted to assist the reading and copying of manuscripts in the monastic scriptoria that were their usual homes.

From about 1500 onwards large and immobile desks of this sort became at any rate less common and instead small and more easily moveable ones multiplied. Some examples, such as the famous Spanish

Sixteenth-century furniture

124 Design for a cabinet by Inigo Jones, wholly unlike any contemporary English piece.

125 Late sixteenth-
century French cabinet,
with fashionable reclining
figures on the pediment.
The form and style are
similar to that from
Azay-le-Ferron.

126 Cabinet of *c.* 1600 in the style of Du Cerceau, from the château of
Azay-le-Ferron.
127 Cabinet of *c.* 1600 in pietro duro, inlaid with miniature portraits and semi-
precious materials, at Stourhead, Wiltshire.

129 South German writing 'till' of the mid-sixteenth century, the biblical scenes upon it inlaid in bone.

130 Antwerp table of mid-seventeenth century, richly ornamented and inlaid with tortoise-shell.

128 (*opposite*) Seventeenth-century vargueño, with marquetry ornament, on its stand.

131 and 132 Two north Italian cassoni of *c.* 1500. The certosina ornament is wholly similar in design and the differences are only in details.

133 Milanese cabinet, ebony veneer with steel plaques damascened with 'antique' ornament and with a central panel of Orpheus charming the beasts.

134 and 135 The Wrangelschrank of 1556, open and closed. The piece is remarkable for the Mannerist scenes upon it in inlay and for the virtuosity of the execution.

137 Headboard of a bed from the Balgatti Valsecchi Collection, Milan, richly carved with religious scenes.

138 Front of a chest of 1584 from the Elbe district. The carving is typical of the period, the subject matter is wholly different from that of contemporary Italian chests.

136 (*opposite*) Early seventeenth-century bed at Berkeley Castle, with a carved and inlaid headboard and with free-standing figures at the foot.

141 Early seventeenth-century English court-cupboard with Anglo-Flemish ornament.

139 and 140 (*opposite above*) Mid-sixteenth-century French chest with quattrocento ornament. Compare with early seventeenth-century cupboard of Dutch origin (*opposite below*), different in both form and ornament.

142 English chest of *c.* 1500 with late Gothic ornament.
143 Early sixteenth-century chest, medieval in form but with quattrocento ornament.

144 Mid-sixteenth-century English chest with quattrocento ornament.
145 Mid-sixteenth-century Italian cassone in the form of a classical sarcophagus.

vargueños, had hinged sides, which let down to form writing platforms [Plates v and 119]; others such as the small press 'with drawing tilles' which once belonged to Henry VIII, and is now in the Victoria and Albert Museum, were without this refinement [Plate 121]. All however were provided with many small drawers and compartments and were placed upon a table or trestles which might be specially made for them, but from which they could always be detached [Plate 128]. That they were not made for monastic scribes, but for educated and wealthy laymen is shown partly by their portable form and partly by the lavish decoration upon so many of them.

Desks of this sort may have been, as the vargueños certainly were, intended to accompany men of affairs on their travels, but side by side with them, and eventually to supersede them, appeared the much larger piece, generally of two stages, which came to be known as a 'cabinet'. In the later Middle Ages some kings and princes had had small rooms called 'cabinets', in which they kept, and often diverted themselves by looking at, a collection of objects which were not necessarily expensive, but were of value for their rarity or beauty or personal or historical associations. The imaginary one which Corrozet described in 1539 held a great number of objects: precious stones, jewellery, cosmetics, drawings and paintings, statues and figurines. Under the influence of the new taste for antiquity it also held

' . . . médailles
Et curieuses Antiquailles'

By that time too this luxury had spread slightly beyond the narrow ranks of royalty and cabinets were owned by duchesses as well as by queens.[14]

Besides the cabinet the very great had sometimes had an 'étude' as well: a small room not always distinguishable from a cabinet but devoted less to the display of curiosities and more to writing desks and bookcases and their accompanying articles. Corrozet called the étude the most important room in the house, comparing its role with that of the spark of life in the human body. The comparison strikes one as strained and far-fetched, but its deliberate exaggeration is probably a sign of a greater appreciation of culture and learning, or at any rate of lip-service to it, among the upper classes. By then études had, like cabinets, become commoner than before and so too had the attitude of mind which had brought them about in the first place. But as more

146 (*opposite*) Late-sixteenth century French cabinet; of a very common form and with the popular wall-niches and pediments

ordinary men acquired the tastes of the greater they had to satisfy them in a less expensive way and the word 'cabinet', like its humbler companion 'garde-manger', ceased to be used of a room and was applied instead to a piece of furniture serving a purpose which in earlier years and at a higher social level had needed a room of its own.

The change may be followed in some detail in France in the late sixteenth century. The 'cabinet' mentioned in the inventory of the Château de Pau in 1561–2 was clearly a room, for it contained several great chests filled with valuables and rarities. A few years later at the Hôtel de Montmorency the word was generally used in the sense of a room, but in one instance the context reveals that a piece of furniture was intended. By 1589 when Catherine de Medici's inventory came to be taken it was normally used in its modern sense. In England cabinets were rare before the Restoration and mentions of them are rarer still, but a reference of the time of Edward VI reveals an up-to-date article in a curiously medieval form: '3 cabinets set in the wall, covered with crimson velvet and garnished with gold and silver.'[15]

The cabinet and the étude had not always been clearly distinguishable when they were rooms, and it is probable that each often served the purposes of the other as well as its own. There was one cabinet in the Hôtel de Montmorency in 1568 which was 'aultrement appellé la librairye', and when the cabinet became a piece of furniture it tended to be a receptacle for curiosities and a writing desk at the same time. For this reason many early cabinets not only have elaborately compartmented interiors, but are given as well a front, or part of one, which hinges downwards and outwards to make a writing surface. Examples are known from many countries and in many styles: a Roman piece made for Pope Paul III (1534–49), ornamented with trophies and vases, incipient strapwork, guilloches and gadrooning; another made for the Emperor Charles V in 1555, probably at Augsburg, with a profusion of terms and architectural motifs; a third example of *c.* 1580 from north Germany with plain panelling but with a central carved motif. In their details the three have little in common, but in form they are nearly identical; all of two stages and with the middle part of the front of the upper stage arranged to fall downwards and serve as a writing table.

These writing cabinets differ from their forerunners not only in their less cumbersome form, but in their wealth of ornament as well. Not all medieval writing desks were plain, some were highly decorated, but as a whole they had no great pretensions: in contrast, lavish ornament is a part of the nature of sixteenth-century cabinets and without it they would hardly be cabinets at all. In one way, of course, this is merely to repeat in other words that they were made for educated gentlemen and not for monkish scribes; in another way it reflects the greater wealth available for household comforts and for domestic furniture in the new homes of many of the upper classes. In the previous century there had been many signs that houses and their contents were acquiring new qualities and some examples of lavish spending upon them were mentioned earlier. All of these, however, although significant in their time and often individually large were of small consequence in comparison with the sum total of the expenditure of the new monarchies and their wealthier subjects upon personal possessions and costly furniture. It is not possible to compare the fifteenth century at all points with the sixteenth, but one comparison is readily available. The late medieval practice of erecting buffets on ceremonial occasions to make a lavish display of prized personal possessions was followed at Fontainebleau in 1545. The buffet erected then was partly intended to mark the signing of a peace treaty with Henry VIII, partly to celebrate the birth of a daughter to Francis I, and wholly to impress the English with the wealth and resources of the King of France. It was built in the form of a pyramid with nine stages and was large enough to show all the royal plate and many antique pieces. A later Frenchman dazzled at the distance of even a hundred years said of it that 'il sembloit qu'icy l'on eust rassemblé l'élite des buffets de tous les Princes de l'Europe'. Attendants were stationed near to it; partly no doubt to keep a watch on it, but partly in order to recount to everyone, and especially to the English, the history and rarity and value of the different pieces. In his show of plate above everything else Francis I was still in the Middle Ages, but in the vast amount of wealth he was able to display, and in the openly political use he made of that display, he was revealing one aspect of those new attitudes which were to lift furniture to the level of esteem that had formerly been reserved for caskets and textiles.[16]

Textiles had been so highly regarded in the late Middle Ages that, as far as their perishable nature allowed, they had often been treated as heirlooms. Lord Bassett at the end of the fourteenth century and Sir Robert Hungerford in the middle of the next both directed that their 'beds', of velvet and cloth of gold, were to go in entail to their heirs male, to those who would bear 'their name and arms'. By the early sixteenth century similar dispositions were being made of furniture, but since by that time both men and furniture were less peripatetic, and more attached to one dwelling than before, favoured pieces were directed to stay for ever in one house rather than to follow the bearer of a name and title. John Colet's will of 1519 ordered that his 'wainscot', which included tables, should remain for ever in his lodging at the Charter-house and in 1607 Gilbert Spence directed that none of the wainscot or wooden furniture in his house was ever to be removed from it. The intention of these directives was stated clearly by a mayor of Newcastle-on-Tyne who died in 1565: 'Also I will that the cupborde wth Sayncte george upon yt wch standeith in my hall shall so remayne still during the life naturell of my welbeloved wife. And after hir deathe I will that the said cubborde and the said george shall still remayne in the house as an hairelome for ev'.' Against this background it is not surprising that outstanding pieces should acquire some popular fame and the 'Great Bed of Ware' [Plate 123] achieved a mention in the *Poetical Itinerary* of Prince Ludwig of Anhalt-Köthen only a few years after it had been made.[17]

Professional designers

Even to contemporaries the Great Bed of Ware was remarkable more for its size than for anything else, but in some quarters furniture was coming to be admired for other qualities. Although Vasari found it necessary to explain and in part even to excuse the employment of famous painters upon the cassoni of the previous century, he still considered some furniture to be worthy of a critic's notice. In his discussion of painting he included an account of the 'trompe l'oeil' effects carried out in intarsia upon the more expensive and elaborate pieces and he was appreciative of the sculptural qualities of some of the carved ornament upon walnut furniture. Montaigne was not inclined to over-value magnificence and when in Rome was quite ready to do without it if he could thereby get his apartments at a lower rent. He had a contemporary's eye for it nonetheless, and if not exactly critical of the Grand Duke of Tuscany's house at Pratolino he was aware that something was lacking: 'the furniture', he commented, 'is pretty but not magnificent'.

In many ways France was the leader of European culture, or at any rate of 'wohnkultur', in the sixteenth century and it is perhaps not surprising that some of the best-known French artists of the time concerned themselves with furniture design. It has indeed been claimed that individually they affected and even helped to bring into being local schools of furniture-makers. Du Cerceau has been seen as the prime inspirer of the style of the Ile-de-France [Plate 126], Jean Goujon as partly responsible for that of Normandy and Hugues Sambin of Dijon as the founder of the distinctive Burgundian school of wood-carving and furniture-making.[18]

Feulner has called Du Cerceau's designs 'the first systematic attempt to produce household furnishings in the spirit of modern art'. Whether any of his ideas were ever carried out is extremely doubtful, and of the three men mentioned above only Sambin can be associated with any known pieces. Although he called himself an architect, and was employed in that capacity by the town council of Besançon, he was a carpenter by origin. Even in France very little furniture, if any, was being designed by recognized artists and one must be careful not to exaggerate their part in the new styles. Nevertheless it is important to know that some of them were concerning themselves with furniture design and there can be little doubt that Du Cerceau's publications helped to spread some knowledge of the new modes and concepts. Many craftsmen consciously imitated illustrious artists and it has been said that 'After Michelangelo designed the Medici tombs it became the ambition of every master and artisan to have reclining figures on the pediments of his furniture' [Plate 125].[19]

In this respect France and Italy were about fifty years ahead of England, where there is no evidence at all before the early seventeenth century of furniture being designed by or even under the influence of artists. This, however, was perhaps not a reflection of an indifference to furniture but of the paucity of artists in Elizabethan England. Once conditions had developed to a point where they permitted craftsmen to develop into artists it was not long before Inigo Jones, the first and most famous of them, was including furniture among the variegated objects of his many-sided genius; and in the Ashmolean Museum at Oxford there is a design by him for a cabinet in the most advanced taste [Plate 124].

In Germany and in Switzerland the designs of the unknown master, H.S., had a wide circulation in the mid-century, and were often copied or adapted by furniture makers. A generation earlier Peter Flötner had been creating finely carved quattrocento ornament, but the later master, both in his designs and his rare surviving works, broke completely with the Gothic tradition and introduced the forms as well as some of the details of Renaissance architecture. His work is richly, but not extravagantly decorated and is most remarkable for a quality lacking in so much furniture of the time: a subordination of the design to the capabilities of the craftsmen and to the practical uses which any piece had to serve.

At the same time there was a very clear understanding that a piece of furniture might be an objet d'art as well as a use-article; might, indeed, be more of the one than the other. Philip Hainhofer, of a patrician family in favour with the Dukes of Pomerania, was a man of some aesthetic sensibility and was instrumental in commissioning the famous 'Pomeranian Cabinet' of 1617. Writing of another cabinet, intended for the Grand Duke of Tuscany, he spoke of it as both a writing desk and a source in itself of intellectual and aesthetic inspiration: '. . . ain herr neben dem nutzen und dienst schöne meditationes und contemplationes an disem schreibtisch haben kann.' He was writing in the early seventeenth century and not in the late sixteenth, but for many years before he put this view into words German cabinet-makers had been practising it in their works.[20]

The decorative and even painterly effects in intarsia to which Vasari had conceded some artistic value were very much in evidence upon the most expensive German pieces, at least in the south. A walnut writing-desk in the Victoria and Albert Museum is richly inlaid in bone with biblical scenes [Plate 129], and the well-known 'Wrangelschrank' of 1556 is only one outstanding example, amongst many other German cabinets, which are richly decorated with inlay in a most up-to-date Mannerist style [Plates 134 and 135]. In eastern Germany, where inlay was rare, the painters had more opportunity and occasionally were able to turn a piece of furniture, such as the cupboard of c. 1590 intended for a member of the House of Anhalt, into a portrait gallery of family connections.[21]

Expensive processes and materials

The north European cabinet of the sixteenth century was in many ways the equivalent of the cassone of fifteenth-century Italy, and the painted portraits upon these east German examples provide perhaps the most obvious but certainly not the most important point of comparison. Of far greater significance are the qualities present upon so many other cabinets: the lavish display of ornament and the fondness for pictorial representation. These, in conjunction with the remark quoted above about 'meditationes' and 'contemplationes', reveal that very commonly, and not merely in exceptional cases, utility was not the only and not always the primary consideration in the manufacture of cabinets. Although this had occasionally been true of other forms of furniture it had been especially true of cassoni, which like cabinets had been treated as vehicles for the display of works of art. Cabinets generally obtained their effects with inlay and marquetry and very rarely with paint and they eschewed the genre scenes so common upon cassoni, but these differences in technique and in iconography cannot disguise the identity of purpose between the two furniture forms.

Nevertheless the differences are also important, for they allow us to see how an aesthetic approach translated from a particular social context in one age into a different context in a later age produced results which in part paralleled those of the place of origin, and in part diverged very far from them. In northern Europe in the sixteenth century the new approach had to work upon forms which were very different from those which had earlier been objects of aesthetic interest; for with the immense increase in the amount of furniture in any house the chest, while not wholly eliminated from important rooms, had been relegated to an inferior position and its place of honour had been usurped by the cabinet. Although in principle it was not impossible for a cabinet to provide as large an unbroken expanse of surface for a craftsman to work upon as a chest, in practice it was most unusual, because the need to provide doors and drawers and falling fronts made this very difficult. In consequence those techniques most suited to small-scale representation, such as inlay, came into their own. Further, the painters who had been happy enough to work upon cassoni in the fifteenth century had risen by the sixteenth to the status of artists and were inclined to consider that decorating the work of craftsmen was beneath their dignity, even when it was not a waste of their talents. The ornamentation of important pieces of furniture was therefore left more and more to the trade itself and in consequence a far greater use was made of such trade processes as inlay and marquetry. This development was the easier because with far more money available for domestic furniture the high cost of those striking but expensive techniques was no longer a major obstacle to their use.

119

The changed position of many of the men who were patronizing the makers of rich furniture in the sixteenth century also had its effect. The magnates at the courts of the absolute rulers of the new states, even of the new state of the Grand Duke of Tuscany, were farther removed from the immediate sources of their wealth and from the active direction of a business than the oligarchs and even the tyrants of the Italian city states of the quattrocento had been. And they were generally anxious to lose what recollections they might still have retained and became far less fond of the cosy and boisterous genre scenes of earlier years. Even in Italy itself where the cabinet never had quite the importance that it attained in northern Europe, and where cassoni continued to be displayed in public rooms throughout most of the century, the nature of the decoration applied to those traditional pieces changed completely and the iconography was much altered.

This change was abetted by developments within the furniture-makers' trade. The cabinet was not the first example of a piece honoured above its fellows, but its predecessors, the casket and the cassone, had owed their prestige, in the main, to the brilliant effects produced by workers in other media. The qualities of the cabinet depended more directly upon the skill of the joiners who made the carcase and applied most of the ornament. These men, working upon furniture of a superior nature, were to become a separate and superior element within their own craft; distinguished by a separate name, 'cabinet-maker' or 'ébéniste'. Employed by a select few, and emphasizing the division between themselves and their fellow-tradesmen, they too lost contact with the sources of older and more popular themes and readily adopted their patrons' concepts as their own.

Aesthetic appreciation of an object is not always clearly separable from, and is often heightened by, awestruck admiration of the vast, and usually exaggerated, sums that it is said to have cost. An Italian who visited England in 1497 was very scornful of the native habit of boasting of the monetary value of precious relics and vestments. Time brought about an odd revenge, and an English visitor to Tuscany in 1605, Robert Dalington, commented upon the Italian fashion of insisting upon the huge sums spent upon some articles of furniture. It may be, however, that this counting-house attitude was not so surprising as it seemed to contemporaries from far-away countries, for in recent years the view has been gaining ground that the great achievements of Italian Renaissance artists were partly due to the opportunities provided for

v (*opposite*) An early sixteenth-century vargueño with the lid raised and the front let down to make a writing platform. The rich ornament of the interior is typical of Renaissance cabinets. vi and vii (*overleaf*) A late-sixteentury century 'Nonsuch chest', richly inlaid with light-coloured woods. The architectural scenes in perspective were a fashionable motif of the time

MVSICA·DISPARIVM·DVLCIS·CONCORDIA·VOCVM

PELLO·LEVO·PLACO·TRISTIA·CORDA·DEOS

DOMINVM·IN·CHORDIS·ET·IN

ORGANO

them by wealthy men who saw works of art as a good investment in difficult times.[22]

This theory shares, or pretends to share, with Marxism a refreshingly down-to-earth attitude towards a subject about which it is delightfully easy to write highfalutin nonsense. It also possesses the advantage over the latter of being readily grasped with very little intellectual effort and of having no undesirable political implications. In many ways it appears to reflect the problems of inflation and taxation which beset the unhappy rich of the twentieth century rather than to describe conditions in the fifteenth and sixteenth. Professor Gombrich has already shown that the art investments of one famous patron, Lorenzo de Medici, were far more in precious antique gems than in the productions of contemporary artists. Nevertheless it may have some truth when applied to furniture. The Pomeranian cabinet mentioned earlier was said to have cost ten thousand gulden and a table and a desk made for the Grand Duke of Tuscany twenty-two thousand and a million ducats respectively. All these figures are probably blatant exaggerations, but all the same those three pieces obviously cost a great amount of money. Further, much of the money spent upon them was spent upon imperishables, for the first was liberally covered with gold and silver and the last two were richly set with precious stones.[23]

Although many other pieces were often richly decorated, it was generally upon cabinets that most money was spent; and in this the sixteenth century was carrying on an old practice in new conditions. In the Middle Ages the exceptionally rich ornament upon caskets had reflected the value of the objects they housed, such as precious relics, jewels and curios. As the cabinet usurped the functions of the casket and began to accommodate its owner's much-prized jewels, objets d'art and antiques so did it simultaneously acquire its predecessor's costly ornamentation, and in its own way revealed upon its exterior the nature of its contents. It may be that the gorgeous ornament upon some musical instruments, for example, the virginals in the Victoria and Albert Museum [Plate VIII], reflects in part the intense love of music among the upper classes. Whether or not there was conscious investment, this magnificence enhanced the status of furniture as a whole, and although most pieces were made with a much sharper eye on economy, nevertheless some of the glory of the few rubbed off upon their numerous fellows.

In discussing some of the very expensive furniture of the time it is

121

VIII (*opposite*) Many among the upper-classes in the sixteenth century were highly skilled in music and the gorgeous decoration upon contemporary virginals reflects their intense love of the art perhaps necessary to get matters into proportion by noting that despite its rise in esteem furniture was still on the whole the object of less lavish spending than textiles. In France in the early years of the century Francis I spent the large sum of 287 écus upon the framework of a bed, but upon the tapestry hangings for it he spent the much larger sum of 1,961 livres. Many years later in Holland, William I spent 936 thalers for the hangings of one bed and 1,100 thalers for those of another. Textiles were still much sought after. The export of Brussels tapestries to Spain began in the fifteenth century and continued throughout the sixteenth in the form of bed curtains and testers, table- and chair-cloths and cushion coverings. In 1583 Hans Fugger, rich enough to indulge his fancy, was importing velvet from Venice to make himself a bed-canopy. As late as *c.* 1630 the Reggia – the principal residence of the Dukes of Milan – was said to have seven sets of hangings for every room in the house. Inventory-makers of the time still followed medieval protocol, beginning their lists with the textiles and working their way round to the furniture later; and it is clear that the latter had not yet risen above the former in glory. Nevertheless, much money was being spent at this time upon providing up-to-date pieces in even quite small houses. When Elizabeth Jenyson of Walworth, County Durham, died in 1604 she left much recently acquired furniture: 'a new great bedstead, a new great press, a long new table in the hall with new forms.'[24]

The larger sums expended in the sixteenth century are partly accounted for by the greater amount of furniture and partly by the wider use of such expensive processes as inlay and marquetry and of expensive materials. Some of these processes were far from new. It will be remembered that intarsia had had some vogue in Italy in the fifteenth century; in the late fourteenth century Charles V of France had owned a casket described as 'marquetré et ferré d'argent' and in 1498 Anne of Brittanny had 'un coffret fait de musaycque de bois et d'ivoire'. These, however, were small objects and their decoration was highly exceptional for their times. In the sixteenth century very large pieces of furniture were so treated, not merely the odd coffer or casket, but many cabinets, table-tops, bed-heads and even chair-backs were inlaid or ornamented in some equally costly way. As a contemporary satirist said, with no very great exaggeration, 'Quant aux meubles de bois, nous voulons qu'ils soient tous dorez, argentez et marquetez … '. Of course, it was neither possible nor desirable to treat all furniture like that, but it was coming to be widely accepted that, ideally, every piece which the gaze of the quality might fall upon should be a thing of beauty.[25]

There were many methods of achieving, or of attempting, beauty through the use of inlays, and craftsmen in Italy, where intarsia had been most widely practised for the longest time, were acquainted with some very varied techniques. In Lombardy in the years around 1500 the use of contrasting light and dark woods had reached a high level, and there and in Venice a form of certosina work – of bone inlay in geometric patterns – was popular throughout the sixteenth century [Plates 131 and 132]. From the other side of the peninsula works in the style known in France as 'façon de Gênes' or 'à la Genevoise' were being widely exported throughout the late-sixteenth and early-seventeenth centuries. The style was an ornate one with many elements, of which one of the more striking was the use of an inlay of paler woods such as lemon within the darker walnut background. German craftsmen had reached a very high standard by then and much of the effect of such magnificent pieces as the 'Wrangelschrank', the 'Pomeranian Cabinet' and those known in England as 'Nonsuch chests' was also due to the use of light-coloured inlays [Plates VI and VII]. Native English inlay was inclined to polychromatic effects with a regular use of holly, box and Irish bog oak; sometimes such out-of-the-way materials as cherrywood were employed and occasionally a bone inlay was used. How far French furniture-makers used different coloured woods for their inlays is not wholly clear, but it is noticeable that many French inventories describe many inlaid pieces as foreign or in foreign taste. In 1550 the Cardinal of Amboise had 'une table de marquetage à l'espagnole' and a resident of Marseilles in 1556 had 'une petite chaise faite de marquetterie à la Genevoise'. Catherine de Medici had tables and cabinets 'marquettée façon d'Allemagne' and a table 'façon d'Indie' which stood upon a pedestal 'marqueté de buys'. On the other hand the inventories rarely describe pieces inlaid with materials other than wood as foreign and it is possible that native furniture-makers were less fond of wood inlays.[26]

More expensive materials than wood were also used for inlay, but not on so wide a scale. Catherine de Medici's use of ebony and ivory has just been mentioned and ivory was sometimes employed upon the interiors of Spanish vargueños. Marble and other coloured stones were often inlaid into table-tops. The late-sixteenth century draw-table, mentioned earlier, at Hardwick Hall was described in an inventory of

123

1600 as 'inlayde with marble stones and wood' and one of the tables which Robert Dalington saw at Florence was 'very curiously wrought and bordered with flowers of their naturall colours (which might be painted for aught I know) howbeit he protested they were all the naturall colours of the stone'. A bed bought for Francis 1 from a Portuguese merchant was 'marqueté à feuillages de nacre de perle' and mother of pearl was used again for a round table which was at the Hôtel de Montmorency in 1568. The same table was inlaid as well with pearls and emeralds and the inlaying of precious and semi-precious stones was not uncommon among Italian furniture-makers. Dalington reported that a table being made for the Emperor in 1604, and which had already cost a vast sum, was 'set with very many and very faire Stones'. At the Reggia the Dukes of Milan at about the same time had one table set all with emeralds, another with sapphires, a third with 'Turkey stones' and a fourth inlaid with amber. A Milanese cabinet with ebony veneer is enriched with steel plaques damascened with mythological subjects [Plate 133]. If sixteenth-century financial geniuses were investing in art at all they were probably putting more money into objects like these than into canvasses.

There was obviously a large market for furniture embellished with expensive stones; and steps were taken to satisfy it. In 1580 the *Opificio delle Pietre Dure* was set up in Florence with the intention of producing vessels and such items of furniture as cabinets and tables made of, or decorated with, agate, sardonyx, jasper, lapis lazuli and similar materials. A cabinet of this type, although not necessarily of Florentine origin, which was made for the Peretti family in the years around 1600 is now at Stourhead in Wiltshire. The frame is of ebony and it incorporates, besides miniature portraits of the Peretti family, ornaments in amber, sapphires, emeralds and semi-precious stones [Plate 127].[27]

The use of inlays and of expensive materials increased many times over in the sixteenth century and the importance of carving declined in proportion; absolutely, however, very much more carving was carried out than ever before. There was far more furniture, and especially luxury furniture, to be ornamented and therefore despite the competition from other craftsmen the demand for carvers was growing. And greater luxury at many levels meant that much furniture decoration which would formerly have kept the painters busy was given to wood-workers instead [Plate 137]. The change from the painted Italian cassoni of the fifteenth century to the carved specimens of the next is well known, but in northern Europe too the supersession of the painter by the carver which had begun in the late Middle Ages was carried further.[28]

Even upon some of those pieces with the most lavish applied ornament there was an equally lavish display of carving. The highly Mannerist scenes in inlay upon the exterior of the 'Wrangelschrank' are matched by equally Mannerist carved figures upon the interior. The ornate 'Pomeranian Cabinet' of half-a-century later was worked upon by twenty different kinds of craftsmen, among whom carvers were prominent. Upon many of the grandiose English beds of the Elizabethan and Jacobean periods inlay upon the head-board is flanked or accompanied by elaborately carved floral or architectural motifs or by engaged or free-standing sculpted figures [Plate 136].

Often the decorative effect was almost wholly obtained by carving. The cabinet made for Pope Paul III (1534–49) has no other form of ornament and with its finely modelled trophies, vases, gadrooning and guilloches achieves a monumental effect. The previously-mentioned two-stage cabinet made for the Emperor Charles V has an upper part carved in the form of classical temples, and another cabinet of later date, now in the Rijksmuseum at Amsterdam and probably of Flemish origin, is profusely carved with caryatides, terms, strapwork and cartouches. Another example of c. 1580 from Kiel is more restrained in its general ornament, but has a central panel carved with scenes from the life of Susanna.

Although chests were no longer very highly prized they were still being made in some numbers, generally with little difference from their medieval predecessors and providing large surface areas for decoration. But because of their now lower status, as compared for instance with cabinets, their makers tended to eschew the more outrageously expensive techniques and to ornament their products, if at all, with carving. In Italy the cassoni were given the most-up-to-date classical motifs and often illustrated some of the most recondite classical themes, but although the old-fashioned painted decoration had been abandoned the modern inlay and marquetry was not embraced; instead the exposed surfaces were covered with carving. In this they differed little from some late-sixteenth century chests from north Germany [Plate 138]. These have a wholly different subject-matter from their Italian cousins but in form and in technique of decoration they are essentially similar. French chests too of the mid-century, and later, often display

125

much classical and classicist ornament, but this is rarely carried out in anything other than carving [Plate 139]. Inlays and other expensive methods were not merely confined to the furniture of the wealthy: they tended to be restricted even within that milieu to the more highly esteemed pieces.

In total amount carved ornament was probably still far and away commoner than inlay and marquetry, and while the latter were probably wholly beyond the reach of ordinary people carved pieces were not unknown amongst them. The north was not the most prosperous region of England at this time, but inventories of men who clearly lived in small houses in those parts often refer to carved cupboards, bed-posts and aumbries. Among such men carved ornament was probably still much less in evidence than paint, but it was becoming ever commoner.

Even without elaborate applied ornament, furniture was getting more costly than before, for rare and exotic woods were being more widely used. In many cases this use perhaps reflects little more than a desire for variety, as for example a cupboard belonging to a German merchant in 1513 with doors of maple and with base and cornice of lime. In England the most noticeable change was the greater use of walnut in place of the formerly dominant oak; in Spain, however, special woods were being imported from the West Indies by the mid-century; and in France at about the same time the author of the *Isle des Hermaphrodites* advised the wealthy to have their furniture, and especially beds, made if not of ivory or ebony, then of rosewood or of cedar or some equally fragrant timber. Doubtless this ironically-offered advice was not always followed, even by the most luxury-loving, but that it should have been proffered is a measure of the standards of sixteenth-century furniture.[29]

Luxury was reflected as well in the great increase in international traffic in furniture of all kinds, far above the earlier level of trade in Flemish chests. In the sixteenth and seventeenth centuries even Spanish furniture, with its very marked national characteristics, fell in some measure under the influence of France and the Low Countries. France itself was an avid importer of foreign wares. The 'deux coffres blancs à la mode de Ytalie' which belonged to the Duchesse de Valentinois and the 'coffre de boys couvert de cuyr en façon de Lombardye' which belonged to Nicholas le Mercier, her valet de chambre, doubtless entered the country in the Duchess' baggage train, but the innumerable

Flemish chests, the 'bahuts de Flandres' were direct imports, just as Catherine de Medici's 'cabinets d'Allemagne' were. Her many cabinets, tables, and chairs in 'Genoese style', in 'German style', in 'Turkish' and in 'Indian style' may in some cases have been imports and in others native copies, but whether the one or the other their popularity testifies to the widespread interest in the products of other countries. 'Flanders chests' were as common in England as in France; 'Flanders bedsteads' were not unknown and 'Danske' and 'spruce' chests from the Baltic were imported widely into northern England, and less widely into the south. Further, not only was furniture being imported from abroad, but some men in the most far-distant counties, less accessible than many foreign parts, were having their furniture sent down to them, presumably in the most up-to-date style, from the capital. That the very wealthy should do this is perhaps not surprising, but even a very ordinary citizen in Durham also had 'two London bedsteads' and 'one new London table'.[30]

The influence of classical architecture

The social and intellectual changes which were producing this revolution in the use of furniture were aided and abetted by a third force; by the effects of the artistic achievements of the Renaissance. The nature and intensity of the relationships between these aspects of an age of transition have long been a subject of dispute and there is at the moment no view which can even claim to be orthodox, still less to be unchallenged. As a result the historian of furniture has to admit that many of his problems are as yet insoluble. Nevertheless, he is on the whole more fortunate than might have been expected, for, whether or not these changes were causally connected, one thing is clear: they accompanied one another in time, and the new furniture of the period reflected, as well as the new despotisms and the new learning, the new artistic creations and theories of the Renaissance.

The most obvious effect of the Renaissance upon furniture was to bring about a transformation, parallel to that in architecture, in the grammar of ornament. The cusping, crocketting, tracery, battlementing, pointed and depressed arches and all the other elements in the repertory of the Gothic style were superseded by contemporary copies and adaptations of ancient forms: by classical columns and pilasters, by dentilled cornices, by egg-and-dart, by guilloches and gadrooning, and by the vases, strapwork and terminal figures which pattern books and architectural writers were to make more and more familiar to more and more artisans.

Examples of the new manner are numerous. In the Rijksmuseum at Amsterdam a chest from the beginning of the sixteenth century and a cupboard from its end serve to illustrate both the change from the old ornament to the new and the further changes which soon occurred within the new itself. The chest is still medieval in form, is divided into small panels and has its ornament organized in a medieval way, but the ornament itself is directly derived from the quattrocento and within the panels, which are divided by classical colonnettes, are grotesques, candelabra and roundels enclosing human busts [Plate 143]. The cupboard on the other hand has abandoned both the form and ornament of earlier years. It is in two stages, with the upper one recessed, and is decorated with strapwork, cartouches, terms and caryatides [Plate 140]. As Lunsingh Scheurleer has pointed out, it is a good example of the influence of one of the most persuasive of contemporary publicists, of Jan Vriedeman de Vries. In France the forms of the Italian Renaissance were wholly triumphant by the middle of the century and Gothic was almost wholly abandoned [Plate 74]. From then onwards French art was ceaselessly employing new elements and although chests were still being made they were usually distinguishable from their predecessors by their fluted bases, strapwork cartouches and terms and caryatides. In England parallel developments occurred and quattrocento ornament superseded Gothic and was itself displaced by the florid Anglo-Flemish style [Plates 141, 142 and 144].

So clear is the change in ornament that it has been held that this alone distinguishes Gothic furniture from that of the succeeding epoch. It is perhaps nearer the mark to note that the difference in ornament, although important in itself, is of most importance as the guise in which other changes first manifested themselves. The new ornament and its accompanying iconography appeared initially upon Italian cassoni, that is, upon forms which were essentially old-fashioned; but long before the end of the sixteenth century, and even before the middle, many new kinds of furniture had been introduced and many old kinds had been modified. The changes which at first affected Italy alone later affected all of northern Europe; but because they came later they came in a more developed way and affected both form and decoration almost simultaneously. In the north there was no long period of

128

IX (*opposite*) During the sixteenth century one of the functions of the Hall was usurped by the Dining Parlour, but the provision of suitable tables and chairs did not come at once and in most houses, as here at Castle Fraser, Scotland, the furniture is of a much later date

Martÿ 12.mo
Anno Domini
1614

No Spring Till

transition, but instead a quick change from a milieu in which the Gothic chest was dominant to one in which it was superseded by the Renaissance cabinet. Indeed, the connection between form on the one hand and ornament and iconography on the other was here sufficiently close for the former to have a direct influence upon the latter. Where the old form survived it was sometimes able to retard other developments and the late-sixteenth century chests from north Germany, although near neighbours in time and space of the 'Wrangelschrank', are notable for their lack of Renaissance ornament and subject-matter.

This intimate connection was made the closer by the enhanced role in building of the architect, the supplanter of the medieval master-mason. The employment of Goujon, of Du Cerceau and of Hugues Sambin upon the design of furniture was cited earlier to show the greater esteem which it had won, but it must also be seen as further evidence of the importance of architecture among the aesthetic interests of the upper classes. Whatever pretensions the rulers of northern Europe may or may not have had to appreciate painting and sculpture in the late sixteenth century, they accounted it as almost a sin to be ignorant of the architectural proprieties according to Vitruvius. England was not a leader of European culture at that time, but almost any upper-class Englishman, with wit enough to be interested in more than horses and women, either owned or was acquiring an architectural library. A German merchant-prince like Hans Fugger was doing much the same and in France the patronage of De L'Orme and Du Cerceau and the popularity of their publications reveal how widespread a knowledge of classical architecture there was in that country. An acquaintance with at least the rudiments of the vocabulary was of sufficient import amongst the élite for affectations to develop, and Montaigne gently ridiculed those who used the high-sounding jargon of the profession in inappropriate contexts.

Because of this, and despite the new prestige of painting and of sculpture, interior decoration was more tightly than ever before under the control of architecture. Schemes of decoration might be planned and executed by painters and sculptors, by Rosso and Primaticcio at Fontainebleau or by Giulio Romano at Mantua, but they were always carried out within a framework determined by architectural canons and with a grammar of ornament derived from the usages of architecture; and, in the circumstances of the time, of classical or classicist architecture. On the other hand, despite the increased prestige of

x (*opposite*) Portrait of 'Lady Scudamore', 1614. As comfort becomes of more importance chairs are upholstered and tables are often covered with a turkey carpet

furniture those who made it were still far from the status of the painters
and the architects. One of the best known of them, Hugues Sambin,
was very particular about calling himself an architect rather than a
furniture-maker, and in consequence of his attitude, and of the attitudes
of many others, there was no force from within the craft itself to
counter the domination of another art. In one sense, therefore, it
might be said that the changes which furniture underwent at the
Renaissance were striking indeed but quite superficial, and amounting
to nothing more than the substitution of the applied details of classical
architecture for those of Gothic.

There was, however, more to it than that. Renaissance furniture
differed from all that had preceded it in an important way; it was not
merely the product of craftsmen copying the motifs of another discipline
but was in many cases the result of conscious design by men who,
whatever their craft origins, were functioning as architects and were
concerned to give their creations an architectural form. In a way there
had been earlier attempts at this, shown by those reliquaries and
caskets fashioned to resemble Gothic churches. That resemblance,
however, had been achieved by a kind of impressionism and the piece
of furniture had never been meant to do more than represent a conventionalized building. In the sixteenth century, and for the first time,
individual items of furniture were designed as architectural compositions.

Because the architect appeared first in Italy so this development
occurred there long before it occurred anywhere else. It began at a
time when the chest had not been wholly eliminated from its leading
position by other pieces and in consequence it affected cassoni very
strongly. The effect upon the ornament and iconography of cassoni
has already been discussed, but their forms were affected as well. This
is revealed in many ways, but most clearly by those examples which
are made to resemble classical sarcophagi and are architectural compositions in themselves. A cassone of mid-sixteenth century date in the
Amsterdam Rijksmuseum illustrates the type very well. It is made of
walnut and is partly gilt, has lions' feet at the corners, a Greek fret to
the base and classical subjects upon the two panels of the front [Plate
145].

By the time that matters had reached this stage outside of Italy the
chest had ceased to be an important piece of furniture and its place had
been usurped by the cabinet. The cabinet was in several respects a more

suitable subject for architectural treatment. It was often made in two or more clearly defined vertical stages and was thus readily provided with superimposed classical columns giving the effect of a storeyed building. Further, at a time when a 'frontispiece' was very popular among builders the cabinet had the added advantage that it could be made in just such a form. One which belonged to the Peretti family, now at Stourhead and mentioned earlier in another connection, is in the form of a triumphal arch and has three orders of superimposed columns, an attic and scrolled pediments [Plate 127]. A common type of French cabinet has two main stages surmounted by niches and a series of pediments [Plates 125 and 146].[31]

That much of this furniture was under the more or less direct control of architects is suggested again by the negative evidence from England. There, it can be argued, the 'architect' hardly appeared at all before the advent in the early-seventeenth century of Inigo Jones; and English furniture of the sixteenth century wholly lacks the qualities of those pieces just mentioned and is architectural only in the narrower and earlier sense that it uses a great amount of applied architectural ornament. On the other hand it is very noticeable, as Feulner has pointed out, how much Italian and French furniture gives the impression that it was designed in stone and translated into timber afterwards. Du Cerceau's designs were at bottom an attempt at producing a programme for the furniture of his age, but despite this they appear as the work of a man who thought in terms of stone and had little concept of the qualities of timber.[32]

By the beginning of the seventeenth century furniture had undergone the necessary changes in form which allowed it to continue to serve new functions; it had wholly transformed its grammar of ornament and its mode of decoration; and it had become the object of design by men who were no longer craftsmen but were looked up to as artists. In some ways it retained many of its old qualities, but it had reached a stage where it was ready for the further changes which would eliminate the last traces of its medieval origins.

5 The seventeenth century: the emergence of modern furniture

The new comforts

In the seventeenth century furniture was at first as much affected as ever by its milieu, but no longer by that alone. From about 1600 onwards other considerations came more into play and by the end of the century the history of furniture was becoming, like that of domestic architecture, a matter, in the main, of stylistic changes. But although western Europe, or some parts of it, had by then reached a level at which this transformation was possible, there were many obstacles in the way of its realization and for many years furniture continued to react more or less directly to social changes. This it did in both old and new ways. In the first place, the steady increase in the amount and diversity of furniture which had begun in the later Middle Ages continued at an even faster pace. At the same time the changes in the way of life and in the modes of social intercourse among the upper classes, which had first shown themselves in the sixteenth century, began to affect not only its amount, but its nature too.

The contrast in the amount and diversity of furniture between the sixteenth and seventeenth centuries is less striking than that between the sixteenth century and its predecessors, but it is none the less real and a few examples may serve to demonstrate it. Even in the best-appointed houses of earlier years chairs, while not uncommon, had still not been plentiful; but in Mme de Rambouillet's 'Blue Chamber' there were no less than twenty; and many articles began to be designed to one pattern [Plate 150]. Cabinets were becoming the pride and joy of connoisseurs in the late sixteenth century and Catherine de Medici was not ill-provided with them. Her collection, though, was small in comparison with that of Cardinal Mazarin sixty years later, for he had no less than seventeen of ebony alone. The evidence of wills and inventories reveals that in late-sixteenth century England men of means were accumulating much furniture, but they yet had far less than their sons and grandsons in the reigns of the first two Stuarts.

The greater diversification of furniture is shown in many ways but perhaps most clearly in the appearance of several kinds of bed. In many wealthy houses a great bed was still part of the furnishings of the Great Chamber or Saloon and was an object of some display [Plates 148 and 149]. Those with a tester overhead and curtains at the sides were to remain the commonest, or at any rate the most long-lived [Plate 162], but by the middle of the century others had become popular [Plates 163 and 164]. One of these was the 'lit-en-housse', provided with curtains which instead of drawing were raised vertically like a blind. When let down during the day-time it had a very neat appearance. One of the earliest recorded belonged to Gabrielle d'Estrées, the mistress of Henry IV, but they were well known among less wealthy and more sober people and are often shown in the engravings of Abraham Bosse, a man of Huguenot origin who depicted the lives and surroundings of the middle classes [Plate 151]. The variety of furniture amongst ordinary men is revealed again in the inventory of the goods of Thomas Chaitor, a gentleman from County Durham who died in 1618. The official who drew up this document was extremely conscientious about his duties and went to some trouble to distinguish between cupboards and linen-cupboards [Plate 147], and between draw-tables, round tables and square tables. He remarked as well on 'embroidered' chairs and on beds and chairs made for children. None of these items was anything very new in itself; what was new and portentous was the presence of so many of them in the home of a man who was no one in particular.[1]

Yet these developments were little more than the continuation and culmination of earlier ones and were of far less significance than the sudden appearance of furniture which was much more comfortable than anything known before. Their importance, indeed, lay less in themselves than in the contribution to comfort which plentiful and varied furniture, even of the old type, could help to provide. It has been said that it was in the course of the seventeenth century that a recognizably modern way of life came fully into existence. If we could be transplanted in time to the years around 1600 we would find an unfamiliar world; in the years around 1700 one essentially similar to our own. Whether or not this judgment will be universally accepted it is certainly true of one aspect of furniture; for in 1600 even those houses with a great amount of furniture had very few pieces which were comfortable in themselves, while those of 1700 had a great many.[2]

Once comfort became a major consideration and furniture began to be made as much for ease as for use or show, there was a rapid change in the nature of those pieces which were made for sitting or lying upon. This is clearly shown by some of the surviving Italian 'sgabelli' of the sixteenth century. They are lightly made and comfort or at least convenience was an element in their design. That it was, however, a very minor one and had to take second place to display is revealed by the carving upon them, elaborate and impressive, but not conducive to ease and rather guaranteed to cause acute discomfort to anyone who ventured to lean his own back against theirs. Some of the expensive armchairs of the period had equally rich and uncomfortable carving upon them and those without it had backs as hard and upright as that of a grenadier; although even a back was something [Plate 152]. There were more comfortable chairs and the so-called 'X-chairs' had been extremely popular. Compared with most others they were indeed luxurious, but again they had limitations. The ease which they provided depended mainly on the cushions placed upon them and their backs were short and straight. In any case, chairs of this kind were in a small minority and most men who had chairs to themselves, and were not relegated to stools and benches, sat in more dignity than their fellows, but not in very much more comfort.

One way of obtaining that quality was to make special types of furniture to suit particular purposes. Of these the so-called 'farthingale' chairs are the best known [Plate 155]. They were expressly designed for the comfort of fashionable ladies of the late sixteenth and early seventeenth centuries, wearing the enormous and cumbersome skirts that went by that name and prevented their owners from sitting down in an armchair or upon a bench. In France these chairs were known by their function from the beginning and Gabrielle d'Estrées had 'neuf chaises de bois de noyer, cinq à vertugadin (farthingale) et quatre à bras'. Farthingale chairs had upholstered or at least covered seats (Gabrielle's were of leather), but it was their purpose and consequent form which distinguished them from others.

134

Of a very different nature but alike in owing their origin to a desire for comfort and convenience were the tea-tables which developed at the end of the century. They were a direct response to the new fashion among the wealthy of drinking tea on some social occasions, and were lightly made that they might be easily moved to that room in the house or that place in the room where the ladies were gathered. They were at the time recent and surprising innovations and John Evelyn contrasted them with all the other kinds of table which he had known in his boyhood, when 'the shovel board and other long tables both in hall and parlour were as fixed as the freehold'.

Comfort, of course, has not always meant the same thing to all men, or women. Gabrielle d'Estrées might perhaps have been accused of extravagance by some people but doubtless herself considered that it was no more than a needful comfort to have six 'litz d'Este' which, presumably to abate the heat of summer, were hung with cloth of silver, chinese taffeta and white lawn. Mazarin is said to have had beds to fit his moods, gaily-coloured when he was happy and sombre when he was not, a whim which must have saved those who had business with him from much anxious speculation.

Not everybody could, or cared to, indulge in the luxuries which were available to acquisitive ministers and to royal mistresses, but in many houses an article of furniture, other than a bed, to recline on in the day-time was appearing. In a way there was again nothing very new in that, for St Louis and Charlemagne before him had occasionally rested on a couch of some sort during the day. But as more men and more women spent more of their leisure in Great Chambers and in salons there was a wider need, or desire, of a special piece for that purpose. By the late sixteenth century it had acquired a name of its own in English and was called a 'day-bed'. Probably it was then still far from common and not yet wholly respectable. Edward IV is described by implication in Shakespeare's *Richard III* as 'lolling on a lewd day-bed' and the pejorative sense of the words, taken in conjunction with Edward's long-lived reputation as a lecher, implies that it was still far from being the kind of article that the strictest moralists could approve of.

Day-beds are not mentioned in the most detailed English inventories of the years around 1600 – those of the Earl of Leicester and of Lord Lumley – and as late as 1613 Sir Thomas Overbury, who was to his cost well-enough acquainted with the ways of the court of James I, spoke of sleeping upon benches in the afternoon rather than upon day-beds. Nevertheless they were not unknown by then for the portrait of Elizabeth Drury painted in 1610, and formerly at Hawsted House in Suffolk, shows her lying upon what is clearly a day-bed; and in Fletcher's *Rule a Wife and Have a Wife* of 1624 they are mentioned as present in every room of a house. The usage of 'lits-de-repos' begins in France in the years around 1630 and when the Prince de Conti was arrested in 1650 he remained 'toujours assis sur le petit lit-de-repos qui étoit dans la galerie'. A description of Henrietta Maria, the exiled Queen of England, at the Château de Chilly in 1656 refers to her as lying on a 'lit-de-repos' surrounded by her ladies.[3]

Furniture of this sort was a comfort in itself, but in the course of the seventeenth century it steadily became more comfortable. Early specimens in England, such as that of *c.* 1600 at Hardwick Hall and that in the Drury portrait, were little more than benches with panelled head-boards and strewn with cushions. By about the accession of Charles I the day-bed had acquired upholstery and an adjustable head-board. On an example at Knole the head-board can be lowered or raised to any desired height [Plate 153], and a later one, now in the Royal Ontario Museum at Toronto, has a head-board which may be set to a number of different positions by means of a chain. A French lit-de-repos of *c.* 1690 has an upholstered head-board at each end and an upholstered back as well. Not every piece had these refinements and some late-seventeenth century ones retain fixed head-boards. Undoubtedly the ways of the aristocracy played a large part in developing the day-bed, but it was a widely-liked piece of furniture and its popularity did not depend wholly upon the tastes and pleasures of courts. There is an example in the Metropolitan Museum at New York, made of maple-wood and probably originating in the years around 1700, whose decorative details show strong Flemish influence, but which is of native American manufacture [Plate 154].

It is probable that the need for day-beds became the less as chairs began to be designed so that their occupants, if not able to recline in them, could at any rate lean back at ease. As late as 1580 a French ordinance recognized nothing but the 'chaire' (the heavy seat of honour of medieval tradition), the 'scabelle' and the 'chair basse appelé caquetoiere'. It was, however, not long before the chair began its evolution into something like its modern form. The typically short and straight back gave way to a longer and often canted one; the high seat,

136

which had forced most users to sit with their legs at attention, was moved to a lower and more convenient position; and arm-rests which had formerly been more for ornament than comfort were made to suit the human frame. England was no more a pioneer in this respect than in others, but a chair in the Victoria and Albert Museum perhaps of a date as early as *c*. 1600 has a wide and sloping back and arm-rests curved up to make a support for the elbows. Another English chair from the end of the century, now in the Toronto museum, shows the full development and has a canted back long enough to support anyone in comfort and a seat which is very low off the ground. Comfort in chairs can never be wholly provided by even the best designed forms, but the un-upholstered chairs of the late seventeenth century had probably come as close to achieving that aim as it is possible to come. [4]

But despite all the ingenuity of carpenters and joiners it was the upholsterer who did the most to raise the comfort of furniture to a level which may be considered modern; and it is perhaps surprising that this occurred so late. As long as the upper classes were peripatetic and constantly on the move from one barely-furnished house to another, they had to carry with them the pillows and cushions which alone could assuage the discomforts of their dwellings. When they took to a more sedentary life they created thereby the opportunity to attach the cushions to the furniture in the form of upholstery. This opportunity they seem to have neglected at first and it was less the change in their way of life than the later and consequent change in their mode of social intercourse which produced this new comfort [Plate XI].

The most commonly upholstered pieces at an early date were the X-chairs so popular in the sixteenth century. Many of them, for example those now at Arundel Castle, were still collapsible and it was not practicable to affix upholstery to the seat, although the sides and arms were often quilted and covered. Despite the origin of X-chairs as portable pieces, many of them were being made in the late sixteenth century with no folding members, and consequently could have upholstered backs and seats; well-known examples are the very richly covered ones at Knole of a date around 1600 [Plate 158]. On the Continent upholstery had become not uncommon some time before then. It will be remembered that the farthingale chairs which belonged to Gabrielle d'Estrées were covered with leather and upholstered Italian chairs from the late sixteenth century survive in some numbers.

In England, it has been claimed, 'no stuffing was upholstered to

137

woodwork before the early part of the seventeenth century'. It is however doubtful whether this view can any longer be maintained. The Ingatestone inventory of 1600 speaks of chairs covered with blue kersey, and well before then the Earl of Leicester had had 'a little chair for a childe, of carnation and green cloth and tinsele'. There are similar references in other inventories and it is unreasonable to suppose that none of these cloth-covered chairs was upholstered. Towards the end of Elizabeth's reign Sir John Harrington was complaining of the hard stools which he had to sit upon at court in contrast with the 'easy quilted and lined forms and stools' to be found in every merchant's house. It is clear that whatever particular techniques he may have had in mind he was thinking of a kind of furniture which, if it was not upholstered, yet had all, or nearly all, the qualities of upholstery. Whether or not 'richly upholstered chairs were becoming plentiful in great establishments' in England towards the end of Elizabeth's reign and were 'rivalling continental standards of luxury and furnishing', it is plain that if England lagged behind the continent at all it was not at a very great distance [Plate x].[5]

There can be no doubt that by the early years of the seventeenth century upholstery was widely known in nearly every country of western Europe, and in a variety of forms. At first leather was more popular or more widely used as a covering than textiles and fabrics. There was, of course, a long tradition to hand of covering chests and coffers, and especially travelling ones, with leather; and the technique employed upon these could be easily adapted for use upon other forms which were to be padded as well as covered. On many coffers the leather had been affixed, and often a very pleasing effect had been obtained, by the use of brightly-coloured large-headed nails, placed partly where need dictated and partly where an engaging pattern could be formed. When it came to the turn of the backs and seats of chairs to be covered with the same material the same technique was used and a similar patterning emerged.

A very early application was the use of gilt nails upon the blue velvet of Queen Mary's X-chair in Winchester Cathedral. Many variations were possible and some of them are aptly illustrated by three chairs now in the Metropolitan Museum. The first, of sixteenth-century date and of Italian origin, has the outlines of the back and of the seat emphasized by closely-spaced rows of small brass-headed nails; the second, a Spanish example of comparable date, has larger

138

and more widely-spaced nail-heads; while the third, which was made
c. 1700 and in America, combines the small nail-heads of the one with
the wide-spacing of the other [Plates 156, 157 and 159]. A resplendent
example, said to have belonged to the Archbishop of Toledo and now in
the Victoria and Albert Museum, is covered in blue velvet [Plate 160].

Leather had however been used for other purposes than covering chests, and methods of decorating it and working directly upon it had been well developed long before this. These techniques too were directly copied and the Italian chair mentioned above has an intricate tooled design on the back in gold, while the Spanish one has a floral design in a Renaissance style embossed upon back and seat.

Makers of fabric coverings had less of a tradition to fall back upon, but at the same time there were possibilities open to them which were not open to their colleagues. Although brass-headed and even silver-headed nails were sometimes used, both to affix the covering and for their ornamental effect, they were less prominent than upon leather; and textile upholstery in the main eschewed contrasts with other materials and an emphasis upon the lines of pieces, and instead set about exploiting its own qualities [Plate XII]. Here again a few examples from the Metropolitan Museum serve to indicate the wide range of fabrics and fabric-designs at the disposal of the furniture-maker by the middle of the seventeenth century. One of the most striking is an English chair of the mid-seventeenth century upholstered in petit point with bright yellow flowers upon a blue background. The covering is in fact considerably later than the chair itself, but it vividly demonstrates the important role of the upholsterer in determining the visual impact of many pieces of furniture. More sober effects were sometimes preferred in other countries and at other times, and an Italian chair of about a hundred years earlier has its seat covered with a red velvet brocade finished at the bottom with a narrow red fringe. Similar to the English example in its richness, but of more muted colour tones, is a French one of *c.* 1700 upholstered on seat and back with a symmetrical and self-sufficient floral design carried out in tapestry [Plate 161].

The decline of classical influence

Although upholstery was a response to the demand for more comfort which followed from the transformation of men's homes, it was at the same time made the more readily acceptable by changes which were

less directly related to social developments. The changes in the educational attainments and intellectual climate of the upper classes,
referred to in the previous chapter, had reached a new level by the
early seventeenth century. In earlier years the humanists had revolu-
tionized much of the ideology of western Europe and had given a vital
impulse to secular learning, but there had been limitations upon their
influence and they were rather the tutors of a very narrow élite than
of all the upper classes. Those highly educated women cited in the
previous chapter were a phenomenon whose importance can hardly
be over-rated, but yet, it must be noticed, they were nearly all the
daughters of kings and princes or of their closest and most trusted
counsellors. In northern Europe especially, where the efficient running
of the new monarchies was demanding the creation of an educated
bureaucracy which the church was unable to supply, humanism was
often patronized for very utilitarian reasons, and classical learning
was pursued by many men because it was, or was thought to be, a
means to political office. Highly educated in the classics and consorting
with and learning from Renaissance artists who, in their own way were
equally conscious of antiquity, the leaders of society and moulders of
taste were drawn to the appreciation of classical architecture, which
was then the only aspect of antique art about which anything very
much could be known and to which any learning at all could be applied.
It was as a result of this that the concepts and motifs of that architecture
came in the course of the sixteenth century to dominate interior
decoration and furniture. By the beginning of the next century,
however, the situation had changed. The impetus of humanism had
carried education into wider circles and the 'classical heritage' was the
common property of all the upper classes.[6]

In spreading its influence more widely humanism had necessarily
spread it more thinly, and the educated gentlemen of the early seventeenth century were less passionately interested in the classical world,
and less likely to regard its practices as unalterable rules, than the
learned statesmen of the sixteenth century had been. At the same time,
they were less inclined to be overawed by the learning of its champions.
They were sufficiently the heirs of their predecessors to regard classical
architecture as in the natural order of things, but yet sufficiently of their
own age to be ready to adapt it to their needs or to eliminate it altogether from some fields. Further, they were less easily imposed upon
than their fathers by the florid Mannerist designs of the German and

Dutch carvers of the late sixteenth century, and they did not turn their backs upon classical columns in order to smile upon caryatides and herms. Amongst these men too there was something of an élite, one not of position or rank but rather of sensibility; a kind of aesthetic intelligentsia. The intelligentsia, a witty American has said, is a social group of which membership is achieved by merely announcing one's arrival; a group therefore which in some circumstances, as in France at a critical time in the seventeenth century, is capable of wide and rapid expansion.

The effect of this development was marked in many fields, and particularly in interior decoration and the treatment of wall surfaces and panelling. Architectural concepts and motifs were still present, but on the one hand the amount of carved ornament in the form of columns and entablatures was smaller, and on the other walls were less often regarded as façades upon which to clap an arcade or a columniation, and the panels within them were more sparingly decorated with blind pedimented windows or with other pieces of sham architecture. Instead, walls were plainly wainscotted or were faced with rich marbles or hung with Flemish or Gobelins tapestries, and carved ornament was supplanted by pictures and ornate mirrors and by curios and ceramics placed upon side-tables. In sympathy with this, the old ornament was steadily eliminated from furniture as well. And not only the details but the forms of classical architecture were less widely employed. The huge constructions which had emulated stone triumphal arches or complete buildings passed out of fashion, and even the smaller pieces with fronts designed in the manner of a two or three-tiered pavilion or frontispiece became ever less common. In their places there appeared furniture built generally upon a smaller scale and given, instead of an aedicular air, an outward form which reflected its purpose.[7]

The rise of the cabinet-maker

Throughout all these changes timber continued to be the almost universal material for furniture and still one of the commonest for wall-coverings, but it had lost much of its old value. Craftsmen no longer strove to obtain artistic effects from working upon it or from exploiting its natural qualities, but rather used it, to employ their own term, as a 'carcase', as a base upon which to affix more brilliant and opulent materials, or else as a foil to other kinds of ornament. The diminution of architectural influence was therefore of importance not only because it freed furniture from the straightjacket of classical motifs and aedicular form, but also because in so doing it ended the Golden Age of the woodcarver, and thereby provided the craftsmen of the late seventeenth century with a large amount of free surface upon which to exercise their own arts of applied ornament. The trade seized the opportunities opening before it, and some of its members took their places as designers alongside the architects and sculptors, who had been unchallenged by craftsmen since the days of the master H.S.

The century was well-advanced before this process came to fruition, but the decline in the esteem of plain unvarnished woodwork, of walnut as well as oak, is revealed by the greater fondness for covering, whether with cheap or expensive draperies, many structural members which had once been richly carved and proudly displayed. The once common great bed, with its posts designed as classical columns with bases and architraves and its head-board decorated with blind arcading, was superseded in many houses by the 'lit-en-housse', covered from top to bottom with fabrics and with no woodwork visible at all, except perhaps an urn at the head of each corner-post; and that too was often replaced by a plume of feathers [Plate 165]. Even the more stately four-poster, which still remained the form of the older type, was wholly covered with drapery, generally of the most expensive sort [Plates 166 and 167]. In this respect beds were reverting to their older form from what may perhaps be thought of as the aberrations of the sixteenth century. Similarly, tables, other than those intended to display objects of interest, were hidden beneath heavy cloths or turkey carpets and the elaborate columniation and arcading which had beautified many earlier examples was rendered superfluous. In Bosse's engravings and in many paintings of Dutch interiors the chairs are often the only pieces with any naked framework [Plate 168], and to judge from the simplicity plainness of many similar ones which have survived, it would seem that and they too were usually intended to be wholly covered with fabric.[8]

Of course, it was neither practicable nor desirable to have every item of furniture draped and many of those which were not, for example cabinets and cupboards, were still given an architectural treatment. In contrast, however, with their predecessors who designed under the influence of such men as Goujon and Du Cerceau, these eschewed purity and correctness and were clumsily robust. They

142

shared a tendency to break and interrupt the clear lines of earlier pieces, to use boldly overhanging members which produced effects of light and shade, to place polished and shining materials against a contrasted background, and in association with all of these, to use dark woods, and especially ebony when it could be afforded.[9]

The use of ebony in the first half of the century is perhaps the clearest symptom of the change which was coming. It had been known in Europe for a long time, since the thirteenth century at least, and Havard has listed several medieval instances of its use; but it was only at this time that it began to be widely popular. Indeed Frenchmen who wished to be in the fashion had at first to import their ebony cabinets from Italy and the Low Countries. The demand, however, was such that before long these were being made in France by native or immigrant craftsmen; and to such a standard that it is not always possible to distinguish between imports and home products. The ebony was generally applied to a carcase in a thick veneer which itself was capable of taking carving, or at least shallow cutting, as on mid-seventeenth-century French examples in the Victoria and Albert Museum and the Kunstgewerbemuseum in Berlin [Plate 169]. The more favoured treatment, however, was to enrich the ebony with highly-coloured inlays of ivory, tortoise-shell, pietro duro, brass and copper. The interiors were equally splendid, generally with inlay but sometimes with well-painted figured scenes in a contemporary style [Plates XIII and 171]. Only the wealthy, of course, could afford much of this, but those seventeen cabinets mentioned earlier as in the possession of Cardinal Mazarin, who at the end of his career was among the wealthiest of all, were inlaid with miniatures, with precious stones and with precious metals.

Some of the outstanding pieces of the sixteenth century had had very rich inlay, but generally in a two-tone colour scheme which was always subordinate to the architectural composition of the whole. Their successors, and especially those of ebony, indulged in bright colours strongly contrasted with more sober and darker backgrounds, and in this way tended to transform any architectural composition into a mere framework [Plate xv]. They thereby gave a further impetus to the initial efforts of the craftsman-ornamentalist to usurp the role of designer-in-chief of furniture.

By the time that Louis XIV was assuming personal power in France the influence of architecture upon furniture was declining, and its end was not far away. Nevertheless, the process was a slow one and the kind of furniture which was to grace Versailles, and its many imitations, was still largely absent from less fortunate milieux, even at the end of the century. In part this was a measure of the backwardness of some other countries in comparison with France, but in part it was a reflection of newly-established differences in taste between the aristocracy and the upper bourgeoisie of the court and the capital on the one hand and the minor gentry of the countryside and the bourgeoisie of the smaller towns on the other. The phenomenon is perhaps clearest in Germany and in France itself. In Germany the decline of interest in carved ornament is shown by the closer rapprochement of the formerly very distinctive styles of north and south. It is apparent as well on a buffet from Basel of 1664 (now in the Kunstgewerbemuseum at Berlin) which has also abandoned the clear lines of the Renaissance styles for a more volume-conscious manner, itself an intimation that the former control of architecture was on the decline [Plate 172]. But all the same, it was declining very slowly. Some Dutch furniture retained a marked architectural character throughout the seventeenth century and as late as *c.* 1700 the massive cupboards in the 'Diele' (the two-storeyed halls) of north German houses were nearly as much architectural constructions as any of their predecessors had been [Plate 174]. In contrast, the petty rulers of that country were by then copying the fashions in furniture of the court of Louis xiv. What was true of some parts and classes of Germany was also true of France itself. The Louis xiii style there was a nation-wide phenomenon, as that of Louis xv was to be later, but throughout the latter part of the seventeenth century most Frenchmen, and especially those in the provinces, failed to follow the lead of Versailles and Paris and clung closely to, or only slightly developed, the early style [Plate 173].[10]

In discussing the development of furniture in the first half of the century one may treat western Europe as a whole and speak of all the major countries as though they were at more or less the same level of development. By about 1700, however, furniture was in many ways under French tutelage. Since French leadership in such matters is not a law of nature but was brought about at this time by historical factors, it is necessary to consider, however briefly and superficially, the cause of this hegemony.

xi (*opposite*) Early-seventeenth century Great Houses were not always as comfortable as they were magnificent. In this room at Knole, however, much of the upholstered furniture is of a comparable date with the house

French absolutism and the salons

It is perhaps with good reason that the age which we see in retrospect as belonging to Locke and Newton was thought of by contemporaries as that of the Roi Soleil, whose power and magnificence cast a far-flung shadow over all his fellow monarchs. This happy state of affairs was not a gift from the gods, however much Louis might feel himself to be their favourite son, but had been brought about by a deliberate and well-calculated strategy. The intentions and achievements of the policies followed by the Bourbon kings in the course of the century were not all of equal effect upon furniture, but one of them may be singled out; the transformation of the French nobility from old feudatories into new courtiers. This was engineered by several means; by force of arms; by isolating them from the petite noblesse; and, of most importance in the present context, encouraging them with extravagant gifts to spend their time in attendance at court. As Saint-Simon put it with all the bitterness of a victim, the monarchy's aim was to beggar everybody by making luxury honourable, even necessary and thus to reduce everyone to complete dependence upon its bounty for their livelihood. The court was yet another of the political instruments of despotism. Of course, by 'everybody' did not mean everybody, but merely the nobility, and to bring them to this state it was necessary to bankrupt them first in order to turn them into grateful or dependent followers afterwards. It seems likely that at this time economic changes were already endangering the financial stability of landed aristocrats, but Louis himself exacerbated their difficulties by setting standards of luxury which he encouraged, and almost commanded, them to follow. As a result, luxury began to turn into its opposite and became a necessity and even a duty.[11]

It would be a distortion to suggest that Louis initiated this policy, for it ante-dated him by many years. To some extent it was inherent in the nature of things in the sixteenth and seventeenth centuries. Long before Louis was born, and at a time when the Valois kings were in the thick of their troubles, Montaigne had written, 'Le reste de la France prend pour règle la règle de la court'. While Louis was still in tutelage under Mazarin, John Evelyn had noticed the predilection for luxury among the French nobility, and had remarked on its effect upon furniture: 'the gentlemen are generally given to those laudable magnificences of building and furnishing their palaces with the most precious

145

XII (*opposite*) An English chair of *c.* 1700, made of beechwood, painted black and upholstered in bright colours, designed for comfort rather than dignity moveables'; he went on to quote the example of one extravagant lady, perhaps to be forgiven because she was a duchess, who had spent 'near a thousand pounds of our money' upon tufts of plumes to decorate a bed. It is clear that French aristocrats, with or without royal prodding, had been developing expensive tastes over a long period; but nevertheless it was only after the defeat of the Fronde and the death of Mazarin that the court was in a position to enforce luxury on a large scale as a weapon in its struggle to control the nobility.

This, however, had a positive as well as a negative side. Seduced or bullied into almost permanent residence at Versailles, the French nobility lost much of the coarseness which it had earlier imbibed from the camp and the countryside, and acquired at the least a veneer of culture. While the court of Henri IV had been more remarkable for the graces which it lacked than for those which it possessed, that of his grandson set new standards of behaviour for the upper classes throughout western Europe.

Those standards were not wholly dependent upon the pursuit of such a policy and at the same time something more than that was needed before a new mode of living and of furnishing could be firmly established. English history provides a useful comparison here. Among the more notable results or accompaniments of Charles I's years of personal rule were the 'Virtuosi', of whom the malicious might have said that they did nothing more useful than hang around a court. There is little evidence that Charles consciously pursued a Bourbon policy; on the contrary, he issued proclamations to the gentry to stay away from London and reside on their estates in the country. Nevertheless, the effect of a court like that of the early Stuarts, a 'fount of honour' and of profit as well, was to attract men of talent and ambition. Once attracted, they often found that boredom was the most constant element of a courtier's life; Mme de Maintenon complained of 'l'ennui qui dévore les grands, et la peine qu'ils ont à remplir leurs journées'. Those who could not be wholly satisfied with the usual diversions of a leisured class sought other pleasures, and amongst them the Virtuosi studied and encouraged the most up-to-date aspects of contemporary art. Their most famous protégé was Inigo Jones, but despite his achievements in many fields, including furniture design, the Virtuosi never managed to impose their views upon their fellows so effectively that the tone of English high society was changed. Their failure may in part be attributed to Charles' fall, but it is probable that something

146

more was necessary than an absolutist court, or even than one successfully pursuing a Bourbon policy.

In France at any rate absolutism did not have to work alone, for the new grace and polish of the court was accompanied, and had been preceded, by the higher status of women and the new culture of the Salons. The most famous of these, that of Mme de Rambouillet, was flourishing before Louis was born. Throughout his reign, and despite his known aversion to Paris and to all it contained, many courtiers absented themselves discreetly when they could from the magnificent halls and chambers of Versailles, and sought other company in the private drawing-rooms of the capital. There they met the habitués of the salons. These latter were not indeed the intellectual leaders of the age, but they were its most successful publicists and they gave to the court the intellectual coverings and comforts that neither the Church nor the University could provide.

Aristocrats who frequented these gatherings mingled there with a far wider range of men than could usually be found at court. To some extent the salons were 'ouverts aux talents' and brought court nobles together with Parisian notables, and both with writers and artists of no social standing at all. In practice the early Bourbons succoured the nobility, once it was ready to submit, and encouraged the haute bourgeoisie, so long as it kept its place, and the salons played a similar role in the realm of ideology, helping to bind together two groups which, for a time at least, had common interests. The two did not necessarily have the same tastes in all respects, but each was open to the influence of the other. The salons, in short, acted as a clearing-house of ideas and aesthetics between two sections of the upper class. This unity was on the one hand to be the basis for new cultural advances, and on the other to bring about the divergence between the art of the court and the capital and that of the rest of the country whose reflection in furniture was noticed earlier.

These relationships were made possible by the long internal peace which France enjoyed under Bourbon absolutism throughout the second half of the century. There was, however, nothing inevitable about this and nothing in her previous history to suggest that it would be France, rather than any other country, which would first emerge from the century-old crisis of western Europe. In earlier years it might well have looked as though some of the German states or England had a brighter future. But Germany was to be exhausted by the Thirty Years War, and in England the potentialities which the Virtuosi represented were cut short by the victory of Cromwell's Ironsides, the bearers of a culture which was at least the equal of that of their opponents, but of a very different kind. The contrasting experience of France was the result of the victory of the French monarchy over all its enemies.[12]

This political success prepared the way for others and the monarchy set about establishing a control over ideology and aesthetics as absolute as that which it exercised over the state-machine and attempted to exercise over the economy. The unity of the country was to be paralleled by a unity, if necessary a uniformity, within the arts; and both were to be achieved by administrative measures. The first tentative step had been taken in 1648 with the founding of the Académie Royale de Peinture et de Sculpture, ostensibly with the object, in part at least, of freeing artists from out-of-date gild restrictions. It was refounded in 1664 with extended powers and privileges and quite openly with the intent of determining 'l'esthétique de l'artiste, comme l'Académie française fixe la langue et comme Boileau va fixer la poésie'. In one way this was a great gain for artists, for they had been given official recognition and protection; and art had become one element in 'une sorte de ligue du pouvoir, des académies, des écrivains et des artistes, dont les chefs furent, sous les auspices de Louis XIV, Colbert, Boileau, Racine, Bossuet et Lebrun.' But if the gain was great the price was heavy: artists were to use their talents to glorify the régime, either blatantly in the sycophantic flattery of Louis Le Grand or more subtly in the adoption of a style of magnificence, of what Sainte-Beuve called 'l'éternel solennel', which should shed an aura of superhuman power and wisdom over the Crown and its minions.[13]

Not content with its organizational control over them, the Crown also established itself as far and away the most important patron and employer of artists, and in the minor arts as well as the great. In some fields France had been backward in the early seventeenth century and at that time her future leadership in furniture design looked as unlikely as her future hegemony in international affairs. It will be remembered that Frenchmen who wanted ebony cabinets had to import them from Italy or entice their makers to emigrate. Italian cabinets figured in the list of customs duties of 1641, and two of the most splendid of all, for which Louis XIV paid 35,000 livres, were made by an Italian. And it was not only Italian craftsmen and their products which were sought after.

148

The names of several immigrants from the Low Countries are known, such as Laurent Stabre from Flanders and Pierre Golle from Holland. Even a native-born worker like Jean Mace of Blois had served his apprenticeship in the Netherlands. Further, very many pieces were imported from Germany. In the 1641 customs list cabinets 'venans d'Allemagne' were rated at only a fraction of the figure of Italian ones, and it may be that they were of painted wood rather than of ebony; but all the same there was a heavy demand for them. And this was not only among the less wealthy, for in the years between 1613 and 1619 the Duke of Lorraine was making many purchases of cabinets in Germany. In Du Colombier's opinion the cabinet – the object of the greatest display of the furniture-manufacturer's skill – was not then indigenous to France, and it may be supposed that, in contrast with some other countries, she suffered from a dearth of cabinet-makers.

Under Louis XIV the monarchy was able both to remedy and to take advantage of this situation, and in the same year that the Academy was founded with Lebrun as its director the Manufacture Royale des Meubles de la Couronne was placed under his control. For furniture-makers there was a double cause for rejoicing, for they were both assured of lucrative employment and given a status which they had never had before. The result was to create in France a highly specialized profession which existed in no other country and which had the opportunities, and with them the abilities, to concentrate upon adopting and perfecting the new techniques which could serve new conceptions of design and new modes of ornament. The effects were spectacular. According to Havard, the furniture industry never had a faster and more spectacular rise nor did it reach such heights in so short a time. A body of craftsmen and designers able to achieve such an immediate and dazzling success was a unifying force in itself and its own innate tendencies were strengthened by the uniformity which pattern-books produced and by the influence upon it of the orthodoxy of the major arts.[14]

That uniformity, however, was not wholly on a par with the orthodox classicism of painting and architecture. For all its importance, furniture was neither so readily nor so usefully employed as those arts in propagating the official ideology. Other forces could therefore work more easily upon it, and among these were the style of decoration which appealed to the court in its festive moods and the freer and more heretical climate of taste of the salons. Consequently, the uniformity of furniture under Louis XIV was manifested not only in its reflection of the dogmas of the Academy, but equally in the concern of a highly centralized craft to develop and exploit to the full these new and improved techniques which lent themselves, above all, to the expression of another and less rigid style. It is true, as Jacqueline Viaux has remarked, that the makers simplified the lines of furniture, eliminated or diminished much of the old heavy and confused ornament, and invested their productions with the classic qualities of 'grandeur, somptuousité, richesse, mais calme mesure et clarté'. But it is also true that many pieces were appreciated for other virtues than an adherence to the canons of the Academy, to which they made but a perfunctory obeisance. As well as uniformity, a dichotomy is also apparent.[15]

The age of Louis XIV is characterized, however, not only by French dominance, but also by the alacrity with which other countries copied French styles and fashions. The gap between France and her neighbours was palpable but not impassable. Western Europe, in fact, was again in a position which it had last been in during the later Middle Ages. At that far distant time much of it had reached a very uniform level of civilization, and the immense differences between one region and another, which had revealed themselves as the Dark Ages passed by, had been more or less evened out. Especially was this so in the realms of ideology and aesthetics, and the advent in the fourteenth century of the 'international style' showed how closely allied, in concept and in execution, were the national arts of most west European countries. This equilibrium, like most others, was of short duration and was disrupted by the Renaissance. The Renaissance too was an international style, but it did not have the same character in every country and neither did it appear everywhere at the same time and develop at the same speed. Instead, 'advanced' and 'retarded' national arts reappeared, paying a greater or lesser respect to classical principles and Italian teachers. The imbalance was as transient as the former balance had been, and by the early seventeenth century another levelling-up was beginning to occur. That process, however, was in some places cut short and was everywhere impeded by the political troubles of the time. It was France which suffered the least from these, or at any rate emerged the soonest, and with the strongest and most centralized government. But as other countries began to work out some kind of a solution to their internal problems, political influences, both direct and indirect, became of less account. In their place those other forces which in England, for example, had bred the Virtuosi, began to reassert themselves, so that by about the end of the third quarter of the century there was in most of western Europe a more or less unified upper class with a common intellectual heritage. Against this background other differences were slight, and the taste of the cultivated in the oligarchical republic of Holland and in the almost equally oligarchical monarchy of England was potentially much the same as that of their fellows under the despotic rule of French kings or German princelings. Other countries necessarily had to yield first place to France because, having taken the lead earlier, she was making all the running; but they were hard on her heels. French fashions were avidly seized on in Amsterdam and London and Berlin because France and Holland and England and Germany were again all at a similar level. To put it another way; French leadership was in a sense accidental, while the bunching-up of all the rest of the field immediately behind the leader was not perhaps 'inevitable', for one may not use that word today, but was at any rate the least surprising result of all the earlier developments.

Fashion and Chinoiserie

The changes in furniture which the French professionals were to help to bring about were immense, but they were not wholly due to happenings within France; and other countries, and especially Holland, made a large contribution. Although the seventeenth century saw the decline of Dutch sea-power in the face of the English advance, nevertheless Holland was probably the most prosperous land in Europe and the standard of comfort in the houses of its oligarchs was unequalled anywhere at a comparable social level. For all the commercial and political rivalry between the two nations it was the Dutch who had the greatest influence upon English furniture; and for a short time upon English architecture as well. In the mid-century Holland was exporting cabinets and cabinet-makers to many countries, and the latter did much to prepare the way for the triumphs of French craftsmen. Peter Golle, for example, had an international reputation for his skill at marquetry long before he was invited to Paris to work and teach.

Golle and the French were in the direct line of descent from their predecessors, but a new and extraneous element in European furniture appeared in the early years of the century, and it perhaps needs to be

151

considered first. The techniques of lacquer-work and japanning and the use of an 'eastern' style are important firstly in their own right, for they were to be popular and long-lived; secondly because their chequered history, in which the French were not pioneers, illustrates that in the absence of favourable conditions no manner of design and ornament could achieve a permanent success; and thirdly because they were instrumental in furthering a movement of which they were themselves a consequence.

Apart from their technique, the most striking aspect of the japanned pieces which began to appear in the very early years of the seventeenth century, was their total lack of any sign of classical influence or of architectural control at a time when these wholly dominated all other furniture. The European technique of japanning was in one way little more than an intensification of the gilded and painted gesso-work of earlier centuries and it has no innate reason for being associated with oriental motifs. In practice, however, and partly because the Asiatic technique was at first far superior to the European, the two usually went hand-in-hand in this period.[16]

The great increase in trade with the Far East at the turn of the century, of which the foundations of the English and Dutch East India Companies are clear signs, certainly provided an easy channel by which oriental art could enter Europe, and there can be little doubt that the oriental vogue of the early years of the century was made possible by contacts with the East. In 1608 the Jesuits presented Marie de Medici with a Chinese cabinet and Sir Thomas Roe made his embassy to the Great Mogul in 1615–18 an occasion to hunt for bargains in orientalia. Throughout much of Europe at this time there was a keen demand among those with money for eastern objects; and prices, often carefully manipulated by the trade, reached a peak in England in 1618.[17]

But diplomatic missions and commercial connections, although they were necessary prerequisites, were not enough by themselves to establish the kind of taste which flourished later in the century. One of the countries with the closest ties with the Far East was Portugal, and Portugal remained aloof from the current interest, despite the use by furniture-makers of oriental woods and the development of an Indo-Portuguese style [Plate 170]. Further, in the middle years of the century, even in those countries most affected by it, the vogue expressed itself in a very emasculated way.[18]

xiv (*overleaf left*) An English lacquer cabinet of the late-seventeenth century. The gold ornament upon a red background is set off by the silver cresting and stand

xv (*overleaf right*) The sombre splendour of much seventeenth century furniture is often achieved, as in this Antwerp cabinet, by the contrast between the dark colour of the carcase and the brilliance of the inlay

152

xiii (*opposite*) A mid-seventeenth century Flemish cabinet painted with scenes of contemporary life. A similar cabinet with mythological scenes in the style of Rubens is shown in Plate 170

To a large extent oriental products were sought after at first as 'curiosities' rather than from a liking for eastern art, and those who could not afford the very expensive genuine article had to be content with a copy. It is probable that even at that early date merchants in the Far East were aware that there was a market for imitations in Europe. Many of the writing-cabinets which came into Europe then – gilded, inlaid with mother-of-pearl, and decorated with birds, deer, trees and floral designs – are very similar to late-sixteenth century German products. They seem to be more or less free renderings in a faintly exotic idiom of European forms, intended to satisfy a European taste. European craftsmen were also aware of potential custom and soon began to turn out their own versions of oriental work. In the Victoria and Albert Museum there is an early-seventeenth century cabinet in black lacquer ornamented in gold, with a design of a highly westernized Chinaman – recognizable, like Bret Harte's 'heathen chinee', by his long finger-nails – against a typically western background with a windmill and a loaded gibbet [Plates 175 and 176]. The Rijksmuseum at Amsterdam has a coffer of similar date lacquered in black with gold arabesques.[19]

Remote as these were from any eastern original, they were yet closer than the 'Chinese' wares which were being turned out from about 1620 onwards. Although inventories of the period often refer to 'Chinese' items or to items 'in the Chinese fashion' it is by no means clear that any of these had any oriental character at all, even of the most debilitated nature. Attempts to identify them have proved almost uniformly unsuccessful and while it is possible that time has discriminated unfairly against them and that nearly all have been destroyed, it seems more likely that their total disappearance is an illusion: that there was nothing oriental about them but their name and that they are today wholly unrecognizable as examples of chinoiserie. To say that much is not entirely guesswork, for some confirmation is provided by the late-twelfth century marriage-casket in Vannes Cathedral. This is decorated with scenes of medieval life in a quite typical contemporary style and there is nothing 'Chinese' or even exotic about any feature of it. Nevertheless, it was described in a list of 1694 as 'peinte à la chinoise'.[20]

In some media, however, in pottery and textiles for example, there was a steady production of more truly 'Chinese' articles. The Delft potteries, founded in 1614, made wares which were at first very close

153

XVI *(opposite)* A late-seventeenth century Dutch cabinet with a naturalistic floral design carried out in inlays of light-coloured woods imitations of Chinese and Japanese porcelain vessels, and which even later, when they had broken away from their prototypes, were still recognizably in an eastern style. Furniture was not one of these media; and nor was architecture. In the 1670s there was something of a mania for chinoiserie at Versailles and perhaps its most notable product was the *Trianon de porcelaine*. Built as a summer pavilion for the king's then reigning mistress, Mme de Montespan, it was fondly imagined to be truly Chinese. In fact, it was designed, in Hugh Honour's words, 'in an uncompromisingly late-seventeenth century classical style, with pilasters between the windows and high mansard roofs.' Whatever fields of art China might ultimately conquer, Architecture was going to be the last to submit, and Architecture's captive, Furniture, could not be the first.[21]

It seems, therefore, that like Palladianism in England the taste for lacquered furniture in Europe got off to a false start in the early seventeenth century. The patronage of the Crown and the talents of Inigo Jones might bring the one into being, and the expansion of trade with the Orient the other, but in the absence of kindly conditions neither could thrive. Until the ground had been properly prepared, until furniture had been liberated from the control of architecture on the one hand, and of the narrowly classical prejudices of official art on the other, there was small scope for a style which was impudently neglectful of both. Under the early Stuarts and Bourbons lacquered furniture was an exotic flower and the climate was against it; by the end of the century the climate had changed while connections with the East had continued and expanded, and it was then that an oriental style flourished in many European countries.[22]

Yet to call lacquer-work with an oriental flavour 'exotic' is perhaps to prejudge another issue and to say too much, for in one way, and the most important way, it was not oriental at all. In a comprehensive survey of lacquer-work in Europe, Holzhausen has distinguished, according to their origins, three categories: European productions which are either direct imitations of, or homespun fantasies upon, eastern themes; oriental creations made to satisfy the European market; and oriental work intended for orientals. The third has almost nothing in common with the other two. On the other hand, those two are not always easily distinguishable from each other. Indeed, the more closely that 'oriental' lacquer-work and furniture is studied, the less oriental it is seen to be; and the more difficult it becomes to decide the origin

of any particular piece. Some were produced by oriental craftsmen at
the instigation of enterprising eastern merchants who thought they
knew what would suit European tastes; some may have been made by
the same craftsmen from patterns supplied to them from Europe; some,
it is known, and it may have been many, were made in the East by a
joiner from Europe and were lacquered by native craftsmen. Whatever
the diversity of origin of the individual articles, the style was in fact a
European one and it was for that reason that it spread rapidly throughout Europe once the necessary pre-conditions had been established.

It was when European furniture had reached the stage at which
japanned wares fitted readily into a sympathetic background of taste
that connections with the Far East became of much greater significance
than they had been earlier. By then the English had won the commercial
and political struggle with their Dutch rivals and were in unbreakable
contact with the Orient. At that time too many among the English
upper classes had thrown off whatever restraints Puritan control and
ideology may once have laid upon them and were ready to indulge in
extravagant spending upon exotic luxuries. For these reasons it is
perhaps not surprising that the earliest evidence of a wide and stable
market for japanned wares should appear in England. It was there in
1688 that John Stalker and George Parker published the first book
intended to assist European craftsmen and amateurs to turn out
passably good imitations of, or substitutes for, the kind of products
which their Asiatic rivals had been profitably exporting [Plate XIV].
There is some evidence that well before 1688 German craftsmen had
been learning the techniques of japanning in England and within a
few years of that date the native industry had become sufficiently
important for a tariff to be imposed upon foreign wares. The designs
in Stalker and Parker's *Treatise of Japanning and Varnishing* were, as
ever, western in inspiration and the single elements were no more
than superficially oriental: human figures, in what was intended for
eastern costume, portrayed in formalized attitudes against an equally
formalized landscape of bamboos and oddly-misrepresented pagodas
[Plates 177 and 178]. For all their display of exotic motifs the designs
were wholly European in composition and many of them were no
more than transliterations of the oak-groves and classical temples of
earlier ornamentalists.[23]

It is possible that developments in England hastened those on the
Continent, and the presence of lacquer-work of undoubted English

origin in Germany, at the Charlottenburger Schloss in Berlin and in the Staatliche Kunstsammlung at Kessel, may perhaps point, and for the first time, to the export of furniture from England to other European countries. Nevertheless, it is neither necessary nor plausible to suppose that the Continent stood in any great need of instruction from the English. The manufacture of lacquered furniture was well-established in some parts of Germany, for example, before the end of the century. As early as 1687 Gerard Dagley had been recruited from the Dutch town of Spa, itself a centre of japanning, to work at the court of the Great Elector at Berlin. Much of his production belongs to the following century, but the beginnings of his Berlin manner may be dated to the 1690s. Where English lacquerers showed a preference for gold upon a red or black background, Dagley's tendency was to use a white background with relief decoration in gold. Many of his designs were copied from engravings, but some appear to be imitations of genuine eastern work and the Duchess of Orleans, for one, was convinced that he was not a European but an 'Indian'. His work was in striking contrast with that of earlier German craftsmen and must have appeared very oriental indeed [Plates 179 and 180]. Typical of their productions is a cabinet, now in the Schloss Ludwigsburg, which has only vaguely exotic motifs and nothing that is noticeably eastern; instead it is reminiscent of Florentine stone intarsia. In Holland as well there was by the last decade of the century a full-blown 'Asiatic' style of which the designs included human figures in Chinese and Indo-Persian costumes against conventionalized oriental landscapes [Plate 181].[24]

Lacquer-work was not the most prominent element in the furniture of the late seventeenth century, but its exploitation of oriental motifs reveals more clearly than anything else the complex circumstances in which the much admired products of the Manufacture Royale were able to come into existence. It has another significance as well. Although its growth was made possible by the aesthetic and intellectual conditions of the time, it had an active role of its own and helped to develop those conditions further through the example set to other branches of the profession by its free use of unconventional motifs. It was the child of the forces which were engendering other new forms of ornament, but it became their ally as well and helped them to break down the rigid conventions of earlier modes of decoration.

Bérain and Boulle

The most important new manner was that perfected by Jean Bérain, who was one of the artists employed on the royal works. He was especially busy in providing the ornament and décor for the balls, fêtes, masques and other 'toys', as Bacon called them at another court, on which Louis XIV and his courtiers were wont to spend much of their own time and of their countrymen's money. Partly perhaps for their own ease, and partly because of the effect upon them of the less solemn attitudes of the habitués of the salons, they tended on these occasions to seek a style of decoration which should be light in spirit and in execution; and it was this that Bérain supplied in full measure. His designs are filled with satyrs and nymphs, with leaping monkeys and chubby children, with exotically clothed human figures, with trailing branches and arabesques, vases and candelabra, and with delicately-framed cupolas and pergolas which seem to float effortlessly in the sky. Over the whole is an airy lightness and a sense of gaiety. There is a marked resemblance to the 'Antique' of a hundred years before, but with a significant difference. The crowded and disorderly composition, 'without Rime or Reason', for which Henry Peacham took that earlier style to task, is replaced by a carefully-controlled symmetry and by the provision of enough elbow-room to allow each element to play its own separate part [Plate 183].[25]

The introduction of Bérain's style was in itself of importance to the development of furniture and its importance was the greater because it assisted the spread of, and was assisted by the taste for, japanning and oriental motifs. Further, this alliance came into being at a time when the forcing-house of royal control and extravagance was encouraging the craftsmen of the Manufacture Royale to raise the techniques of furniture-making and of applied ornament to a level unknown before. As a result there was to hand a body of workers able to impose upon furniture the new conceptions which the intellectual and aesthetic changes of the age were beginning to bring forward.

The furniture so produced is not homogeneous, but its most typical pieces are those generally associated with the name of André-Charles Boulle, master-ébéniste to the Crown, with workshops in the Louvre. Although he was a painter and sculptor as well as a furniture-maker, Boulle usually worked to other men's designs, or at any rate in their spirit. Occasionally he was dependent upon Lebrun or the Le Pautre

brothers, but more often, and increasingly in his later years, upon
Bérain.

'Boulle' has come to be used as a generic term for furniture, which
may or may not have been made under Boulle's supervision, but is
characterized by a marquetry technique wherein a metal, usually
brass or copper, is used in association with other materials, of which
the most favoured were tortoise-shell and mother-of-pearl. The
combination had been known earlier and in other centuries [Plate 182],
but never before had it been used on such a scale and with such skill.
The method was to glue together a thin sheet of metal and another of
tortoise-shell and to trace a pattern upon one or the other of them. The
pattern was then cut out, the sheets were separated, and the tortoise-
shell was inserted into a metal ground and the metal into a tortoise-shell
one. The result was two panels of marquetry identical in pattern but
wholly different in appearance, which were generally used side by side.
On some rare occasions ebony or silver was used. The style was a rich
one in itself and was made richer by the need to protect the vulnerable
edges of thin sheets glued to flat surfaces. This was done by surrounding
them with a rim, or other ornamental framework, generally of gilt
bronze mountings held in position by screws. If the whole carcase was
covered with a veneer then the easily damaged corners were protected
with similar mountings.[26]

The distinctive contribution of Boulle himself was essentially one of
technique; in other matters he was firmly held within the conventions
of his age and his style changed as they changed. Nowhere is this
clearer than in his use of decorative motifs. In the mid-century furniture-
makers were turning out work in the technique of marquetry and
counter-marquetry described above, but using different coloured woods
or mother-of-pearl or tortoise-shell rather than metal, and in a style
which was very much influenced by naturalistic floral designs [Plates
184 and 185]. Excellent examples of this are the cabinets and commodes
from the Château de Montargis now in the Victoria and Albert
Museum and a Dutch cabinet in the Rijksmuseum with vases of tulips,
lilies and roses [Plate xvi]. In his earlier years Boulle tended to employ
a very similar style in his own very different technique and an early
cabinet of his in the Wallace Collection may be compared in this
respect with those just mentioned [Plate 186].[27]

Later, however, as Bérain began to affect the nature of interior
decoration and to give it, or some of it, a less naturalistic and more

festal air, the motifs upon Boulle's productions changed in character and, while never quite achieving the same airy effects, took on many of the features of Bérain's style. A cabinet now in the Musée des Arts Décoratifs in Paris and probably of the 1670's, is an early and very splendid example. It is of ebony and stands upon a plinth ornamented in gilded and carved bronze; the main panels are of marquetry with tinted and shaded woods upon a ground of brown tortoise-shell and the subsidiary ones are of copper and bronze set in blued tortoise-shell. The motifs are graceful and delicate vases, bouquets, birds and butterflies.[28]

But if much of the ornament of Boulle's later work is a reproduction of the gayer elements which Bérain introduced into interior decoration, its form is still strongly under the influence of the stately manner of the court. This was not an idiosyncrasy of Boulle's. On many pieces of the time there is a marked contrast between the light-hearted decoration and the massive and imposing form [Plate 187]. Further, Boulle turned out much carved, gilded and silvered work and it was this which was most often to the designs, or under the influence, of Lebrun and the Lepautres. And this contrast, since much furniture was still of ebony or was lacquered in black, is paralleled by the accompanying contrast between the dark background and the brilliance and richness of the decoration placed upon it. The result is highly effective and is a striking example of a unity created by opposites.

The effect of these contrasts was heightened by another. Unless a pointless waste of time and labour was to be indulged in, the inevitable result of such a technique as that described above was to produce a symmetrical composition in which each element was both the exact partner and also the exact antithesis of another; a design in which balance and unity was obtained by the juxtaposition of reflecting opposites. In the words of G. Yver: 'Toujours symétrique dans ses ornements comme dans sa construction, le meuble semble un reflet du *Discours de la Méthode*. La raison, la logique, l'équilibre se retrouvent dans une oeuvre d'un ébéniste comme André-Charles Boulle.' The direct comparison between Boulle and Descartes – who belonged to a much earlier generation and was a long way from being the philosopher of the French Establishment – may seem far-fetched, but the general truth of this characterization of French furniture of the later years of Louis xiv's reign is plain enough.[29]

There was, however, more to it than that, for furniture was not meant to be seen by itself but against the background of the room it was in. Its qualities, themselves contrasting enough, made a further contrast with the dominant mode of interior decoration. A recent writer has well described the effect: 'Thus to the black, gold and silver of the ébéniste and menuisier is added the brilliant red, green and yellow of lacquer from the Orient. If we add also a handsomely parquetted floor, walls faced with rich marbles or hung with tapestry, and a sculptured and painted ceiling, we get a very good idea of the taste of people of fashion in France in the last quarter of the seventeenth century.' Much furniture and especially pieces which lined the wall – other than the fashionable side-tables – remained heavy in form in sympathy with the heavy and often grandiose décor of its milieu. But just because the form was heavy, the brilliant ornament upon it was on the one hand saved from being gimcrack and on the other thrown into more effective relief. To quote Mr Watson: 'The contrast between the dark colours of the ebony and shell and the brightness of the brass inlay, the emphasis provided by the gilt bronze mounts on the essentially architectural structure of the heavy severe forms combined to produce an effect of sober splendour'. As before, the qualities of furniture were partly determined by the character of the room it was in, but they were no longer controlled by it. Furniture was ceasing to be a consequent and subordinate element of interior decoration and was becoming instead an equal and distinctive partner; no longer additional to the architectural scheme, but complementary to it. [30]

It was some time before such pieces were common in other countries, and at least until the end of the century they were not indigenous. In England, as far as is known, Gerreit Jensen was the only craftsman producing anything remotely comparable to Boulle's work and a cabinet at Windsor Castle veneered in ebony and olive-wood and with marquetry of engraved brass and pewter may reflect the kind of producing anything remotely comparable to Boulle's work, and a princelings of French pieces into Germany that country was not in any very advanced state. The old concepts of furniture decoration, however, were being eroded not only by the style of Boulle and Bérain in France, but equally by the increasing presence of japanned wares and exotic designs in other lands. Both within France and outside of it, therefore, artistic changes were moving in different ways towards one end. If each had been working separately perhaps neither would have achieved much, but because of the homogeneous nature of western

The seventeenth century

147 *The Linen Cupboard* by Pieter de Hooch. The provision of a cupboard for one purpose alone, and that to hold linen, reveals the profusion of furniture of all kinds by the mid-seventeenth century.

148 and 149 Two engravings of wealthy households by Abraham Bosse. In Plate 148 a family meal is being prepared; in Plate 149 the ladies are at a dinner-party from which their husbands have been excluded. In both cases the bed is a prominent feature of the room.

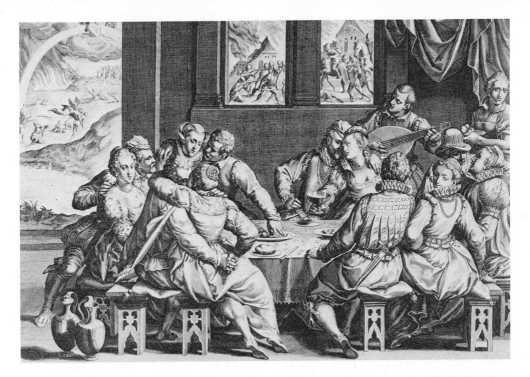

150 Mid-seventeenth-century engraving by T. B. Barentz. The diners sit upon short benches all made to the same pattern.

151 *The Schoolmaster* by Abraham Bosse. The schoolroom contains, as well as desks, tables and benches, the schoolmaster's 'lit-en-housse' with its tightly drawn curtains.

152 Painting by Pieter Breughel the Younger to illustrate the proverb, 'falling between two stools'. The left-hand stool has been given a rudimentary back by prolonging the rear leg upwards and adding a cross-piece.

153 (*opposite above*) Upholstered seat of English origin, early seventeenth century. By means of a ratchet the sides could be lowered to any desired height and the piece could be used as a day bed.
154 (*opposite below*) Late seventeenth-century day-bed, Flemish in style but of North American manufacture.

155 English chair of so-called 'farthingale' type, early seventeenth century.

156 Sixteenth-century Spanish chair, covered with tooled leather with large ornamental nail-heads.

157 Late seventeenth-century leather-upholstered chair of North American origin, the leather affixed with ornamental nail-heads.

158 Early seventeenth-century upholstered X-chair at Knole. It is similar in form but shows an advance in comfort upon the one in Winchester Cathedral (Plate 3).

159 Sixteenth-century Italian chair, upholstered in gilt tooled leather with ornamental brass nail-heads.

160 Seventeenth-century Spanish chair ornamented with enriched nail-heads, said to have belonged to the Archbishop of Toledo.

161 Late seventeenth-century French upholstered armchair covered with tapestry in a floral design.

155

156

157

159

162 (*above*) In this early seventeenth-century engraving by Crispin de Passe the bed still has a sixteenth-century form, with the framework as important to the effect as the drapery.

163 and 164 Two mid-century engravings by Buran and Bosse. The frame of the bed is now wholly subordinate to the drapery and variations are achieved by the decoration on the tops of the posts and the manner of drawing the curtains.

165 Four-poster bed at Knole with the tester surmounted by plumes of feathers. Although imposing it is smaller than the great state beds of the late seventeenth century and is less richly decorated and apparelled.

66 Late seventeenth-century Dutch bed, the frame of the tester exposed and moulded and painted.

168 Painting of a mid-seventeenth-century Dutch interior by Terborch. A lit-en-housse is in the background, a Turkey carpet covers the table, and very little woodwork is left exposed.

169 Mid-seventeenth-century ebony cabinet in the Kunstgewerbemuseum, Berlin.
Notice the shallowness of the carving upon the ebony veneer.

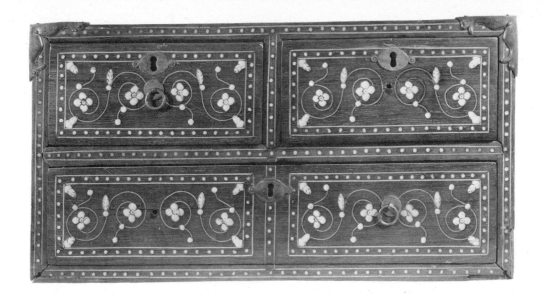

170 Seventeenth-century Indo-Portuguese cabinet in teak and rosewood. Despite its origin and the use of an eastern wood, the cabinet is wholly immune from the fashionable 'oriental' style.

171 Mid-seventeenth-century Flemish cabinet, the insides of the leaves and the fronts of the interior compartments painted with scenes from classical mythology in the style of Rubens.

172 (*opposite*) Buffet of 1664 from Basel, now in the Kunstgewerbemuseum, Berlin. Despite the lavish use of architectural details the piece is less of an architectural composition than many of those of the sixteenth century.

173 Late seventeenth-century cupboard from south-west France. It shows no sign of any concern with contemporary Paris fashions, but continues in the style of the early part of the century.

174 North German 'Diele' cupboard of *c.* 1700. These huge cupboards were meant to stand in a lofty hall, a Diele. The influence of classical architecture is still to be seen in the heavy moulded cornice.

175 (*opposite*) Early seventeenth-century lacquer cabinet of Western origin.
176 Detail of Plate 175. Despite some exotic elements the design is patently European.

177 and 178 Designs from Stalker and Parker's *Treatise of Japanning* of 1688. They were intended to assist professional and amateur in producing 'oriental' lacquer-ware, but essentially they are European compositions in eastern fancy-dress.

179 and 180 Two cabinets of *c.* 1700 by
Gerard Dagley. As these examples show,
he approached closer than any of his
orientalizing contemporaries to the
sources of their inspiration.

181 Dutch lacquer cabinet of *c.* 1700. In contrast with Dagley's work, the crowded orientalizing motifs proclaim at once that this is a European product.

182 Seventeenth-century Portuguese table, with elaborate moulding and turning and affixed metal ornament.

183 Centre of a door panel of a cabinet of *c.* 1700 with a design in the style of Jean Bérain.

184 (*opposite*) English marquetry cabinet of the late seventeenth century, with naturalistic floral designs.

185 Mid-seventeenth-century Dutch cabinet, the marquetry carried out in walnut, satinwood, rosewood, ebony and ivory upon a deal carcase.

186 Mid-seventeenth-century French cabinet by André Charles Boulle.
The stand has been adapted to fit the top.

European society and culture at the time, they worked in partnership or at any rate in involuntary association. As a result, they did more than free the ornament of furniture from the hegemony of architecture and of interior decoration; they transformed it into a force for promoting or abetting stylistic changes in other media. [31]

It may be an exaggeration to say, as one writer has, that imported lacquer-wares had the most important single part in transmuting baroque into rococo; but if so it is no more than an exaggeration, or rather an over-emphasis of the role of one of the parties in an alliance. Certainly it would seem to be true that 'a blend of the exotic with the traditional European grotesques and in particular, the currently popular decorative creations of artists like Bérain . . . was to produce the later eighteenth-century continental Rococo.' This change from one style to another was common in many fields and is not to be attributed solely, or even mainly, to the example of furniture decoration: but it is clear that that decoration had a hand in the matter. For the first time furniture was exerting its own influence upon other arts and no longer passively accepting theirs. [32]

If a sufficiently long-term view is taken, the development up to the years around 1700 is seen to have three phases. In the first, which more or less corresponds with the Middle Ages, furniture directly reflected the way of life of its owners and the impact of that way of life upon their houses. In consequence it was scanty and its decoration was controlled by the concepts of Gothic architecture. In the second phase the influence of the house upon the objects it contained was less, and furniture-forms were partly determined by new modes of social intercourse. But because those modes coincided in time with the Renaissance, and were one facet of the forces which that movement also reflected, the authority of architecture persisted; no longer Gothic but classic, it wholly dictated the ornament and to a large extent the design of furniture. Finally, as a classical education and a conscious appreciation of art became the hallmark of the leaders among the upper classes, and as attendance at court and in drawing-rooms became the principal occupation of many of them, the nature of furniture was affected mainly by notions of comfort and convenience, and its decoration no longer by architecture alone but by current taste in other and often quite unconnected media. To sum up: as European society became more complex, as an intellectual and aesthetic élite appeared among the ruling class, and as the relationship of that class with the

161

187 (*opposite*) Later Boulle cabinet showing the influence of the designs of Jean Bérain

immediate producers of wealth grew more remote, so social influences worked ever more indirectly and furniture appeared to develop, and sometimes did develop, quite independently of them; and those influences continued to dominate only among the classes whose homes still closely reflected their role in production.

Notes

Any study of the history of European furniture must be heavily indebted for French and English material to T.H. Turner's and J.H. Parker's pioneer-work, *Some Account of Domestic Architecture in England* (3 vols. Oxford, 1851–9); to the monumental *Dictionary of English Furniture* (3 vols. 2nd ed. 1954) by P. Macquoid and R. Edwards; and to a publication which one has to call monumental for want of a stronger word, H. Havard's *Dictionnaire de l'Ameublement* xx (4 vols. Paris, 1887–1890). To avoid over-burdening the text with footnotes, references to these volumes have been made only when there might be some doubt about the source of a statement. Similarly, other much-used works have been cited only at their first occurrence.

1 The Middle Ages

1 Childe, V. G., *Ancient Dwellings at Skara Brae*, 1933; Bruce-Mitford, R.L.S., *Recent Archaeological Excavations in Britain*, 1956, pp. 167–96; Thomas, F.W.L., 'Beehive Houses in Harris and Lewis', 'On the Primitive Dwellings of the Outer Hebrides', *Proceedings of the Society of Antiquaries of Scotland* iii (1857–60), pp. 127–44; vii (1866–8), pp. 153–95.
2 The existence in Italy of the hall with an open hearth fire has been disputed, but the evidence assembled by A. Schiaparelli (*La casa fiorentina*, 1902) shows clearly that it was common in many parts of the country. An ingenious attempt to circumvent some of its inconveniences was made at the Rathaus in Göttingen in 1369–71, when a kind of hypocaust was installed: Heyne, M., *Das deutsche Wohnungswesen* (Leipzig, 1899), pp. 243–5.
3 The open hall lasted in some districts of Denmark into the nineteenth century: Michelsen, P. and Rasmussen, H., *Danish Peasant Culture* (Copenhagen, 1956).
4 Smith, P. and Lloyd, F., 'Plas Ucha, Llangar, Corwen', *Transactions of the Ancient Monuments Society* N.S. xii (1964), pp. 97–116.
5 Perroy, E., 'Social Mobility among the French Noblesse' *Past and Present* No. 21 (April

1962), pp. 25–38; Du Faïl, N., *Contes d'Eutrapel* (Paris, 1856), p. 284; Rossetti, W.M., *Italian Courtesy Books* (London, 1869), p. 57. For the use of the hall as a kitchen and general living-room in French 'manoirs' of the sixteenth century see De Vaissière, P., *Gentilshommes campagnards de l'ancienne France*, (Paris, 1903).

6 *Rotuli Parliamentorum* (London, 1767) i; pp. 228–38, 243–65. K. Hahm states that German peasant furniture did not appear until peasant houses had developed to a stage where the beasts were accommodated separately from the human beings: *Deutsche Bauernmöbel* (Jena, 1938), pp. 16–17. Undoubtedly this played an important part, but the sharing of quarters by men and animals was not universal among west European peasantry in the Middle Ages, while the paucity of furniture was. For the low housing standards of the French peasantry, for example, see Defourneaux, N., *La Vie quotidienne au temps de Jeanne d'Arc* (Paris, 1952). For Neckham's 'De Utensilibus' see Wright, T. *Volume of Vocabularies* (London, 1857). René of Anjou's dogs had clearly been sneaking advantages; the more usual place for them was under the benches in the hall, where straw was spread.

7 The author of the English version of *The Brut*, writing c. 1200 and describing the court of King Arthur, was conscious that the more intelligent of his readers might wonder how Arthur and his knights were able to take their famous and immense Round Table on all their journeys. He got over the difficulty by supposing that having been made by a Cornishman it was miraculously light. (Loomis, R.S. *The Development of Arthurian Romance* (London, 1963), pp. 42–3. Later magnates, living in a world whence magic had departed and where plastics had not yet arrived, had no such easy solution to hand.

8 Frati, L., *La Vita Privata di Bologna* (Bologna, 1900), pp. 20, 225–8; Zdekauer, L., *Life of Old Siena* (London, 1914), pp. 35–6; Luthmer, F., *Deutsche Möbel der Vergangenheit* (Leipzig, 1902), pp. 26–7.

9 Burr, G.H., *Hispanic Furniture* (New York, 1941), p. 18; Barley, M.W., *The English Farmhouse and Cottage* (London, 1961), p. 53. Harrison's bias was pointed out long ago by T. Wright, *Homes of Other Days* (London, 1871), p. 415.

10 Coulton, G.C., *Social Life in Britain* (Cambridge, 1956), pp. 75, 386.

11 Coulton, G.C., *Life in the Middle Ages* (Cambridge, 1954) iii, p. 81.

12 Raine, J., *Wills and Inventories of the Northern Counties of England* (London, 1835), p. 35; Turner and Parker, ii, pp. 111–12.

13 Bonnaffée, E., *Voyages et Voyageurs de la Renaissance* (Paris, 1895), p. 56; Domenech, R. and Bueno, L.P., *Mueblos Antiguos Españoles* (Barcelona c. 1921), p. 4.

14 Feulner, A., *Kunstgeschichte des Möbels* (Berlin, 1927), pp. 12–13; Müller-Christensen, S., *Alte Möbel vom Mittelalter bis zum Jugendstil* (Munich, 1957), pp. 9–10; Luthmer, F., *Deutsche Möbel der Vergangenheit* (Leipzig, 1902), p. 5; Von Falke, O., *Deutsche Möbel des Mittelalters und der Renaissance* (Stuttgart, 1924), p. 6; Viaux, J., *Le Meuble en France* (Paris 1962), p. 34.

15 The cupboards at Bayeux and Noyon figure prominently in nineteenth-century literature, but the first is much mutilated and the second disappeared during the 1914-18 war.

16 Bonnaffée, E., *Inventaire des Meubles de Cathérine de Médicis en 1589* (Paris, 1874).

17 The Frankish casket was excavated at Weilbach near Wiesbaden in 1950–1; *Germania*, No. 31 (1953), pp. 44–50.

18 For a full discussion of ivory caskets see Loomis, R.S., *Arthurian Legends in Medieval Art* (London and New York, 1938).

19 The high technical level of carpenters in south-east England has been emphasized by Hewitt, C.A., 'Structural Carpentry in Medieval Essex', *Medieval Archaeology* vi–vii (1962–3), pp. 240–71.

20 Because they were often portable, chests remained easy objects of plunder for a long time. In an angry poem 'Aganis the Thievis of Liddisdale' Sir Richard Maitland numbered

'kists' and 'arcs' among the household goods stolen by Anglo-Scottish border raiders in the late sixteenth century. 'Arc' was a widespread medieval term for a chest with a rounded or canted top. *The Paston Letters* (Everyman ed. 1956), p. 111.

21 For Genoese conditions see Lopez, R.S., *Studii sull' Economia Genovese nel Medio Evo* (Turin, 1936), pp. 183–226.

22 The Countess of Leicester's Roll is printed in Turner, T.H., *Manners and Household Expenses of England in the Thirteenth and Fifteenth Centuries* (London, 1841).

23 Schulz, A., *Deutsches Leben in XIV und XV Jahrhundert* (Vienna, 1892), p. 162.

24 The Spanish chest was exhibited at Madrid in 1912: *Catalogo de la Exposicion de Mobilario Español* (Madrid, 1912), plate 111.

25 Origo, I., *The Merchant of Prato* (London, 1957), p. 228; Molmenti, P., *Venice* (trans. Brown, H., 1906), part I. vol. ii, p. 110; Salzman, L.F., *Building in England* (Oxford, 1952), p. 159.

26 Hillenbrand, K., *Bemalte Bauernmöbel aus wurtembergisch Franken* (Stuttgart, 1956). Montaigne seems to be referring as much to the simple application of paint as to its use for ornament.

27 Salzman, p. 166; Turner and Parker, i. 210, 223; Frati, p. 22.

28 The 'beds' in medieval hospitals were generally nothing more than mattresses laid upon the floor or upon low stands. In 1330 an inmate of the del Ceppo had a vision of the Virgin while lying upon this bed, which became in consequence a holy relic. It is probable that he had only a pallet to lie upon and that the present framework was made to hold the pallet, and was painted in commemoration after the event.

29 Schmitz, H., *Das Möbelwerk*, (Berlin 1942) xiv; Hallweg, F., *Die Geschichte des deutschen Tischlerhandwerks* (Berlin, 1924), p. 38.

30 Fox, L., *Leicester Castle* (Leicester, 1944), p. 22; Sharp, S., *Letters from Italy* (London, 1767), pp. 238–9.

2 The survival of primitive forms

1 Gage, J., *History and Antiquities of Hengrave* (London, 1822), p. 42; Nutting, W., *Furniture of the Pilgrim Century* (Framingham, Mass. 1924), p. 19.

2 Dudley, P. and Minter, E.M., 'The Medieval Village at Garrow Tor, Bodmin Moor, Cornwall' *Medieval Archaeology*, vi–vii (1962–3), pp. 272–94.

3 Michelsen, P. and Rasmussen, H., *Danish Peasant Culture* (Copenhagen, 1956), pp. 45–6.

4 Henne am Rhyn, O., *Kulturgeschichte des deutschen Volkes* (Berlin, 1892) i, 351–2. The now-destroyed Millichope is illustrated in Wright, T., *Homes of Other Days* (London, 1871), pp. 150–1.

5 For the wide distribution of box-beds in western Europe see Eriksson, M., 'Bed-shelves and two-storeyed bedsteads', *Acta Ethnologica*, 1936, pp. 65–84. Box-beds were common in Brittany throughout the eighteenth century and into the nineteenth. They were known as well in Auvergne, Dauphiné, Lorraine and Normandy; Bayard, E., *Les Meubles Rustiques Régionaux de la France* (Paris, 1925), pp. 22–9.

6 Hodgson, J., *History of Northumberland* (Newcastle-on-Tyne, 1827) part II, vol. 1, p. 189.

7 Enlart, C., *Manuel d'Archéologie Française*, ii (1904), p. 66; Picard, R., *Les salons littéraires et la société française* (New York, 1943), pp. 27–9.

8 Raine, J., *Wills and Inventories of the Northern Counties of England* (London, 1835); *Durham Wills and Inventories*, Surtees Society cxlii (1929).

9 Bonnaffée, E., *Inventaire de la Duchesse de Valentinois* (Paris, 1878), items 518, 639; Corrozet, G., *Les Blasons Domestiques* (Paris, 1865). 'A closed chair where the scented musk lies among folded linen.'

10 Babeau, A., *La vie rurale dans l'ancienne France* (Paris, 1883), pp. 36–7.

3 The end of the Middle Ages

1 Waley, D., *Later Medieval Europe* (London, 1964), p. 176; Ottokar, N., *Il commune di Firenze alla fine del Dugento* (Turin, 1962); Imperiale, C., *Jacopo d'Orio e i suoi annali* (Venice, 1930), p. 305.

2 Trevor-Roper, H. R., 'Doge Francesco Foscari', *Penguin Book of the Renaissance* (ed. J. H. Plumb, London, 1964), pp. 245–60. Professor Trevor-Roper confined himself to the political situation; his editor, however, (p. 236) points out that: 'The patricians found that they could tap the riches . . . of the Lombardy plain, far more easily than they could the Oriental trade, rich as it was'. In interpreting the later Middle Ages as a period of relative, if not of absolute, economic decline I am, I think, in agreement with most modern historians; even with those such as Baron and Cipolla who think that recent writers have painted too dark a picture.

3 A study of the Florentine upper class is provided in some detail by P. J. Jones: 'Florentine Families and Florentine Diaries', *Studies in Italian Medieval History* (ed. P. Grierson and J. Ward Perkins, London, 1956), pp. 183–205. Among Italians the Genoese were exceptional; the merchants 'had little taste for buying land, while the aristocratic landowners of Liguria played scarcely any part in the city's business life'; Waley, D., loc. cit. Genoa made the smallest contribution to the Renaissance of all Italian cities of comparable importance, although its upper classes showed a fondness for the new style of Flemish painting. I owe the information about Shrewsbury to Mr J. T. Smith.

4 Coulton, G. C., *Life in the Middle Ages*, iii 52–3; Pantin, W. A., 'The Merchants' Houses and Warehouses of Kings Lynn', *Medieval Archaeology*, vi–vii (1962–3), pp. 173–87.

5 In describing the bed itself as adorned with statues of Philosophy and the Liberal Arts Baudry was very much indulging his fancy; but the form which his fancy took is instructive; Raby, F. J. E., *History of Secular Latin Poetry of the Middle Ages* (Oxford 1934) i, pp. 347–8.

6 Lunsingh Scheurleer, T., *Van haardvuur tot beeldsherm* (Leyden, 1961), p. 25.

7 Einhard described three silver tables – 'mensae' – and a gold one, ornamented with scenes of Rome and of Constantinople, which were presented to Charlemagne: Buchner, R., *Ausgewählte Quellen zur deutschen Geschichte* (Berlin, 1956) v, p. 208. It is however very far from certain that these were tables in a modern sense and not plaques meant to be affixed to a wall for decoration. The Salisbury table is so well preserved that it must come under suspicion as a modern fake. It has features which suggest that it is in the main original: the gesso under the modern paint, the methods of jointing. But whether it is a fake or not is of no great consequence to anyone but a collector; for if it is not original then it is a very close copy of another table which was formerly in the Chapter House. This was published by Turner and Parker and in 1808 was illustrated by Buckler in a water colour now in the Museum at Devizes. Unless current ideas about the history of the Gothic Revival are erroneous, it is unlikely that there was anyone alive before 1808 capable, or desirous, of concocting a Gothic fake which would deceive Buckler.

8 Burr, G. H., *Hispanic Furniture* (New York, 1941), p. 18; Raine, J., *Wills and Inventories*, p. 13.

9 La Curne de Saint-Palaye, *Mémoires sur l'ancienne chevalerie* (Paris, 1826) I, pp. 189–95.

10 Furniture occurs occasionally in earlier English wills, but of a more utilitarian nature; for the Duchess of York's chair see Nicholas, H., *Testamenta Vetusta* (London, 1826) I, p. 423.

11 Hallweg, F., *Die Geschichte des deutschen Tischlerhandwerks*, (Berlin, 1924), pp. 38–43.

12 The Pistoia agreements are cited by Schiaparelli, pp. 253–5; the bedstead for Henry VIII by Turner and Parker, iii, 106.

13 Many French reliquaries are illustrated in *Les Trésors des Eglises de France* (ed. J. Taralon, Paris, 1965).

14 It is likely that intarsia appeared earlier upon panelling than upon furniture, but the

earliest evidence for linen-fold seems to be the buffet depicted in Hubert van Eyck's miniature, *The Birth of St John*.

15 There are valuable discussions of national and regional characteristics in the previously cited works of Feulner and Müller-Christensen and in H. Halbgewachs, *Der Sudwestdeutsche Schrank des 16. und 17. Jahrhunderts* (Kaisers lautern, 1936).

16 Masons from northern Europe were often called upon for advice at Milan Cathedral, the greatest Gothic building in Italy, and they were rarely at much pains to dissemble their opinion of their Italian colleagues. In 1400 the Frenchman, Jean Mignon, in the course of an acrimonious dispute declared his readiness to welcome advice from German, French or English masons, but not from Italians. (Ackerman, J.S., 'Gothic Theory of Architecture and the Cathedral of Milan', *Art Bulletin*, No. 31 (June, 1949), pp. 84–109.

17 The Danish chest was not influenced by cassoni, for the treatment of the subject is wholly different; *Ting* (Vendsyssels Historiske Museum, Hjørring, 1964), pp. 52–3. It will be clear that I lean heavily here upon P. Schubring's magnificent *Cassoni* (Leipzig, 1923).

18 That the single-handed defeat of Milan by Florence in 1402 allowed all Tuscany to breathe again, and initiated a 'civic humanism' which was an essential element of the Renaissance, was first expounded by Hans Baron in *The Crisis of the Early Renaissance*, (Princeton, 1955) and has won wide acceptance. It has recently been challenged by J.E. Seigel, who attempts to show – what the cassoni themselves may be thought to demonstrate – that there was no sharp break in Florentine development between the late fourteenth and the early fifteenth centuries.

19 This is in startling contrast with the developments in northern Europe, where painting upon furniture was becoming old-fashioned and was being superseded by elaborate carving.

20 The very secular nature of education in Italy throughout the Middle Ages, in contrast with that in most other countries, has been stressed by, among others, R.R. Bolgar (*The Classical Heritage and its Beneficiaries*, Cambridge, 1954) and E.R. Labande (*L'Italie de la Renaissance*, Paris, 1954). This secularism is partly reflected in the humanism of the later Middle Ages; and it affected the arts, sometimes very directly. It was, for example, the re-discovery of Vitruvius by the philologists in the late-fourteenth century which permitted the architects to practise, or to justify, their theories in the fifteenth: Ciappono, L.A., 'Il "De Architectura" de Vitruvio nel primo umanesimo', *Italia medioevale e umanistica*, v (1962), pp. 59–99.

4 The sixteenth century: modern men and modern homes

1 Luthmer, F., *Deutsche Möbel der Vergangenheit* (Leipzig, 1902), p. 28; Bonnaffée, E., *Etudes sur la vie privée de la Renaissance* (Paris, 1898), p. 101. In a few parts even the peasantry were affected. In south-eastern England, which in this respect may well have been unique throughout western Europe, there survive from the late Middle Ages very many substantially-built dwellings which are probably to be ascribed to rich peasants. During the sixteenth and seventeenth centuries nearly all of these were radically transformed by the insertion of floors and chimneys in the open hall. At the same period in most of England south of the Trent 'yeoman' houses, wholly different from any earlier rural dwellings, were being built in large numbers.

2 In the early seventeenth century a gentleman in County Durham had a 'stand' bedstead in his hall, and as late as 1745 the best house in Inverness – the home of Lady Mackintosh and the headquarters successively of the Young Pretender and the Duke of Cumberland – had only one room without a bed in it.

3 Cust, L., 'The Lumley Inventories', *Walpole Society Annual Volume*, vi (1917–18), pp. 15–35; Raine, *Wills and Inventories*, p. 247.

4 de Vaissière, P., *Gentilshommes campagnards de l'ancienne France* (Paris, 1903), pp. 76–7; Du Faïl, *Contes d'Eutrapel*, p. 284; Lunsingh Scheurleer, T., *Van haardvuur tot beeldscherm*, (Leyden, 1961), pp. 36–7.

5 Raine, *Wills and Inventories*, p. 250.

6 For a valuable discussion of this point see Symonds, R., ' "The Dyning Parlor" and its furniture', *Connoisseur* cxiii (1944), pp. 11–17.

7 Mirot, L., *L'Hôtel et les Collections du Connétable de Montmorency* (Paris, 1920), pp. 100–1. 'Four dozen escabelles serving for all the house – eight demi-tables serving both for the said chamber of the king and for elsewhere.'

8 As so often, some of the best evidence about medieval practices comes from eighteenth-century Scandinavia. Travellers of that period describe heavy benches with swivelling backs which permitted the occupants to face different ways at different times.

9 Rodocanachi, E., *La Femme Italienne à l'époque de la Renaissance*, (Paris, 1907), pp. 3–6. Women of fashion in Naples continued to receive company in this way on these occasions in the late eighteenth century; Sharp, S., *Letters from Italy* (London, 1767), p. 109.

10 On this point see Verlet, P., *Frick Collection Catalogue* xi (New York, 1956).

11 Bourciez, E., *Les Moeurs polies et la Littérature de la Cour sous Henri II* (Paris, 1886), p. 149; Thielen, P.G., *Die Kultur am Hofe Herzog Albrechts von Preussen* (Göttingen, 1953), p. 182.

12 Mornet, D., 'La signification et l'évolution de l'idée de la préciosité en France au xviie siècle', *Journal of the History of Ideas* i (1940), pp. 225–31.

13 Siegel, P.N., 'Milton and the Humanist Attitude towards Women', *Journal of the History of Ideas* xi (1950), pp. 42–53.

14 The small one-stage cabinet still had a role to play throughout the seventeenth century A Dutch example of *c.* 1680 in Amerongen Castle differs little in form from its predecessors of the early sixteenth century. This is probably because it still 'served the master of Amerongen as a desk cabinet on his numerous official missions abroad'; Lunsingh Scheurleer, T., *Apollo*, No. 80 (1964), p. 367.

15 *Inventaire des Meubles du Château de Pau* (Société des Bibliophiles françaises, Paris, 1892).

16 Dan, P., *Le Trésor des Merveilles de la Maison Royale de Fontainebleau* (Paris, 1642), pp. 226–7.

17 Symonds, R.W., 'The Bed through the Centuries', *Connoisseur* cxi (1943), pp. 34–5; Nicholas, *Testamenta Vetusta*, pp. 11, 568; Surtees Society cxlii, pp. 19–20; Raine, *Wills and Inventories*, p. 385.

18 *Le Meuble* (ed. A. Léjard, Paris, 1941), pp. 34–5.

19 Odom, W., *History of Italian Furniture* (New York, 1919), p. 316. A full account of Sambin's activities is given by A. Castan, *L'Architecteur Hugues Sambin* (Paris, 1891).

20 Lessing, J. and Brüning, A., *Der pommersche Kunstschrank* (Berlin, 1905), p. 10.

21 Möller, L., *Der Wrangelschrank und die verwandten süddeutschen Intarsien Möbel des 16. Jahrhunderts* (Berlin, 1956); Holst, N.W., 'Die Ostdeutsche Bildnismalerei des 16. Jahrhunderts' *Zeitschrift fur Kunstgeschichte* i (1932) pp. 41–2, fig. 17.

22 Malfatti, C.V., *Two Italian Accounts of Tudor England* (Barcelona, 1953), p. 31; Dalington, R., *A Survey of the Great Duke's State of Tuscany* (London, 1605), pp. 40–1. Dalington was inclined to be sceptical about the vast sums alleged to have been spent, and qualified many of his statements with 'as they say' or 'as they dare affirme'.

23 Gombrich, E.H., 'The Early Medici as Patrons of Art', *Italian Renaissance Studies* (London, 1960), pp. 279–311. The gems in the Medici collection were valued at 400–1,000 florins and the Tazza Farnese at 10,000; in contrast the average painting by masters of the highest standing cost about 50–100 florins.

24 Lunsingh Scheurleer, *Van haardvuur . . .*, pp. 35–6; De Prada, V.V., in *Annales : Economies, Sociétés, Civilisations* Année 10 (1955) 41; Lill, G., *Hans Fugger und die Kunst* (Leipzig, 1908), pp. 154–5); Odom, W., *History of Italian Furniture*, pp. 229–30; Surtees Society cxlii, p. 5.

25 Artus, T., *L'Isle des Hermaphrodites* (Cologne, 1724), pp. 59–60. 'As for wooden furniture, we want it to be all decorated with gold, silver or marquetry.'

26 It is noticeable that in some German-speaking districts, as in Italy very much earlier, inlay was also used in wall-decoration. A panelled room of 1548 from Schloss Haldenstein in Switzerland, now in the Kunstgewerbemuseum in Berlin, has a deep frieze ornamented with architectural scenes in inlay. These were carried out by the master H.S. and resemble those on a chest of 1557 which is also his work.

27 Honour, H., 'Pietro Duro and the Grand Tourist', *Connoisseur* cxli (May, 1958), pp. 212–5.

28 There were exceptions to this rule. In the late fifteenth century Sienese chests had been painted, gilt or stuccoed; in the late seventeenth century Sienese furniture was very richly painted.

29 Other woods such as plane and cypress were being used in northern England, and a red wood from Cuba was mentioned in a French-Spanish phrase-book of the mid-century.

30 'Bahut de Flandres' seems to have meant to the French exactly what 'Flemish chest' meant to the English, for the one was described in 1589 as 'barrés de bandes de fer' and the other in 1575 as 'bandyd wth. iron'.

31 A frontispiece was a highly decorated entrance in a façade of which it formed a part, but within which it was a self-sufficient composition.

32 Du Cerceau's designs are perhaps most easily available in the *Oeuvres*, published by E. Baldus (Paris, 1884–91). The fantastic quality of some of them, such as the bed in the shape of a sphinx, does not detract from the essentially serious nature of the whole.

5 The seventeenth century

1 For a survey of Bosse's work see Blum, A. S., *Abraham Bosse et la société française au 17ᵉ siècle* (Paris, 1924). *Durham Wills*, Surtees Society cxlii, pp. 85–6.

2 Hill, C., *The Century of Revolution* (Edinburgh, 1961), pp. 1–4.

3 The now-lost portrait of Elizabeth Drury is reproduced by Cullum, J., *The History and Antiquities of Hawsted* (London, 1784), p. 146.

4 The ordinance of 1580 is quoted by Du Colombier, P., *Le Style Henri IV – Louis XIII* (Paris, 1941), pp. 57–8.

5 The denial of upholstery in England before 1600 was made many years ago by P. Macquoid in *Shakespeare's England*, (1916) ii, p. 122. It is fair to say that this has not yet been positively disproved, but nevertheless very convincing contrary evidence has since been brought forward. Much of it is assembled in M.S.C. Byrne's *Elizabethan Life in Town and Country* (London, 1954), pp. 25–6, and in the second (1954) edition of Macquoid and Edwards, i, pp. 232, 233, 236, 313.

6 Bolgar, R.R., *The Classical Heritage and its Beneficiaries* (Cambridge, 1954) ch. viii.

7 The role of mirrors and pier-glasses in interior decoration in the late seventeenth century was very great indeed. The inventory of an architect who died in 1706, leaving a house in Paris and another in the country, lists a mirror in every room; and in every room a mirror heads the list: Duby, G. and Mandrow, R., *A History of French Civilisation* (London, 1956), pp. 326–7.

8 For an elaboration of this point see *Le Meuble* (ed. A. Léjard, Paris, 1941), p. 35. In many of the English 'courtier' portraits of the early seventeenth century, obsessed with depicting the subjects amid fashionable and opulent surroundings, a richly-draped table is the most prominent accessory of the background.

9 Cheaper woods were sometimes doctored to give them a rich appearance: Evelyn condemned those tradesmen who had perfected a technique to 'black and polish (beech) so as to render it like ebony'. Du Cerceau's influence was not wholly over by the early seventeenth century. His engravings circulated for a long time amongst provincial

artisans, who sometimes managed to give them a Louis XIII air: Du Colombier, pp. 15–16.

10 Gauthier, J.S., *La Connaissance des meubles régionaux français* (Paris, 1952), p. 14. For the architectural treatment of late furniture in Holland see Lunsingh Scheurleer, T., in *Apollo* No. 80 (1964), pp. 363–4.

11 Picard, R., *Les Salons Littéraires et la société française* (New York, 1943), pp. 19–20: St Simon, *La Cour de Louis XIV* (ed. C. Sarolea, Edinburgh, 1911), pp. 384, 371.

12 Evelyn, J., 'The State of France (1652)' in *Miscellaneous Writings* (ed. W. Upcott, London, 1825), p. 81. There were, of course, deep-seated reasons for the success of the Bourbons and the contrasting failure of the Stuarts, but for the future development of furniture it was the success, and the failure, which were to be decisive.

13 Rocheblave, S., *Le Goût en France* (Paris, 1914), p. 64; Lemonnier, H., *L'Art Français au Temps de Richelieu et de Mazarin* (Paris, 1893), p. 39. Artists who were not ready to pay the price had to take the consequences. The Le Nain brothers 'persevered in patient obscurity and their art was recognized only in the days of the Academy's decline'; Pierre Mignard 'dissimulated, encouraged disaffection and bided his time'; while Bosse was 'hounded out of Paris'. (Chambers F.P., *The History of Taste* (New York, 1932), p. 99. The unedifying story of the virtual banishment of Bosse from the capital is told at length by Blum.

14 The importance of an organized profession of furniture-makers has been emphasized by John Harris in *Burlington Magazine* cii (1960), pp. 535–6.

15 Mme de Rambouillet's famous 'chambre bleue', decorated in silver and blue, was a declaration of independence in itself and a wilful defiance of the current orthodox use of red and gold.

16 The opening chapters of W. Holzhausen's *Lackkunst in Europa* contain a succinct account of earlier lacquer-work in Europe.

17 Du Colombier, p. 55; Honour, H., *Chinoiserie The Vision of Cathay* (London, 1961), p. 43; Irwin, J., 'A Jacobean Vogue for Oriental Lacquer-work', *Burlington Magazine* xcv (1953), pp. 193–5.

18 As early as 1563 there were said to be 900 Portuguese in Macao: Chang, T-T., *Sino-Portuguese Trade from 1514–1644* (Leyden, 1934), p. 97.

19 The import of genuine oriental products, however, still continued, and Dieppe and St Germain were well-known markets in the mid-century: Huth. H., *Europäische Lackarbeiten 1600–1850* (Darmstadt, 1955), p. 5.

20 The argument of this paragraph is drawn from Hugh Honour, *Chinoiserie*. For the Vannes casket see Taralon, J., *Les Trésors des Eglises de France* (Paris, 1965), p. 180. Taralon suggests that it was perhaps the use of the technique of Limoges enamel upon this casket which won it a 'chinese' label.

21 Eastern craftsmen were aware, and wary, of this architectural domination. Their earlier exports looked more like Buddhist shrines than anything else, but later they often included 'European' architectural elements.

22 J. Irwin has pointed out that in Jacobean England the vogue almost exactly coincided in time with the East India Company's ten years of direct trade with Japan from 1613 to 1623. The ending of that connection may well have done something to stifle further developments in England; but it can hardly have affected Europe as a whole, for she was not dependent upon England for contacts with the East, nor yet for any leadership in aesthetics.

23 The *Treatise of Japanning* has been published in a facsimile edition: edited by H.D. Molesworth, London, 1960. Whether or not the book was originally meant for amateurs rather than for professionals, japanning by the end of the century was one of those accomplishments which taste and leisure allowed, or compelled, elegant young ladies to acquire. There was, however, a market for books for professionals as well. In 1688 Nicolas

Woltmann of Bremen was claiming that he had worked in England for eleven years on 'rare Vernisarbeit' and he was admitted by the Town Council because 'kein Künstler in Bremen solchen Arbeit machen könne': Huth, pp. 7–8.

24 The Duchess did not use 'Indian' in any precise sense: most Europeans of the time were uninterested in, or incapable of, distinguishing between the different countries of the East and spoke indiscriminately of 'Indian', 'Chinese' and 'Japanese'.

25 For a full account of Bérain and his work see Weigert, R.A., *Jean Bérain* (Paris, 1937).

26 There were at one time many pieces made wholly of silver or of timber plated with silver. Most French examples went to the melting pot to finance the megalomania of Louis XIV, whose 'wars brought nothing about'.

27 For an analysis of this style see Windisch-Graetz, S., *Le Meuble Baroque et Rococo* (Brunswick, 1949).

28 In fairness to Boulle it should be said that Bérain himself never achieved quite the same lightness in furniture design as in interior decoration; perhaps because official art still exercised a greater influence upon furniture than upon the whimsies which he was usually called on to decorate.

29 *Le Meuble* (ed. A. Léjard, Paris 1941), p. 36. A needlessly expensive English marquetry cabinet of *c.* 1675, upon which no piece of decoration was duplicated, was probably a test piece for a mastership, and outside the normal run of the mill: Cescinsky, H., in *Burlington Magazine*, No. 77 (1940), pp. 88–93. 'Always symmetrical in ornament as in construction, furniture seems to be a reflection of *The Discourse on Method*. Rationality, logic, balance, are found in the work of a cabinet-maker like André-Charles Boulle.'

30 Packer, C., *Paris Furniture of the Master Ebénistes* (Newport, Monmouthshire, 1956), p. 7; Watson, F.J.B., *Wallace Collection Catalogues – Furniture* (London, 1956), p. xxv.

31 In the Queen's New Bedchamber at Kensington Palace in 1697 there were 'two tables, looking glasses and stands the frames all inlade with mettle . . . bespoke by the Queen . . . from Mr Johnson' (Lunsingh Scheurleer, T., 'Documents on the Furnishings of Kensington House', *Walpole Society Annual Volume*, xxxviii (1960–2), p. 34. G.F. Laking, *The Furniture of Windsor Castle* (London, 1905), pl. 11, p. 31, commented on the 'stunted' nature of the Windsor piece and suggested that it had been 'made in England, probably by French workmen'.

32 Thorpe, W.A., 'A Group of Chinese Secretaries', *Apollo* xxiii (1936), pp. 323–8; Molesworth, H.D., *Treatise of Japanning* (facsimile edition 1960), p. vii.

Select Bibliography

The following bibliography is mainly intended as a guide to further reading. It lists, I hope, all the most important books upon furniture, together with those books and articles which I have found most illuminating upon the relationships between furniture and its milieu. I have not attempted to list works of wider historical concern but some of the more immediately relevant will be found in the notes.

Babeau, A., *La vie rurale dans l'ancienne France*, Paris, 1883.

Baretti, G., *Manners and Customs of Italy*, London, 1769.

Barley, M.W., *The English Farmhouse and Cottage*, London, 1961.

Bayard, E., *Les Meubles Rustiques Régionaux de la France*, Paris, 1925.

Beckwith, J., *Caskets from Cordova*, London, 1960.

Blum, A.S., *Abraham Bosse et la société française au 17ᵉ siècle*, Paris, 1924.

Blunt, J.J., *Vestiges of Ancient Manners in Italy*, London, 1823.

Bode, W.M., *Italian Renaissance Furniture* (translated by M.E Herrich), New York, 1921.

Bonnaffée, E., *Le Meuble en France au 16ᵉ siècle*, Paris, 1887.
   Voyages et Voyageurs de la Renaissance, Paris, 1895.
   Etudes sur la vie privée de la Renaissance, Paris, 1898.

Bourciez, E., *Les Moeurs polies et la littérature de la Cour sous Henri II*, Paris, 1886.

Brackett, O., 'The Influence of Du Cerceau on French Renaissance Furniture', *Burlington Magazine*, XV (1909), p. 357.

Brown, H.R.F., *Studies in the History of Venice*, London, 1907.

Burr, G.H., *Hispanic Furniture*, New York, 1941.

Byne, A., and Stapley, M., *Spanish Interiors and Furniture*, 3 vols. New York, 1921–5.

Byrne, M.S.C., *Elizabethan Life in Town and Country*, London, 1954.

Castan, A., *'L'Architecteur' Hugues Sambin*, Besançon, 1891.

Cescinsky, H. and Gribble, E.R., *Early English Furniture and Woodwork*, London, 1922.

Champigneulle, B., *Le Règne de Louis XIII*, Paris, 1949.
    Le Règne de Louis XIV, Paris, 1943.
Coleselli, F., *Alpenhäuser und ihre Einrichtung*, Frankfurt am Main, Innsbruck, 1963.
Corrozet, G., *Les Blasons Domestiques*, Paris, 1865.
Cotchett, L.E., *The Evolution of Furniture*, London, 1938.
Coulton, G.C., *Life in the Middle Ages*, Cambridge, 1954.
    Social Life in Britain, Cambridge, 1956.
Cust, L., 'The Lumley Inventories', *Walpole Society*, VI (1917–18), p. 15.

Defourneaux, N., *La vie quotidienne au temps de Jeanne d'Arc*, Paris, 1952.
De Vaissière, P., *Gentilshommes campagnards de l'ancienne France*, Paris, 1903.
Domenech, R. and Bueno, L.P., *Muebles Antiguos Españoles*, Barcelona, *c.* 1921.
Duby, G, and Mandrow, R., *A History of French Civilization*, London, 1956.
Du Cerceau, Jacques Androuet, *Oeuvres*, 2 vols., Paris, 1884–91.
Du Colombier, P., *Le Style Henri IV–Louis XIII*, Paris, 1941.

Eberlein, H.D. and Ramsdell, R.W., *Italian, Spanish and Portuguese Furniture*, Philadelphia, 1927.
Enriquez, M.D., *El mueble español en los siglos XV, XVI, y XVII*, Madrid, 1951.
Eriksson, M., 'Bed-shelves and two-storeyed bedsteads', *Acta Ethnologica*, 1936, p. 65.
Erixon, S., *Folklig Mobelkultur i svenska bygder*, Stockholm, 1938.

Falke, O. von, *Deutsche Möbel des Mittelalters und der Renaissance*, Stuttgart, 1924.
    Deutsche Möbel des Barock und Rococo, Stuttgart, 1923.
Fastnedge, R., *English Furniture Styles from 1500 to 1830*, London, 1955.
Félice, R. de, *French Furniture in the Middle Ages and under Louis XIII* (translated by F.M. Atkinson), London, 1923.
    French Furniture under Louis XIV (translated by F.M. Atkinson), London, n.d.
Feulner, A., *Kunstgeschichte des Möbels*, Berlin, 1927.
Franklin, A., *La vie privée d'autrefois : La vie de Paris sous Louis XIV*, Paris, 1902.
    La civilité, l'étiquette, la mode, le bon ton du XIIIᵉ au XIXᵉ siècle, 2 vols. Paris, 1908.
Frati, L., *La Vita Privata di Bologna*, Bologna, 1900.

Gauthier, J.S., *Le Mobilier des vieilles provinces françaises*, Paris, 1933.
    Les Maisons paysannes, Paris, 1951.
    La Connaissance des meubles régionaux français, Paris, 1952.
Giedion, S., *Mechanisation takes command*, New York, 1948.
Gloag, J., *The Englishman's Chair*, London, 1964.
    A Social History of Furniture Design from 1300 BC to AD 1960, London, 1966.
Gombrich, E., *Norm and Form*, London, 1966.
Gudiol Ricart, J.M., *The Arts of Spain*, London, Milan, 1964.
Guimaraes, A., *Mobiliario do Paço Ducal de Villa Vicosa*, Braganza, 1949.

Hahm, K., *Deutsche Bauernmöbel*, Jena, 1938.
Halbgewachs, H., *Der südwestdeutsche Schrank des 16. und 17. Jahrhunderts*,
    Kaiserslautern, 1936.
Hallweg, F., *Die Geschichte des deutschen Tischlerhandwerks*, Berlin, 1924.
Havard, H., *Dictionnaire de l' Ameublement*, 4 vols. Paris, 1887–90.
Henne am Rhyn, O., *Kulturgeschichte des deutschen Volkes*, Berlin, 1892.
Heyne, M., *Das deutsche Wohnungswesen*, Leipzig, 1899.
Hillenbrand, K., *Bemalte Bauernmöbel aus württembergisch Franken*, Stuttgart,
    1956.
Hirth, G., *Das deutsche Zimmer der Gothik und Renaissance*, Munich, Leipzig,
    1899.
Holmes, U.T., *Daily Living in the 12th century*, London, 1953.
Holzhausen, W., *Lackkunst in Europa*, Brunswick, 1959.
Honour, H., *Chinoiserie: The Vision of Cathay*, London, 1961.
Howard, C., *English Travellers*, London, 1914.
Huth, H., *Europäische Lackarbeiten*, 1600–1850, Darmstadt, 1955.

Irwin, J., 'A Jacobean Vogue for Oriental Lacquer-work', *Burlington
    Magazine*, XCV (1953), p. 193.

Jacob, E.F. (editor), *Italian Renaissance Studies*, London, 1960.
Jonge, C.H. de, *Hollandische Möbel und Raumkunst 1650–1780*, Stuttgart, 1922.
Jourdain, M., *English Decoration and Furniture of the Early Renaissance*, London,
    1924.
    Stuart Furniture at Knole, London, 1952.

Labande, E.R., *L'Italie de la Renaissance*, Paris, 1954.
Laking, G.F., *The Furniture of Windsor Castle*, London, 1905.
Leinhaus, G.A., *Wohnräume des 15. und 16. Jahrhunderts*, Berlin, 1901.
Léjard, A. (editor), *La tradition française: le meuble*, Paris, 1941.
Lemonnier, H., *L'Art Français au Temps de Richelieu et de Mazarin*, Paris, 1893.
Lessing, J.A. and Brüning, A., *Der pommersche Kunstschrank*, Berlin, 1905.
Lill, G., *Hans Fugger und die Kunst*, Leipzig, 1908.
Longnon, H. and Huard, F.W., *French Provincial Furniture*, Philadelphia,
    London, 1927.
Loomis, R.S., *A Mirror of Chaucer's World*, Princeton, 1965.
Lunsingh Scheurleer, T., *Van haardvuur tot beeldscherm*, Leyden, 1961.
    'Documents on the Furnishings of Kensington Palace', *Walpole Society*
    XXXVIII (1960–2).
Luthmer, F., *Deutsche Möbel der Vergangenheit*, Leipzig, 1902.

Macquoid, P. and Edwards, R., *Dictionary of English Furniture*, 3 vols.
    London, 1954.
Maillard, E., *Old French Furniture and its surroundings* (translated M. Percival),
    London, 1925.
Martorell, J., *Interiores*, Barcelona, 1923.
Michelsen, P. and Rasmussen, H., *Danish Peasant Culture*, Copenhagen, 1956.
Mitchell, A., *The Past in the Present*, London, 1880.

Möller, L., *Der Wrangelschrank und die verwandten süddeutschen Intarsienmöbel des 16. Jahrhunderts*, Berlin, 1956.

Molmenti, P.G., *La vie privée a Venise*, Venice, 1895–6.

Mongrédien, G., *La vie quotidienne sous Louis XIV*, Paris, 1948.

Müller-Christensen, S. *Alte Möbel vom Mittelalter bis zum Jugendstil*, Munich, 1957.

Neckham, Alexander, 'De Utensilibus', printed in Wright, T., *Volume of Vocabularies*, Vol. 1, London, 1857.

Nutting, W., *Furniture of the Pilgrim Century 1620–1720*, Framingham, Mass,. 1924.

Odom, W., *A History of Italian Furniture*, 2 vols., New York, 1918–19.

Oswald, E., *Early German Courtesy Books*, London, 1869.

Packer, C., *Paris Furniture of the Master Ebénistes*, Newport, Mon., 1956.

Pedrini, A., *Il Mobilio del Rinascimento in Italia*, Florence, 1948.

Picard, R., *Les Salons littéraires et la société française*, New York, 1943.

Poitiers, Alienor de, 'Les Honneurs de la Cour', printed in La Curne de Saint-Palaye, *Mémoires sur l'ancienne chevalerie*, Paris, 1826.

Rocheblave, S., *Le Goût en France*, Paris, 1914.

Rodocanachi, E., *La Femme Italienne à l'époque de la Renaissance*, Paris, 1907.

Roe, F., *Ancient Coffers and Cupboards*, London, 1902.
History of Oak Furniture, London, 1920.

Rossetti, W.M., *Italian Courtesy Books*, London, 1869.

Rye, W.B., *England as seen by Foreigners*, London, 1865.

Salomonsky, V.C., *Masterpieces of Furniture*, New York, 1953.

Sandao, A., *O movel pintado em Portugal*, Barcelos, 1966.

Schade, G., *Deutsche Möbel aus sieben Jahrhunderten*, Leipzig, 1966.

Schiaparelli, A., *La casa fiorentina e i suoi arredi nei secoli XIV e XV*, Florence, 1902.

Schmitz, H., *The Encyclopaedia of Furniture*, London, 1936.
Das Möbelwerk, Berlin, 1942.

Schottmüller, F., *Wohnungskultur und Möbel der italienischen Renaissance*, Stuttgart, 1928.

Schubring, P., *Cassoni*, 2 vols., Leipzig, 1923.

Schulz, A., *Deutsches Leben in XIV. und XV. Jahrhundert*, Vienna, 1892.

Shaw, H., *Specimens of Ancient Furniture*, London, 1836.

Singleton, E., *Dutch and Flemish Furniture*, London, 1907.

Sluyterman, K., *Ancient Interiors in Belgium*, London, 1915.

Stalker, J. and Parker, G., *A Treatise of Japanning and Varnishing* (facsimile edition, Molesworth, H.D.), London, 1960.

Symonds, R., ' "The Dyning Parlor" and its furniture', *Connoisseur*, CXIII (1944), p. 11.

Taralon, J. (editor), *Les Trésors des Eglises de France*, Paris, 1965.

Thielen, P.G., *Die Kultur am Hofe Herzog Albrechts von Preussen*, Göttingen, 1953.

Thorpe, W.A., 'A Group of Chinese Secretaries', *Apollo*, **XXIII** (1936), p. 323.

Turner, T.H., *Manners and Household Expenses in the 13th. and 15th. Centuries*, London, 1841.

and Parker, J.H., *Some Account of Domestic Architecture in England*, 3 vols., Oxford, 1851–9.

Verlet, P., *Le mobilier royal français*, 2 vols., Paris, 1945–55.

Viaux, J., *Le meuble en France*, Paris, 1962.

Villa, N., *Le XVIIᵉ siècle vu par Abraham Bosse*, Paris, 1967.

Vogelsang, W., *Le meuble hollandais*, Amsterdam, 1910.

Wallin, S., *Nordiska Museets mobler*, Stockholm, 1931–5.

Weigert, R.A., *Jean Bérain*, Paris, 1937.

Le style Louis XIV, Paris, 1941.

L' époque Louis XIV, Paris, 1962.

Weisbach, W., *Francesco Pesellino*, Berlin, 1901.

Windisch-Graetz, S., *Le Meuble Baroque et Rococo*, Brunswick, 1949.

Wright, T., *History of Domestic Manners in England*, London, 1862.

Homes of Other Days, London, 1871.

Zdekauer, L., *Life in Old Siena*, London, 1914.

Index

179

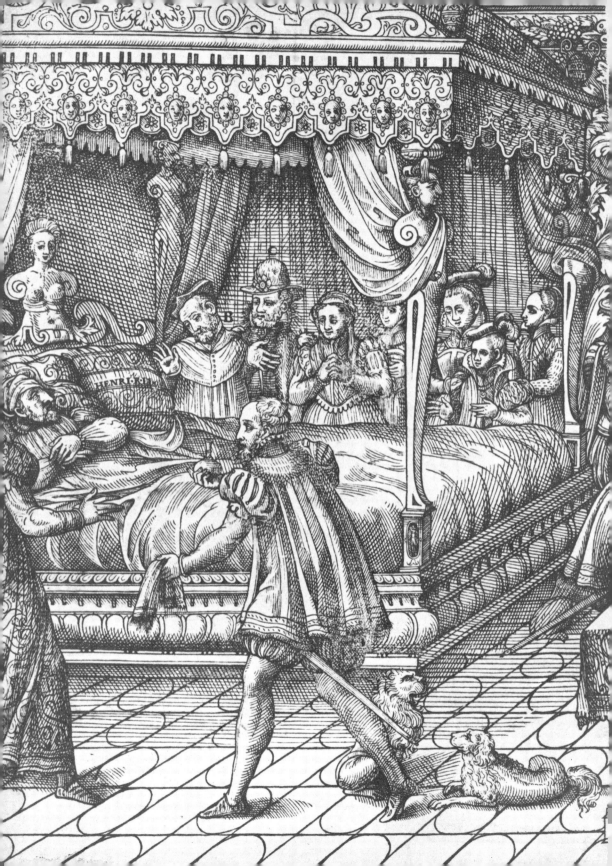